METROPOLITAN COLLEGE OF N.
LIBRARY, 12TH FLOOR
431 CANAL STREET
NEW YORK, NY 10013

Megabank Consolidations in the United States

MEGABANK CONSOLIDATIONS IN THE UNITED STATES

The Enigma Continues

Ashford Maharaj

iUniverse, Inc.
New York Lincoln Shanghai

Megabank Consolidations in the United States
The Enigma Continues

Copyright © 2005 by Ashford Maharaj

All rights reserved. No part of this book may be used or reproduced by any means, graphic, electronic, or mechanical, including photocopying, recording, taping or by any information storage retrieval system without the written permission of the publisher except in the case of brief quotations embodied in critical articles and reviews.

iUniverse books may be ordered through booksellers or by contacting:

iUniverse
2021 Pine Lake Road, Suite 100
Lincoln, NE 68512
www.iuniverse.com
1-800-Authors (1-800-288-4677)

ISBN-13: 978-0-595-35640-9 (pbk)
ISBN-13: 978-0-595-81419-0 (cloth)
ISBN-13: 978-0-595-80116-9 (ebk)
ISBN-10: 0-595-35640-0 (pbk)
ISBN-10: 0-595-81419-0 (cloth)
ISBN-10: 0-595-80116-1 (ebk)

Printed in the United States of America

CONTENTS

LIST OF TABLES ix

LIST OF FIGURES xiii

PREFACE xv

ACKNOWLEDGEMENT xix

CHAPTER 1: The U. S. Banking Industry in Retrospect 1
    The Early Beginnings of US Banking 2
    Federal Deposit Insurance 5
    Bank and Financial Holding Companies 7
    Major Issues of the Post 1980 Period 11
    Savings and Loan Associations Crisis 13
    The Enigma Continues 15

CHAPTER 2: Megabank Consolidations: Problems, Issues, and Methodologies 18
    Background of the Problem 18
    Purpose of the Study 24
    Theoretical Framework 28
    Research Problem 33
    Specific Research Questions 33
    Hypotheses to be Tested 35
    Significance of the Study 37
    Assumptions and Limitations of the Study 38
    Outline of the Study 39

CHAPTER 3: Review of Bank Consolidations: Trends, Theories, and Hypotheses 41
  Recent Trends in Bank Mergers and Acquisitions 41
  Review of Merger-Related Theories and Hypotheses 43
    Growth Maximization Group of Theories 44
    Value Maximization Group of Theories 47
    Concluding Comments on Hypotheses and Theories Reviewed 51
  Review of Research Methodologies in Mergers and Acquisitions 52

CHAPTER 4: Research Methodology for the Study 57
  Goals of a Public Business Organization 58
  Goals in Managing the Banking Business 60
    The Optimum Goal 60
    Conclusion 61
  Value and Market Efficiency 61
    The Basic Valuation Process 61
    Market Efficiency 63
  Basic Event Study Methodology 64
  Theoretical Constructs 66
    The Independent Variable. 68
    The Dependent Variable 69

CHAPTER 5: Research Design 72
  Sample Selection 73
  Hypothesis 1: Megabank Acquirers and Abnormal Return on Equities 76
    The Dependent Variable: Abnormal returns. 76
    The Independent Variable: Event window period. 79

Hypothesis 2: Mergers of Equals In-market Megabanks 79
Hypothesis 3: Acquisition Premium and Megabanks 82
    Purchase price to book value. 83
    Market price to trailing-four-quarters earnings per share. 83
    Acquisition premium as a percentage of book value. 84
Threats to Validity 85
Threats to Validity: A Summary 87

CHAPTER 6: Results and Discussion of Value Creation for Acquirers Hypothesis 89
    Test Results of Value Creation for Acquirers 90
    Threats to Internal Validity Analysis 99
    Value Creation for Acquirer Shareholders: A Synthesis 102

CHAPTER 7: Results and Discussion of Merger of Equals Hypothesis 103
    The Analysis 104
    Discussion of the Results 116
    Mergers of Equals: A Synthesis 116

CHAPTER 8: Results and Discussion of Premium Paid to Integrate with Megabanks: Price Offered to Book Value Approach 119
    Price Offered to Book Value Approach: The Basis 120
    The Data 121
    Price Offered to Book Value Approach: The Results 124
    Price to Book Value: A Synthesis 133

CHAPTER 9: Results and Discussion of Premium Paid to Integrate with Megabanks: Price to LTM Eps Approach 134
    The Results 135

A Discussion of Premium Payments to Integrate with Megabanks 145
Price Offered to LTM Eps Approach: A Synthesis 147

CHAPTER 10: Bank Consolidations: Implications for the Future 148
Summary Results of Bank Consolidations in the U.S. 149
Practical and Theoretical Implications 153
Contemporary Consolidation Issues and Future Research
Initiatives 155

REFERENCES 161
APPENDIX A: Definition of Important Terms 169
APPENDIX B: Mathematical Explanations 175
ABOUT THE AUTHOR 181
INDEX 183

LIST OF TABLES

Table 1.1	Top Ten Bank Holding Companies in the United States as of June 2002 Measured in Terms of Deposits Held and Headquartered by State	8
Table 6.1	Mergers and Acquisitions Involving Megabanks in the United States for Period 1990 to 1997	91
Table 6.2	Average and Cumulative Average Excess Returns Calculated Over the 41-day Event Window with Applicable t Statistic	94
Table 6.3	Acquirers Grouped by Classes of Excess Returns, Frequency, and Cumulative Percentages (%) Over the Event Window	97
Table 6.4	Results of Recent Studies on Stock Market Reaction to Acquirers in Mergers and Acquisitions Covering the Period 1978 to 1997	98
Table 7.1	Excess Returns for Acquirees and Acquirers for Period t (-5, 5) with Signed Rank Values for Matched Pairs	110
Table 7.2	Summary of Wilcoxon Signed Rank Sum Test for Paired Samples Over the 11-Day Event Window for Merger of Equals' Megabanks	113
Table 8.1	Number of Megabank Mergers and Acquisitions with Percentage Spread for Period 1990-1997	122
Table 8.2	Data Showing Number of Small Banks Per Year in the Small Bank Category for which Reliable Data Were Available with Appropriate w_i	123
Table 8.3	The Estimated Values of d Over the Period 1990-1997 for Price Offered to Book Value	125
Table 8.4	Proportionate Sample (n_i) Allocated to Strata Based on Weight of Stratum (w_i) in Sample n for the Price Offered to Book Value Approach	126

Table 8.5	Single Factor ANOVA Test for within and Between Groups for Acquirees with Asset ³ $5.0b Price to Book Value	129
Table 8.6	Single Factor ANOVA Test for within and Between Groups in the Acquirees £ $0.1b Category Price to Book Value for a Proportionate Stratified Random Sample	130
Table 8.7	F-test for Sample Variances between Acquirees in Megabank and Small Bank Categories for the Price Offered/Book Value Variable	131
Table 8.8	T-test Assuming Unequal Variances on the Price Offered/Book Value Variable for Megabank and Small Bank Categories	132
Table 9.1	The Estimated Values of d Over the Period 1990–1997 for the Price Offered to LTM Eps Approach in the Small Bank Category	136
Table 9.2	Proportionate Sample (n_i) Allocated to Strata Based on Weight of Stratum (w_i) in Sample n for the Price Offered to LTM Eps Approach for Banks in the Small Bank Category	138
Table 9.3	Single Factor ANOVA Test for Within and Between Groups for Megabanks with Asset ³ $5.0b in Price to LTM Eps Variable	141
Table 9.4	ANOVA Single Factor Test for Price Offered / LTM Eps for Small Bank Acquirees with Assets £ $0.1b. at Announcement	142
Table 9.5	F-test for Sample Variances between Megabank and Small Bank Categories for the Price Offered / LTM Eps Variable	143
Table 9.6	T-test Assuming Unequal Variances on the Price Offered/LTM Eps Variable for Megabank and Small Bank Categories	144

Table 9.7   T-tests of Merger and Acquisition Premium Payment Hypothesis for Banks in the Megabank and Small Bank Categories: Summary Results 146

Table 10.1   Summary of the Results for the Hypotheses Tested in this Study 150

LIST OF FIGURES

Figure 1.1	Changes in Number of Institutions FDIC-Insured Commercial Banks	9
Figure 1.2	Failure Rates for Banks in the United States 1934 to 2002	10
Figure 1.3	Number bank mergers over the period 1934 to 2002. FDIC (2002).	11
Figure 2.1	Market concentration continuum.	21
Figure 4.1	Asset price adjustments to new information	64
Figure 6.1	Graph of AER and CAER	96
Figure 6.2	Graph of cumulative frequency distribution of the average excess returns in the acquirers' megabank category.	99
Figure 6.3	Graph showing frequency distribution of the data points representing Average Excess Returns (AER) in the megabank category.	100
Figure 8.1	Histogram depicting price offered to book value in the megabank category.	127
Figure 8.2	Frequency distribution curve showing price offered to book value for banks in the megabank category.	127
Figure 8.3	Histogram showing price offered to book value in the small bank category.	128
Figure 8.4	Frequency distribution curve depicting price offered to book value in the small bank category.	128
Figure 9.1	Histogram showing price offered to LTM Eps for banks in the megabank category.	138

Figure 9.2 Frequency distribution curve depicting price offered to LTM Eps in the megabank category. 139

Figure 9.3 Histogram showing price offered to LTM Eps for banksin the small bank category. 139

Figure 9.4 Frequency distribution curve depicting price offered to LTM Eps in the small bank category. 140

PREFACE

Published works on bank consolidations through mergers and acquisition are relatively rare when compared to the writings on integrating activities in other industries such as chemical, manufacturing, and consumer goods industries. More so, the new phenomenon of "merger of equals" is hardly ever investigated. By investigating merger of equals among megabanks there is little doubt that, in this work, I have ushered-in, what may be a new and interesting area of finance that would require the expending of huge amounts of intellectual and physical resources. This book attempts to fill a void in the area of business consolidation with an emphasis on megabank consolidations and merger of equals among megebanks. It is hoped that other researchers will want to further illuminate merger and acquisition issues among banks and to ascertain whether the variable, shareholders value, is indeed increasing, decreasing, or having no impact as bank consolidations continue in the first decade of the new Millennium.

In the light of this new impetus to compete more keenly, banks are again seeking to grow in leaps and bounds as they come face-to-face, with the reality of an increasingly harsher global environment and the purposeful realization that large firms could enhance each other's financial performance. Thus, as bank consolidations among themselves seemed to be picking up the pace, after slowing down in the late 1990s and early 2000s, decision makers, academicians, policy makers, and students of finance are once more diligently looking for "what is out there." Discovering bits and pieces of the enigma will no doubt guide renewed interests, understandings, and decisions relating to aspects of integration among financial business units.

The structure and functioning of financial intermediaries in the United States are quite similar to those found in other parts of the world. In general, financial institutions provide ubiquitous functions, such as holding deposits of consumer funds, promoting savings, packaging and selling financial claims, providing liquidity in the financial system, and being major players in channeling funds from surplus savers to deficit saving units and individuals. However, unlike most other countries where only a few large banks dominate the entire banking industry, in the United States numerous banking entities dot the financial landscape. In fact, there are scores of large banks and thousands of smaller commercial banks, savings and loan associations, credit unions, and mutual saving banks that seek to fulfill the banking needs of consumers, investors, and federal, state, and local governments. In more recent times, and especially during the decade of the 1990s, the competitive paradigm of a relatively huge number of suppliers of financial services gave way to a limited measure of collusion, vertical and horizontal integration, and hostile acquisitions in the banking industry. Consolidations among financial intermediaries were undertaken with the expectation that economies of scope or scale will be realized, thereby increasing the probability for increased profit margins from the resulting operating and financial synergies.

The question of whether consolidations among financial intermediaries do result in value creation for shareholders is still a contentious issue. The research done for this book and the findings derived from the analysis do confirm that such a vacillating question is real and will need further theorizing and analyzing by banking professionals and academicians. Additional resources need to be directed towards the bringing about of a greater radiance or perhaps closure to the issue of shareholders' value creation among consolidating financial intermediaries. Another issue examined in this book is to test whether megabanks that integrate on a merger-of-equal basis do create the relatively conventional value creation for shareholders of target (acquiree) banks. A final and very important but less contentious issue dealt with in this book is related to the question of premiums paid by acquirers for the right to integrate with small versus that which is paid for the right to integrate with the very large banks. I have argued and provided the evidence to support the contention that consolidation premiums are quantitatively higher for big banks vis-à-vis smaller banks.

On my first encounter with the United States financial markets, I was fascinated by what was taking place in the pits of the New York Stock Exchange (NYSE). This was the 1990s and wealth generation seemed endless in that it was seen then, that by holding assets in stocks one was likely to see his or her investment portfolio grew in leaps and bounds. The technological explosion in communication supported by concerted technological innovation in manufacturing and a favorable geopolitical climate facilitated by the rise of emerging markets at the end of the Cold War witnessed runaway bull markets. Financial experts believed that their models to predict the behavior in financial markets were sound and financial opinions on buying and selling securities were plentiful. As we all now know, the post Cold War economic order was to have been greeted by a Y2K projected technological doomsday which never really materialized, but was instead surpassed by a catastrophic Nine-Eleven bewilderment.

The seemingly unpredictable Nine-Eleven (9/11) shock and awe may have been the substitute for the unrealized Y2K catastrophic events. In other words, there seemed to be no escape from a world's event of colossal proportion to replace a dwindling Cold War. Analogous to the disruption of the booming financial markets immediately preceding World War I, so too was the disruption of the booming 1990s and early 21st century being confronted this time, however, by an assault on the major financial and military institutions in the United States. The attack on the World Trade Center and the Pentagon and the financial uncertainty that followed convinced many analysts that an economic recession was more real than apparent. Striking at what may be the heart of the United States financial and military complexes virtually brought the United States economy to a standstill. There was never a time in modern American history that financial markets ceased to operate for one week and so too were major activities in what is essentially the financial capital of the world, the island of Manhattan.

Prior to Nine-Eleven and preceding the once envisaged Y2K disruptions that didn't really happened, the grand finale in financial sector liberalization was a piece of federal legislation known as the Financial Services Modernization Act of 1999. Such a legal document took down barriers that prevented the close affinity between commercial and investment banking and presented windows of opportunities and cross-selling financial claims at what seemed to be financial supermarkets. Simultaneously, financial liberalization was taking place internationally thereby allowing international banking consolidations between banks such as Deutsche Bank of Germany and Nations Bank of the United States, Credit Suisse of Switzerland acquiring American financial intermediary, DLJ among many other extraterritorial consolidations. Founded in 1959 and headquartered in New York City, DLJ maintained offices in 13 cities in the United States and 16 cities in Europe, Latin America, and Asia. The investment banking business of DLJ has been integrated into Credit Suisse First Boston, with much of the asset management business incorporated into Credit Suisse Asset Management. The huge amount of money thrown after so many deals suggested that the financial wisdom behind bank consolidations were not yet fully understood.

The chapters that follow will attempt to clarify shareholders value creation among the banks identified and will measure shareholders value creation among identifiable mergers and acquisitions. Perhaps hubris may be also had been a motivation factor given that many of the banking sector's mergers and acquisitions destroyed shareholders value especially for the acquiring banks. Chapters 1 and 2 have identified and described the historical underpinnings of a United States banking system that are still evolving and perhaps, only now coming to grip with the dynamics of a global environment. It is interesting to note also that the United States banking structure has only recently settled many of the protracted issues involving interstate rigidities. A review of bank consolidation was undertaken in chapter 3, where the focus was on trends, theories, and hypothesis by which I have attempted to explain bank consolidations through mergers and acquisitions. Two groups of theories were identified in chapter 3 namely, growth maximization and value maximization. In chapter 4, I focused on research methodologies for studying business consolidation and started with goals of a business undertaking and zeroed-in to the unique goals of a banking organization. In addition, chapter 4 examined the concepts of market value and market efficiency and in so doing presented a full examination of basic event study methodology, of which was derived from the capital asset pricing model.

The design of the research for this book was described in chapter 5 including identifiable research problems supported by testable propositions. Chapter 6 presented the result and discussion of value creation for shareholders of acquiring banks, while chapter 7 did the same for megabanks that integrate on the basis of mergers of equals. Chapters 8 and 9 presented the results and discussions of the issue of premiums paid for the right to integrate with the very large banks versus premiums paid for integrating with relatively smaller banks. The variable, *price to book*, was the choice for an independent variable in chapter 8, whereas in chapter 9 *price to LTM Eps* was the independent variable that had influenced the dependent variable. The conclusions drawn from the study were highlighted in chapter 10 together with a crystal ball gaze into the future where some of the impending issues, problems, situations, and the underlying implications for further research were also intimated.

ACKNOWLEDGEMENT

I wish to thank all those who helped me to re-examine the theories of financial risk and return ensuring that I stay focus on the dynamics of and ever changing financial landscape of the United States. To my many students at Berkeley College, from both the Westchester and New York City campuses, who often "peppered" my utterances on financial matters with questions that repeatedly forced me to go back to the drawing board to rethink my various pronouncements on matters pertaining to the study of finance.

I am grateful to my former employer, Chase Manhattan Bank (now J.P. Morgan Chase and Company), for granting me financial assistance as I proceeded to collect data for some of the chapters of this book, while being a Ph. D. candidate. I am also grateful to Professor Aswath Damodaran of New York University, New York, NY and Dr. James Brown of Walden University, Minneapolis, Minnesota. I am indebted to Professor Damadoran for his helpful advice and comments especially in areas of financial analysis of the data for this book and Dr. Brown, my academic advisor, who ensured that I stay on "message" with my academic writings. I am also very grateful to Dr. William Brent of Howard University, Washington D.C. for his profound interest in seeing that I aspire to achieve acceptability in the scholarly community.

Special mention must be extended to my wife, Leah and children, Hansen and Mark for their understanding and waiver of demands on my time for them, as I sought to complete this book in the shortest time possible. I am also grateful to iUniverse, and especially Ron Amack, for guiding my efforts toward the final publication of this work. Last, but in no way least, I wish to thank Professor Luisa M. Feriera of Berkeley College, White Plains Campus for reading certain parts of this manuscript and making corrections as she saw fit. For all remaining errors in this book, I claim full responsibility.

Ashford Maharaj Ph.D.
Finance Professor
Berkeley College
White Plains NY 10601

CHAPTER 1

THE U. S. BANKING INDUSTRY IN RETROSPECT

The structure and functioning of financial intermediaries in the United States are quite similar to those found in other parts of the world. These financial institutions provide ubiquitous functions, such as holding deposits of consumer funds, promoting savings, packaging and selling financial claims, providing liquidity in the financial system, and being major players in channeling funds from surplus savers to deficit saving units and individuals. However, unlike most other countries where only a few large banks dominate the entire banking industry, in the United States, numerous banking entities dot the financial landscape. In fact, there are scores of large banks and thousands of smaller commercial banks, savings and loan associations, credit unions, and mutual saving banks that seek to fulfill the banking needs of consumers, investors, and federal, state, and local governments. In more recent times, and especially during the decades of the 1990s, the competitive paradigm of a relatively huge number of suppliers of financial services gave way to a limited measure of collusion, vertical and horizontal integration, and hostile acquisitions in the banking industry. Consolidation among financial intermediaries were undertaken with the expectation that economies of scope or scale will be realized, thereby increasing the probability for increased profit margins from the resulting operating and financial synergies.

The question of whether consolidations among financial intermediaries do result in value creation for shareholders is still a contentious issue. The research done for this book and the findings derived from the analysis do confirm that such a vacillating question is real and will need further theorizing and analyzing by banking professionals and academicians. Additional resources need to be directed towards the bringing about of a greater radiance or perhaps closure to the issue of shareholders' value creation among consolidating financial intermediaries. Another issue examined in this book is to test whether megabanks that integrate on a merger-of-equal basis do create the relatively conventional value creation for shareholders of target (acquiree) banks. A final and very important less contentious issue dealt with in this book relates to the question of premiums paid by acquirers for the right to integrate with small versus the very large banks.

During the decade of the 1990s, CEOs of financial intermediaries exhibited the resoluteness to expend greater resources by way of paying higher premiums for the right to integrate with large banks, vis-à-vis smaller ones. This issue is diligently pursued in this book and the findings dealing with the question of premiums paid to acquire the very large banks in the United States will also be documented in later chapters. Inherent in some of the questions addressed is an issue of psychological warfare, where the urge to integrate may be driven by hubris (Roll, 1981). Hubris tends to essentially suggest an "ego trip" or sales maximization on the part of CEOs of banks, irrespective of diseconomies in the unit cost of production. Thus, it is sometimes likely that CEOs of acquiring entities (acquirers) go after market share increases by the merging or acquiring in-market competitors, as the former seek to close deals prior to any announcement of competitive bids by lurking white knights.

The Early Beginnings of US Banking

The modern day banking system owes its beginning to a bank known as the Bank of North America, which was officially chartered in Philadelphia, Pennsylvania in 1781, with the authorization to operate as a commercial bank (New York Public Library, 1997). Such a bank, as was envisaged by early financiers, grew to be a proven success and as a result other banks were established along that model. However, given the unique situation in which the early republic had found itself, forging a "united states" among the many colonial states sometimes appeared to be insurmountable. Documented sources referencing the birth and development of the United States are littered with federal-states controversies over questions such as who has jurisdiction to grant bank charters and who has the right to oversee the banking system.

Given the success of the early banks among the states, the federal government, rather than resorting to an undesirable warfare concerning the chartering rights over banks, pursued the conception of establishing their own federally chartered banks. Thus, it was no surprise that a bank known as the Bank of the United Stated was given a federal charter to operate as a full-fledged commercial bank in the year 1791 (Mishkin, 2003). Such a federally chartered bank, in addition to serving as a commercial bank, became a central bank of the federal government with responsibilities such as overseeing the supply of money, credit expansion, and other germane duties consequential to a financial public bureaucracy. Resulting from this federal-state dichotomy originated a system of dual banking structure in the United States, which has proven to be a peerless characteristic of commercial banking vis-à-vis, the rest of the world.

The first Bank of the United States, in a relatively short period of time, did find itself mired in controversies and was challenged by the powerful interests among rural farmers and other investors involved in the habitation of lands west of the Mississippi River. These new settlers in the westward movement harbored a persistent distrust for the federalists and view the latter as having a bias for the money-centered bigger cities in north/eastern United States. The new rural settlers also perceived the federalist's centralized power, which accompanied the establishment of a central banking facility, as not in the best interests of the former. Thus, the federalists capitulated to the pressure placed on them by the states, especially those of the south, thereby rendering the first bank of the United States a defunct entity by the year 1811. However, the centralized banking initiative resurfaced again at the onset of the British-American Wars, which began in 1812 and ended with the Battle at New Orleans in 1815 (New York Public Library, 1997).

In the aftermath of a war-ravaged economy, the federal government was experiencing a period of acute shortage of funds, and the absence of a government's bank was a luxury that the post-war economy of the United States couldn't withstand much longer. Therefore, in 1816 the Second Bank of the United States was established under a federal charter. The re-chartering of a second bank of the United States usurped the roles of being the fiscal agent of the United States government and as such, issued banknotes that were used as federally-backed currencies redeemable in fixed quantities of gold.

When the war ended in 1815, the combatants for and against the centralized banking system resumed their rivalry, especially in the light of the founding of the Second Bank of the United States. The tenacious conflict between state and federal banking powers came to an end with the elevation of Andrew Jackson to the presidency of the United States. President Jackson, a strong promoter of states' rights, vetoed a re-chartering of the second Bank of the United States in 1832 (New York Public Library, 1997). The National Banking Acts of 1863 and 1864 created the platform for the establishment of a uniform national currency, but the absence of a central bank suggested that regulation of the currencies in circulation was aloof of the federal authorities. Up to this point, however, as commercial banks were state-chartered banks empowered with the right to issue their own banknotes, which could have been redeemed in gold. It was no colossal surprise therefore, when many of these banks failed, and in so doing, the banknotes issued by such failed banks became worthless intangible assets.

Strength returned to the banking system when the aforementioned Acts of 1863 and 1864 became law, and as a result, state-chartered banks were indirectly supervised by the United States government's Comptroller of the Currency. Using its power to tax, the federal government levied a tax on banknotes of state-chartered banks, leaving the federally chartered national banks free of taxation. State banks eventually found the right avenue to soundness, and a great majority of them finally decided to build their businesses around the mobilization of savings from their customers, many of whom were holding federal banknotes. In addition, the 10% tax levy on the banknote issues of state banks was a heavy incentive for them to do business in federal banknotes. Therefore, rather than issuing their own banknotes, a great number of state banks began doing business in banknotes issued by the federal authorities within a relatively short period of time.

The National Banking Acts of 1863 and 1864, although being successful at securing a uniform national currency, lacked the missing regulatory framework, which could have only been provided by a central bank. For example, vital roles provided by a central bank such as regulating the amount of money in circulation, overseeing the amount of M1 money available in the economy, having monetary controls over the banks' credit and safety, and general soundness of the financial system could not be realized in the absence of a centralized financial institution. In addition, a central bank was also required to perform the clearinghouse function for the banking system and to essentially be the bank for all banks. The United States endured financial crises in 1873, 1878, 1893, and 1907, when convertibility was suspended; that is, banknotes could not have been converted to gold and hence, traces of banking panics occurred during those years (Calomiris, 2000; Burton, Nesiba, & Lombra, 2003). It was not until 1913, the year in which the Federal Reserve System was created by the United States Congress, that the United States entered an era when bank panics and monetary instability were considerably reduced. It was clear, however, that despite a reduction in incidences of bank panics and occurrences of insolvency, the scope and power of the Federal Reserve System did measure up to the task of dealing with a rapidly industrializing United States.

A main function of the Federal Reserve System (FRS), as enshrined in the Act of 1923, was to provide an elastic currency and be a lender of last resort to the commercial banks. However, it was clear that the FRS became financially sound and panic-proof enough to avoid a "run on the banks" during the early 1930s, when some 8,000 banks became insolvent. Interstate branching was not allowed for even federally chartered national banks, a situation that was perhaps motivated by the FRS intention to reduce concentration in the banking industry including any stifling of competition among banks. The McFadden Act of 1927, which was abrogated in 1994, ensured that national banks conform to state laws, which *inter alia*, directed that state banks be forbidden by a given bank's home state from opening branches across state lines.

Resulting from the crises of the Great Depression, there is hardly any doubt that the Federal Reserve System essentially became a central bank. Hence, the Banking Reform Acts of 1933 and 1935 were introduced to empower the Federal Reserve

System to, in addition to being a banker's bank, facilitate the attainment of the economic and financial goals, including the promotion of the overall health and stability of the United States economy. It seemed quite plausible, that during the Great Depression era the failure of many banks was as a result of the unwillingness of commercial banks to de-link investment from commercial banking activities. Investment banking activities during that period would have included investing in all kinds of financial claims, such as securities and stock market-related investment activities, while commercial activities would have involved the taking of deposits, facilitating payment transactions, and the granting of loans.

The lacking distinction and clarity of banking activities forged the basis for the enactment of the (in)famous Glass-Steagall Act of 1933, which is a piece of federal legislation that sought to prohibit the integration of the investment and commercial functions of banks. Despite repeated intimation by The U.S. Congress to repeal this act on the grounds that it was breeding unfair competition among commercial banks vis-à-vis nonbank financial entities, conformity with the Glass-Steagall's guidelines remained intact. In fact, the political establishment seemed unable to muster the collective will to amend such seemingly archaic legal business restrictions. Restrictions pertaining to the separation of commercial and investment activities including the trading in insurance products placed American banks at a disadvantage relative to those banks outside the United States. However, with the conglomerate merger in 1998 between Citicorp, a commercial bank, and Travelers Group, an insurance business, the ball fell heavily in the court of the political power brokers to act. And act, they did, in that the 1999 Gramm-Leach-Bliley Financial Service Modernization Act replaced the essentially antiquated Glass-Steagall Act of 1933, thereby setting the stage for banks to legally engage in insurance, securities, and real estate underwriting activities. The Gramm-Leach-Bliley Act also paved the way for the creation of financial supermarkets, in that the once prohibited investment and commercial banking and insurance activities under the proverbial "one roof," could now consolidate under a common organizational structure.

Federal Deposit Insurance

The Great Depression years of 1930 to 1933 engendered an unprecedented level of bank failures as the United States sought to chart the course for a unique banking system. During the same period, some 9000 banks failed and in the process decimated the savings of millions of banking customers. The banking cataclysm during the Great Depression was primarily due to the absence of a pre-existing institutional arrangement or some concrete policies that could buffer the negative effects pertaining to the depleting confidence in the banking system. Compounding this catastrophe was the absence of an appropriate monetary mechanism to respond to the evolving calamities in the areas of banking and finance. In order to prevent losses of hard-earned savings of the citizenry and the resulting bank failures, the federal government, in 1933, created the Federal Deposit Insurance Corporation. There is little doubt that, had it not been for the economic hardship attributed to the Great Depression of the 1930s, risk insurance for bank deposits may not have been brought to fruition. However, Insurance for bank deposits did not begin with the introduction of the 1933 federal legislation in that some states experimented with deposit risk insurance prior to 1933. In fact, by the year 1920, there were some eight state-type insurance schemes existing among some half-a-dozen or so states. States like Indiana, Michigan, Iowa, New York, and Vermont, at one time or another, experimented with some form of deposit insurance (Calomiris, & White, 2000). These experiments at developing insurance to insulate the effects of excessive withdrawal of deposits, which could have resulted in bank panics, excessive risk taking, and unscrupulous management of financial intermediaries proved invaluable in promoting the soundness of the financial system in the United States.

The creation of the Federal Deposit Insurance Corporation, popularly known as FDIC, owed its origin to the Glass Steagall Act of 1933. In reality, the FDIC was created as a federal agency entrusted with a portfolio of responsibilities, one of which was the insuring of bank deposits held by commercial banks for a maximum amount currently set at $100,000 per account. The Glass-Steagall Act of 1933 required that banks of the Federal Reserve System purchased FDIC insurance for deposits held. Other banks were given the option of purchasing insurance, an opportunity which almost all banks took advantage of, over a relatively short period of time. In 1989 deposit insurance was given the full faith and credit obligation of the federal government, which essentially was a guaranteed protection that was not offered in earlier years. Thus, between the period 1933 to 1988, FDIC insurance was to the individual banks as private insurance was to individual consumers.

During the 1990s the catalyst for creating value for shareholders in the financial services sector was to merge with or acquire other financial institutions. Consolidation pressure was high on the agenda of CEOs, and virtually every bank in the industry became a takeover or merger target. However, big banks targeted other relatively large financial intermediaries, and when the legal impediments were removed, big banks went after nonbank financial institutions. For example, Citicorp of New York merged with Travelers Insurance Group in 1998. The case for financial deregulation, which was intended to give the banking industry in the United States the edge it needed to stay competitive in the global environment, is a continuous battle being waged by members of the banking community, politicians, and academicians. The competition for clients among banks, nonbanks, and other financial intermediaries, both domestically and internationally, implied that the U.S. financial regulators had to destroy the firewalls, which have restricted the connectivity between banking and nonbanking financial institutions. The polemic issue of having a large number of small banks, which could promote competition and provide competitive services and financial products at reasonable prices, vis-a-vis having a few large banks that could reap economies of scale or scope. Whether or not greater competition among financial institutions that could result in higher consumer surplus, will continue to be a hotly contested debate among banking professionals, policy makers, and academicians.

Bank and Financial Holding Companies

The historical underpinnings of the of banking system in the United States have been grounded in the theory that the very existence of competition indicated that the banking interests of consumers were best served with the presence of a large number of banks and fierce competition among in-market financial intermediaries. Such a competitive environment, it was believed, would result in high-quality financial products at reasonable prices. However, despite the political desire for greater competition, the presence of legislation restricting intrastate and interstate branching ensured that the status quo was maintained. Banking services available to a rural community were very often provided by only one bank, given that there were no other banking facilities within a reasonable geographic area. Therefore, the existence of a large number of banks couldn't foster competition given the prevailing mode of transportation, such as wagon trains, river boats, and steam-powered trains in the United States during the 18th and early 19th Centuries. The popularization of anti-branching sentiments among the politically powerful rural farming community, coupled with the support of politicians who endeavored to uphold the concept of anti-branching, resulted in the proliferation of bank holding companies.

A bank holding company is essentially a corporation that owns several different companies with at least one of them being a bank, while the others could be engaged in activities that are very much related to banking. Given a more comprehensive spread in financial product offerings, such as brokerage, credit bureau services, assets management, and so on, bank holding companies could reduce the risks associated with the limited scope of commercial banking. A bank holding company, as conceived many decades ago, was the convenient form of a financial service establishment that would facilitate the circumvention of the strict intrastate and interstate banking laws. Most of these laws, however, are virtually repealed today, and therefore, bank holding companies may have outlived their main usefulness as conceived in 20th Century America.

A recent configuration of holding companies gave rise to a new form of financially related corporation known as a *financial holding company*. The Gramm-Leach-Bliley Act of 1999 legitimized the financial holding company, which essentially is an umbrella organization for embracing bank holding companies, insurance companies, securities firms, and other financial institutions. Financial holding companies are empowered to hold up to 100% of commercial banks and nonfinancial businesses so long as ownership is for investment purposes only and not for day-to-day management of any of the institutions, which constitute the aggregation. Ascribing the status of a financial holding company allowed the business to engage in a broader array of financial and nonfinancial services vis-à-vis the conventional bank holding companies of the pre 2000 era, given that the Gramm-Leach-Bliley Act was not in effect during that period. Today, almost all the large banks are still under the rubric of bank holding companies as compiled data on the relatively new "one-stop shopping" financial holding companies are not yet available. Table 1.1 gives the 10 largest bank holding companies in the Unites States as of 2002 measured in terms of assets.

Table 1.1
Top Ten Bank Holding Companies in the United States as of June 2002 Measured in Terms of Deposits Held and Headquartered by State

Rank	Name	State Headquartered	Deposits ($M)
1	Bank of America Corporation	North Carolina	326,268
2	Wells Fargo & Company	California	189,505
3	Wachovia Corporation	North Carolina	173,207
4	J.P. Morgan Chase & Co.*	New York	170,132
5	Citigroup Inc.	New York	146,390
6	Bank One Corporation	Illinois	146,141
7	Fleet Boston Financial Corporation	Massachusetts	110,527
8.	U.S. Bancorp	Minnesota	104,397
9	Suntrust Banks, Inc.	Georgia	69,043
10	National City Corporation	Ohio	56,072

Note. From FDIC (2002). "Top 50 bank holding companies by Total Domestic Deposits." Retrieved 12/20/03 at http://www.fdic.gov/sod/sos/SumReport.asp?
*J.P. Morgan Chase and Bank One Corporation, in 2003, have announced their intention to merge into a single entity.

Almost all the large banks in the United States are bank holding companies, where deposit liabilities are measured by aggregating the funds placed in these banks by individuals, businesses, and governments. Deposits are essentially financial claims against the banks, which must be astutely managed according to sound banking business practices. The top 10 banks as shown in Table 1.1 hold approximately 31.5% of the deposits of all FDIC-insured commercial banks in the United States, while the remaining 7,877 banks hold 68.5% of these funds. The shrinking number of banks has been quite observable in recent times, in that, it seemed as though, after an unprecedented period of stability in the banking system from the mid-1930s to mid-1980s, the number of banks began declining sharply in the latter half of the 1980s. The declining trend continued until the year 2000, when the speculative bubble bursts and in the process stifled the urge to merge among businesses. Figure 1.1 depicts the number of banks registered in the United States between the years 1934 to 2001 and does show a declining trend, especially from the latter half of the 1980s.

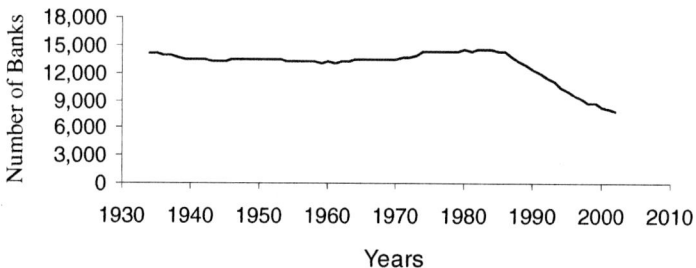

Figure 1.1. Changes in Number of Institutions FDIC-Insured Commercial Banks United States (50 states and DC). Data retrieved 12/20/03 from http://www.fdic.gov/hsob/hsobRpt.asp

As can be seen in Figure 1.1, after a slight drop in the post-Great Depression era, the number of banks remained constant from around 1940 to the early 1980s. However, the lateral movement in the number of banks was interrupted around the early 1980s, when the number of banks declined dramatically. The decline in the number of banks was by and large a result of three main factors. One such factor was the harsh economic realities of the Great Depression of the 1930s, when many businesses went "belly up" and catapulted many banks along the way. A second factor was the savings and loan associations crises of the 1980s, when many of these financial entities fell victim to faulty risk assessment and unsound business practices. The third and final factor was the propensity of banks to integrate with other banks especially large banks, an occurrence that may have been fuelled by the need for global comparability and elements of hubris. Elements of hubris suggests an inflated ego of the acquirer bank's CEO, who manifests a lavish presumptuousness as he or she proceeds to enlarge the business irrespective of the debilitating influence on shareholders' value. Figure 1.2 depicts the failure rate for banks, which is presented as a percentage of the number of banks per given year in the banking industry.

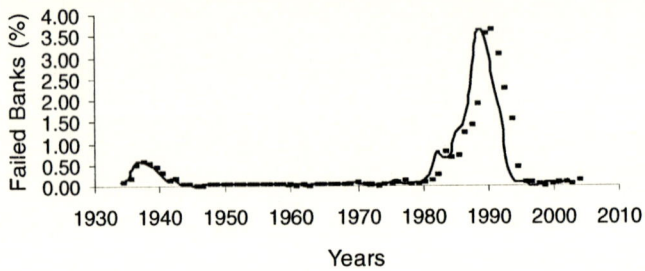

Figure 1.2. Failure Rates for Banks in the United States 1934 to 2002. Calculated from "Changes in Number of Institutions FDIC-Insured Commercial Banks United States (50 states and DC)." Retrieved from http://www.fdic.gov/hsob/hsobRpt.asp

---

While many banks did fail, such an occurrence was only a smaller part of the enigma in the declining number of banks. The other part of the dilemma was that banks were consolidating at unparalleled levels in the United States banking industry. Figure 1.3 depicts merger activities over the period 1934 to 2002, thus highlighting the fact that merger activities became radiantly obvious during the decades of the 1980s and 1990s. It was more so during the 1990s, however, that the very large banks went prowling for other large banks with the hope of accelerating the pace towards achieving megabank status, and in the process, endeavored to achieve economies of scope and scale.

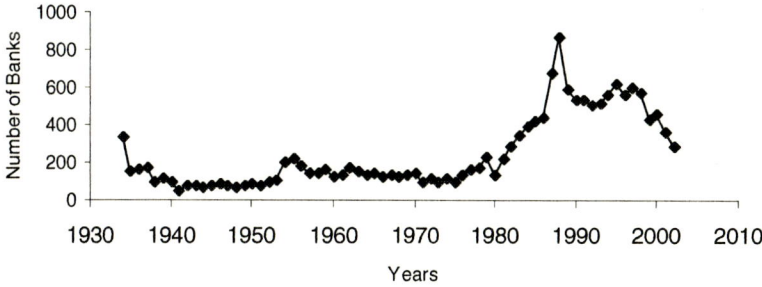

Figure 1.3. Number bank mergers over the period 1934 to 2002. FDIC (2002). "Changes in Number of Institutions FDIC-Insured Commercial Banks in the United States (50 states and DC)." Data retrieved on 12/20/03 from http://www.fdic.gov/hsob/hsobRpt.asp. Note. Mergers over the period consisted of banks categorized as "unassisted" and "Failed" Mergers.

In retrospect, it seems as though the acute impetus for bank integration was more or less driven mainly by the savings and loan associations' crises of the 1980s (see below) and the desire by banks in the 1990s to reap economies of scale or scope, as indicated above. In addition, other motives such as hubris, which is the inflated ego of acquirer CEOs, who are desirous of catapulting their banks into being a comparatively large player on the global scale, may have positively impacted the sharp increase in integrative activities, especially among the very large banks. Given the drive by the CEOs of the very large banks to target other very large banks as take-over or merger targets, it was quite possible that premiums paid to integrate with other megabanks were at historically high levels. The issue of premiums paid for the right to integrate with megabanks will be addressed in later chapters of this book.

Major Issues of the Post 1980 Period

The concepts of *adverse selection, asymmetry of information,* and *moral hazard* have impacted the banking industry to the extent that there is now, a deeper understanding of the basic environment in which banks generally operate. Adverse selection occurs when the people who are most undesirable, from the other party's viewpoint, are the most likely to vigorously seek to be parties to the given financial transaction, suggesting that the most undesirable may be selected.

From a banker's perspective, the less desirable borrower of funds may vigorously pursue and be chosen for a given loan transaction. Thus, the banker will be very concerned about the fact that the least creditworthy applicant will pursue a loan more diligently, and hence, may receive the loan, which could result in a greater exposure to default risk on the part of the lender. Asymmetry of information suggests that one party to a transaction may have more information about the given transaction than the other party. For example, a party to a loan, such as a borrower, may have more information about a potential project to be funded than the lender, who would have less first-hand knowledge about the project and may even rely on the borrower for some of the pertinent information. In this situation, the borrower will have a decided advantage over the lender in terms of information about a project that requires funding.

Moral hazard suggests there is a risk that one party to a transaction will exhibit a behavior that may be deemed repulsive, from the other party's point of view. For example, when a borrower receives a loan, he or she may engage in activities that are more risky (hazard) than the approved project, thereby improving his or her chances for a higher return. The downside to this situation is that the lender would not have factored-in the reward for such a higher risk and hence, would have received a lower return (immoral) than would have been for a riskier undertaking. Theories of finance do dictate that higher returns necessarily involve greater risks and by implication a greater probability for the realization of negative returns. Therefore, from a banking perspective, a bank that is supported by a FDIC insurance, or even a government's supported policy of bailouts for the banks that may be exhibiting insolvency tendencies, may not be subjecting themselves to the strict disciplines of the marketplace. After all, such banks will magnify the moral hazard problem in the midst of escalating levels of risk. Consequently, a bank may seek out greater risk (hazard) than it may otherwise have had intended, in the absence of a government- or FDIC-supported program of limited indemnity.

Faced with the reality that a government is desirous of having a healthy financial environment and is also being confronted with the need to prevent bank failures (especially the very large banks) has given rise to a too-big-to-fail policy. Because of a major financial disruption that will likely occur when a large bank fails, bank regulators have an intrinsic interest in megabanks' failure avoidance. The failure of a megabank could lead to a major financial disruption; thus, an infusion of an appropriate amount of capital by the FDIC or the by the federal government through an insurance body such as the FDIC may circumvent a potential run on the banks. Consequently, the FDIC will be interested in pursuing the "purchase and assumption" method, which suggests that the insolvent bank will be the beneficiary of a large infusion of funds supported by the provision of a willing merger partner. One of the main responsibilities of the merger partner (when found) is to assume all the liabilities of the financially distressed bank, the end result being that the financial claims of customers will be fully honored.

Savings and Loan Associations Crisis

There is no doubt that with the advent of the Federal Deposit Insurance Corporation a good deal of financial stability was brought into the banking industry. Prior to the year 1934 bank failures were regular occurrences (Mishkin, 2003). In fact, the years between the "great crash of 1929 and the introduction of the FDIC in 1933, some 8,000 banks failed (Burton, Nesiba & Lombra, 2003). Stability in the banking industry was brought about when the FDIC became an effective player among financial intermediaries; and hence, failure rates were reduced from almost 1% to approximately 0.16% of the total number of banks the United States. What went wrong in the banking industry during the 1980s and 1990s deserves a little attention or alternatively, what was done right so as to bring about the relatively stable banking years between 1934 and 1980? The problem arose from what is commonly referred today as the S&Ls crises of the 1980s.

The savings and loan associations were originally established to fund homeownership among members, who joined such a financial intermediary with the expressed purpose of pooling their savings and in return receiving financial assistance in the construction or purchase of existing (already built) houses. These S&Ls functioned like the modern day mutual funds, where members pool their funds and purchase mortgages within specific geographic locations. With the passage of time and perhaps changing circumstances, the function of "saving" and "loan" became separate activities, and so members of a given S&L were not necessarily the same persons who did the savings and the borrowings. Given that S&Ls were moving closer to operate like commercial banks, it follows that in a matter of time, these financial intermediaries were subjected to regulations similar to commercial banks. In addition, banking regulators gave the S&Ls the option to insure or not to insure customers' deposits. As a matter of fact, most of them did purchase insurance to cover their deposit holdings. Thus, in the post World War II era, S&Ls proliferated, and in so doing fulfilled the request for the much-needed funding in a growing housing market.

During the decades that followed World War II, financial innovations abounded in the banking sector and the S&Ls wanted to be part of the banking industry's expanding scope of operations. Ingenious financial products, such as Negotiable Order of Withdrawal (NOW) accounts, money market mutual funds, commercial paper, junk bonds, and other financial instruments, were some of the new product lines pursued by the S&L financial intermediaries. In addition,

S&Ls sought after and traded in, other highly volatile new financial instruments, such as financial futures, swaps, and mortgage-backed securities. The extension of deposit insurance to S&Ls invited the moral hazard problem as increases in the scope of operations and financial experimentation led to higher risk-tolerance levels. The expanded legal framework in 1980, which facilitated a deregulated banking sector, also indirectly engendered the taking of higher risk by banking entrepreneurs.

The S&Ls managers made sure that they indulged in added innovative risk with the overall desire aimed at securing greater profitability. Thus, the repeal of Regulation Q, a regulation which previously established interest rate ceilings on deposits, coupled with the increase in federal deposit insurance from $40,000 to $100,000 per account, indicated that rapid growth in assets and riskier projects could be tolerated. Soon, the S&Ls found themselves in one crisis after another; and that, these crises were generally rooted in financially indiscreet scenarios such as funding long-term assets with short-term liabilities in an escalating interest rate-sensitive environment and superficial gap and duration analyses.

During the late 1970s and early 1980s, the S&Ls did not yet fully developed the financial techniques such as adjustable rate mortgages and securitization that were vehicles for the management of interest rate risks. Therefore, as interest rates rose, the value of long-term assets, such as mortgages fell, and so a problem that began in the 1970s escalated during the 1980s, when the depository institutions' deregulation exacerbated the problem. The result was that hundreds of S&Ls failed or were taken over by other banking entities and in the process, billions of taxpayers' dollars were spent in an unsophisticated attempt by the fed at staving off an impending unhealthy and unstable financial environment.

In hindsight, it is possible that money could have been saved, assuming that the U.S. Congress had acted earlier and in a more sophisticated way. Rather than injecting funds earlier, when the funds were more acutely needed in order to minimize further financial losses, Congress responded instead by granting S&Ls the right to deal in new and innovative product lines. In addition, the reserve ratios for S&Ls were reduced from 5% to 3% of assets, resulting in additional investments undertaken with higher risks and hence, losses escalated even further up to a point where many S&Ls went broke. Congress, in 1986, made $10.8 billion available to the Federal Savings and Loan Insurance Corporation (FSLIC), the agency that insured the S&Ls' deposits, with the aim of bailing out the ailing S&Ls (Burton, Nesiba, & Lombra, 2003). Banking regulators, by retarding the decision to close out failing banks and assuming outstanding liabilities, engaged in *regulatory forbearance*. Regulatory forbearance, in this context, implies that the regulators were sidestepping their obligations to act in an appropriate and timely manner. Therefore, an appropriate and efficient decision-making process by banking regulators could have thwarted the escalating closure costs and simultaneously could have impeded any further incidences of the moral hazard problem.

The Enigma Continues

Back in the early 1990s many of the merger and acquisition deals launched by the very big banks seemed excellent as size, in terms of assets, continued to soar. Mergers involving megabanks such as Chemical Bank and Manufacturers Hanover Trust (*Mani Hani*), Bank of Boston and Shawmut Bank, First Union Corp and Dominion Bank Share, and NationsBank Corp and MNC Financial are some of the early 1990s consolidating experiments among the very large banks. Banking deregulation and the savings and loan associations crises of the 1980s seemed to suggest that financially strapped multi-state banks could be bought out at relatively cheap prices. Banking executives were growing in confidence, given that in their view, a magabank with one-stop shopping capacity for financial products was the answer to evade the curse of the competitive market at both the domestic and international levels.

The notion of one-stop shopping enticed banking professionals to postulate that large market share and geographic diversification could produce economies of scale or scope by cross-selling a multiplicity of financial products. Thus, "small is beautiful" must give way to "bigger is better", especially when "bigger" implies technological efficiency and decreasing unit cost per service provided. Exorbitant prices were also paid for large banks, measured by way of relatively high premiums, for the right to integrate with megabanks. For example, Bank One paid 143% of market value for First USA; NationsBank paid 137% for Barnett Banks Inc; and First Union paid 118% of market value for CoreStates (Kover, 2000).

Paying hefty premiums, as seemed to be the practice among the very large banks, suggest that the acquirer shareholders value may very well be on the decline, at least in the short run, if not in the long run. Contrast these situations involving exorbitant premiums with that of, the Citigroup-Travelers merger. Citigroup paid 100% of market price for Travelers stocks indicating that there was no ostensible reallocation of value from the acquirer' to acquiree' shareholders as part of the merger arrangement. A merger or an acquisition premium is the value paid for the acquiree's stocks by the acquirer in excess of the pre-merger or -acquisition price. But why would an acquirer pay a premium for an acquiree's stocks? Two major reasons are offered here. The first reason is that an acquirer would pay a merger or acquisition premium ahead of the perceived cost savings that would be realized in the post-consolidation period. The second reason is that a premium should be offered in order to stave off competition by any party to a *white knight* tender offer. A white knight situation will arise when a counter offer is made for an acquiree's business, usually at the request of the latter. For example, assume that bank A is interested in merging with or acquiring bank B. Bank C (or other interested acquirers) may enter a counter offer at the request of bank B, the result being that bank B receives a competitive value by way of a greater premium for its common equity.

Previous studies have shown that there is no significant relationships between merger or acquisition premiums paid to acquirees by acquirers and the creation of positive financial value in the post-consolidation period (Agrawal, Jaffe, & Mandelker, 1992; Sirower, 1997; Higson & Elliott, 1998). From a financial perspective resources allocated up front for a merger or an acquisition suggest a financial discounting and probability considerations must enter into the cost-benefit configuration. Therefore, crucial to cost-benefit analysis and premium paid to integrate among banks is the resulting (expected) cash flows with uncertainty (risk) and discounting factored into the analysis over a specified post-consolidation period. Inherent in such an analysis are the discounted expected free cash flows and the accompanying risk analysis over a given post-consolidation period using an appropriately factored expected growth rate in the model (see Appendix B #8).

In summary, unlike most other countries where only a few large banks dominate the entire banking industry, in the United States there are numerous banking entities that dot the financial landscape. Currently, there are dozens of large banks and thousands of smaller commercial banks, savings and loan associations, credit unions, and mutual saving banks that seek to fulfill the banking needs of consumers, investors, and federal, state, and local governments. In recent times, the competitive paradigm of a relatively huge number of suppliers of financial services gave way to a limited measure of collusion, mutual integration, and hostile acquisitions in the banking industry.

Consolidations among financial institutions were undertaken with the expectation for efficiency in terms of economies of scope and scale and any resulting profits from synergies. Additional resources need to be directed towards the bringing about of a greater radiance or perhaps closure to the issue of shareholders' value creation among consolidating financial intermediaries. The question of whether consolidations among financial intermediaries do result in value creation for shareholders is still a contentious issue. In the following chapters, an effort is directed towards lending further explication to this enigma with the result being, that an addition will be made to the existing inventory of knowledge in the area of bank mergers and acquisitions in the United States.

Inherent to the continuing enigma is the seemingly fragmented banking system in the United States where small banks have historically been vulnerable to runs and panics. With runs on banks, the psychology is not on what the true picture is about the banks but what is believed to be the perceptive truth about the actual state of the banking sector. Hence, there are elements about a self-fulfilling prophecy when it comes to run on a bank. Thus, assuming that consumers define a situation as "true" such a situation will be true its consequences. It follows that a rumor of a bank's insolvency could trigger action by customers of a given bank and insolvency will inevitably result. There is therefore, an incentive to be among the first group of customers to withdraw savings from a bank given that customers who seek funds later will endure the greatest risk when runs on banks seem to be in the making.

Given the way runs on banks work, there is a propensity for a run on one bank to impetuously bring about runs on other banks. When one hears that a particular bank might be heading for trouble it is not unreasonable to assume that others may follow as customers have grown leery about a banks' balance sheets. Policy makers and banking professionals are very concerned about this contagion effect which could give rise to bank panics. Such a domino effect no doubt would give rise to the need for increased regulations aimed at controlling systematic risks. A few failing banks could threaten a run on the very solvent ones and so, here is where "bigness" kicks in. A consensus of opinions in the literature on the size of banks is that small banks are more susceptible to runs and panics than the larger banks as the latter could enjoy the benefits of operational and reputational economies, which will serve to repel bank runs over an extended period of time (Kohn, 2004). And hence size, as a matter of maintaining the perception of solvency, may be a motivating factor behind mergers and acquisitions among financial intermediaries.

The process of consolidation in the banking industry involves banks merging with one another or banks acquiring one another. In a merger, the shareholders of the merging entities give up their equities in exchange for equity holdings of the merged company. In an acquisition situation the acquirer purchases the stocks of the acquiree. Such a consolidation was made possible by the existence of a well-functioning public equity market. Increasing competitive pressures and the need to create greater shareholders value have given rise to increased consolidation activities in the financial industry. In addition, to relish the need to become a world class financial organization size will matter as banks in Europe, Japan, and Canada were significantly larger than banks in the United States in the pre-1990 American banking era.

CHAPTER 2

Megabank Consolidations: Problems, Issues, and Methodologies

The tearing down of barriers to inter- and intra-state banking have ushered in a new and dynamic structure among financial intermediaries in the U.S. banking industry. In addition to the removal of those long-standing barriers, the reality is that banking's scope of operations has expanded to include once outlawed dealings with insurance agencies, securities underwriting and other complementary financial activities that are not contrary to the safety and soundness of the financial system. The expanding role of banks and financial deregulation of the banking industry suggest that competition among financial intermediaries will be greater and keener with the possible realization of greater industrial concentration among banks. The origin of bank holding companies and the newly permitted financial holding companies, in effect, guaranteed that the one-stop shopping for financially-related products will be the new reality of the banking structure in the United States. In this chapter, the problems and specific research questions addressed in this study will be described, analyzed, and theorized against a backdrop of assumptions and limitations.

Background of the Problem

The banking industry in the United States, similar to other industries, seemed to have enjoyed favorable economic successes on the various investment portfolios during the period 1990 to 1997 (Allen, 1997; Johnson, 1995). For banks as a whole, these favorable economic results were not surprising in that interests paid on deposits were relatively low, growth in the loan portfolio was strong, and the interest rate spreads were generally large. In addition, the legal framework, which previously inhibited operations in areas such as insurance, relationships with mutual funds, and other financial products, was relaxed (Spiegel, Gart, & Gart, 1996). In the light of these new developments, the dilemma facing the banking industry in the first decade of the new millennium is whether to exploit the advantages it already possessed or to leverage the new, open and less-restrictive fields of operation towards a horizon of insulation from persistent bank failures. Spiegel, Gart, and Gart intimated that such bank failures characterized the banking industry especially during the first half of the 20th century. One possible way for banks to insulate themselves from the vagaries of future economic misfortunes is to adopt an aggressive growth path through systematic mergers and acquisitions activities.

For many banks, merging with a partner bank or by acquiring the assets of another bank will most likely result in tremendous savings in overhead costs, especially in cases involving in-market mergers and acquisitions (Allen, 1997). For purposes of this study, an in-market refers to the consolidation of two or more banking entities that do business within identical markets and, or geographical areas. Therefore, in-market mergers and acquisitions are within the purview of the horizontal form of integration. Identical markets are those markets where each consolidating party trades along similar product lines, whereas geographical areas may involve physical proximity, but different product lines. The merger between Chase Manhattan and Chemical Bank in 1995 is an example of geographic areas, whereas the 1997 merger between First Union Corporation of North Carolina and CoreStates Financial of Pennsylvania is essentially an example of identical markets.

Commercial banks are favorably poised to wield great economic power within the financial sector of the United States economy by virtue of their ability to dictate the loan amortization process, despite the presence of a highly competitive operating environment (Allen, 1997). The banking industry's sphere of influence is further enhanced by having an effective service distribution network by way of bank branching, the proliferation of automated teller machines (ATMs), roving teller services, and excellent franchises built around customers' inertia. Such powers of influence, however, are minimized in the light of fully functional quasi-banks such as finance houses, money stores, credit unions, and mutual fund entities. In addition, large corporations operate parallel captive finance departments that raise capital and make loans to customers for the purposes of purchasing the corporations own products. General Motors Acceptance Corporation (GMAC), Toyota Motor Credit Corporation (TMCC), and General Electric Small Business Solutions are examples of parallel consumers' financing entities. In addition, these large corporations have the wherewithal to raise their own capital by way of commercial paper, corporate bonds, and debentures, thereby affording them the luxury of circumventing the demand for bank loans from the banking industry.

The shifting competitive environment has forced some banks to look for more competent ways to positively impact their bottom lines and boost the return on equities (Johnson, 1995). Clearly one of the best ways to become more efficient is to increase market share, while simultaneously holding down costs to a ratio less comparable to the gains in market share. In their search for economies of scale, or more particularly in the case of banking costs function, economies of scope, a quick way to drive down unit costs and boost income is through operating and financial synergies (Gaughan, 1996). Synergy will occur under the assumption that the existing customer base will continue to patronize the new entity or that the new entity will produce a net addition to the customer base. Economies of scope imply the ability of a bank to produce a broader range of outputs from a given set of inputs (Kolari & Zardkoohi, 1987). When banks merge they can spread the fixed costs associated with technology, operating infrastructure, on-line services and so on, over a broader range of service offerings such as financial advisement, trusts, loan services, and so on. In addition, financial products comprising Certificate of Deposits (CDs), Money Market Deposit Accounts (MMDAs), and Individual Retirement Accounts (IRAs) may be offered as differentiated product lines.

In addition to the economies of scope (scale) motive for mergers and acquisition, there are three other considerations or goals that may influence a decision to integrate with another business entity. These are diversification, horizontal integration, and vertical integration. Diversification occurs when one business entity acquires or merges with another, the latter being involved in a different industry with the resulting entity being sometimes referred to as a "conglomerate" (Cooley, 1988, p. 859). For example, the 1996 acquisition of Life Insurance Co. of Virginia, an insurance business, by General Electric Co., a manufacturing undertaking, is, in effect, a diversified or conglomerate integration (Mergers & Acquisition, 1996). Diversified mergers or acquisition involving banks are not legally allowed under United States law, but combinations between finance related businesses are permitted. For example, the 1998 merger between Citibank, a commercial bank, and Travelers Group, an insurance business, is perhaps the nearest to a diversified integration. A merger between insurance and banking may best be described as an out-market merger, since both types of businesses belong to the finance industry with the product lines being more or less differentiated. Whereas, in-market integration may involve banks along identical or very similar product lines or geographic areas, out-market mergers may involve differentiated markets with related (financial) products.

Horizontal mergers and acquisitions take place between companies in the finance industry and may include both in-market and out-market combinations. Horizontal mergers and acquisitions, in a strict sense, involve firms merging with or acquiring a rival in identical or related markets, the likely end-results being, increased market share and increased market power (Gaughan, 1996). Economic theories suggest that there are two extreme forms of market structures. On one end there is the pure competitive form resting on assumptions such as numerous buyers and sellers, perfect information, homogeneous products and so on.

On the other extreme there is the monopoly form, which rests on the assumptions of being a single seller with the almost unrestricted ability to set a price-output combination that maximizes its profits. Horizontal integration involves a movement from the purely competitive end of the spectrum to the monopoly form at the other end. Along the way, however, may be found other differentiated market structures such as monopolistic competition (many firms with differentiated product lines), oligopoly (only a few firms), and duopoly (only two firms). Figure 1 depicts a continuum line of a hypothetical industry that can move from the so-called purely competitive market form, comprising of a huge number of firms, to a monopoly situation comprising of only a single seller.

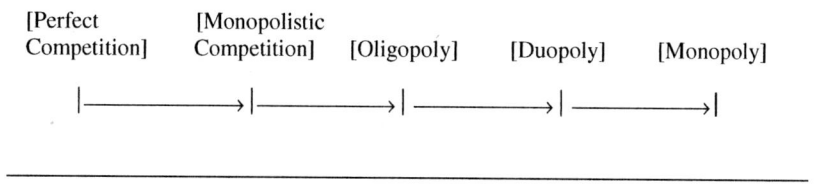

[Perfect   [Monopolistic
Competition]   Competition]   [Oligopoly]   [Duopoly]   [Monopoly]

|——————→|——————→|——————→|——————→|

Figure 2.1. Market concentration continuum.

One of the major problems with mergers leading towards the monopoly end of the spectrum is that monopolies can cost society. Economic theories suggest that activities such as mergers and acquisition can result in dead weight or welfare loss, that is, losses involving both consumer and producer surpluses. The basis for such dead weight or welfare losses hinges on the fact that the monopoly situation ultimately leads to higher price and lower industrial output and possibly greater profits for the single seller. Whether the banking industry within the United States will move closer to even an oligopoly situation is anyone's guess. However, there is a tendency for the number of banks that are servicing a growing United States market to be on the decline.

In the 1990s shrinkage in the number of commercial banks was mainly due to the dynamic nature of a competitive environment (Spiegel, Gart, & Gart, 1996), changes in the legal and operating frameworks (Johnson, 1995), and transformation within the global, economic, and capital markets (Allen, 1997). In 1980 there were some 14,400 commercial banks, while in 1990 that number was reduced to 12, 250. By 1997 the number of independent commercial banks operating was approximately 9,360 (U.S. Bureau of Census, 1998). According to

Johnson (1995), the shrinkage is likely to continue rapidly and may flatten out when the number reaches approximately 5,000 commercial banks.

The movement around merger and acquisition activities reveals an interesting pattern of behavior with respect to assets size. Taking the categorization of banks as proposed by financial information expert, SNL Securities LC which categorizes large banks as those banks with assets of $1 billion to $5 billion and medium-size banks as those with less than $1 billion, this study will consider megabanks as banks with assets of $5 billion or more. Data available for the period 1990 to 1995 reveal that there were some 71 mergers and acquisitions in the $1 billion to $5 billion asset category which constitute approximately 17% of banks from that group. In the megabank category, in which case assets are in excess of $5 billion, mergers and acquisitions involved some 68 banks or approximately 18% of all banks within that group (SNL Securities LC, 1998). However, by 1997 the number of banks involved in mergers and acquisitions in the megabank category was very much close to 80 (Mergerstat Review, 1997, 1998).

Two important effects originated from the changes to Regulation Q that took place during the 1980s and paved the way for the favorable economic climate in the banking industry, inclusive of the merger and acquisition impetus, for the period under review (Johnson & Johnson, 1989). First, banks could compete for deposits among themselves and other quasi-banks and related financial institutions. Second, the changes allowed banks to counter the disintermediation problem, which manifested itself in situations where consumers withdrew cash deposits from banks and invested these funds directly in various financial products, thereby attracting higher returns on their investments.

Regulation Q, however, facilitated the disintermediation problem faced by banks while simultaneously setting the ceiling on interest that banks can pay on liabilities such as demand deposits, negotiated order of withdrawals, checking accounts, and other similar bank liabilities. The repeal of Regulation Q was a necessary condition for the banking industry to seriously afford the luxury of growth and value maximizations that can be generated directly from bank mergers and acquisitions.

The period covered by this study was also characterized by low interest rates, given that the Federal Reserve Board continuously monitored these rates and took action by way of moral suasion and direct intervention in order to prevent the interest rates from escalating too rapidly (Allen, 1997). Given that the caps on interests paid to various types of deposits had been removed, the funds placed in banks were more rate-sensitive. One of the main funds management techniques attributed to banks was the ability to maximize the gap between interest income on assets and interest expense on liabilities. A bank sought to maximize its total income by carefully managing and periodically adjusting its mix of assets and liabilities based upon speculation of the interest rate movements (Hatler, 1991).

Banks that possessed the capabilities to anticipate interest rate movements and manage interest rate gaps in a timely manner experienced higher profitability ratios and abnormal stock returns. It is no surprise, therefore, that the decade of the 1990s provided most commercial banks with safe operating margins and relatively high returns on equities (Johnson, 1995; Allen, 1997).

Statistics compiled by the United States Bureau of Census revealed that the net income of commercial banks moved from a low of $14 billion in 1980 to a moderate $16 billion 10 years later (U.S. Bureau of the Census, 1996). By 1995 net income had grown to a massive $49 billion, attesting to the fact that the first half of the 1990s was an economically fertile period for commercial banks. In addition to very favorable economic returns, the build-up of capital impacted the returns on equity as the capital to asset ratio continued to improve. Capital to asset ratio strengthened from 5.8% in 1980 to 6.5% in 1990 and to 8.1% in 1995. This ratio continued to climb and in so doing increased to 8.2% in 1996 and 8.3% for the year 1997 (U.S. Bureau of the Census, 1998). The progression in capital strength tended to suggest that banks may seek to either increase dividend pay outs, initiate stock buybacks in order to increase balance sheet leveraging, or explore opportunities for consolidation through mergers and acquisitions (Johnson, 1995). Bank consolidation may be a preferred choice for many banks based on the assumptions that synergy and greater market share may be the end results (Spiegel & Gart, 1996). Banks with limited balance sheet leveraging ability opted for either protecting their market share, finding a suitable partner to merge with or sell to the highest bidder. In many cases selling to the highest bidder may be the best or only option facing some banks.

A cursory look into the future for the banking industry tends to suggest three major influencing factors that will determine to what extent banks, as a whole, will overcome the daunting challenges that lay ahead in the new millennium. First, as previously indicated, mergers and acquisition, especially among the very large banks, will be one way for banks to stay competitive and boost shareholders' value in the new millennium. The integration of previous arch-competitors in the financial market into a single organizational entity will precipitate the need for a new breed of managers to address cultural differentiation issues and "old organizational" ties among long established working friends and colleagues.

Second, non-bank competitors will increasingly become "fierce invaders" into the traditional core marketing areas for banks (Allen, 1997, p. 210). The search for scale or scope may best be achieved, as this study has sought to show, through in-market integration. But banks may seek to merge with non-banking entities in related financial fields and hence, such "out-market" mergers and acquisitions may seem attractive and plausible as well, as is evident by the 1998 merger of Citibank, a commercial bank, with Travelers Group, an insurance business. The eventual success of the Citibank-Travelers merger suggests that out-market mergers and acquisitions could be attractive investments for speculators, in a market that embraces merger and acquisition activities.

A final influencing factor that will shape the future of the banking industry is the posting of transactions of a bank's clientele to the general ledger in real time. Real-time general ledger postings imply the instantaneous processing of a customer's transaction whereby the customer sees the debits, credits, and other transactional activities in his bank accounts within moments. Bringing this real-time processing to fruition will be the whole new area of banking facilitated by uses of the Internet. Internet banking is increasingly becoming the way of doing business, especially for the very large banks that are seeking to serve an expanding group of curious Internet users, who seem quite ready to accept the challenges of cyberspace. This idea of virtual banking suggests that transactions between the customers and their banks occur in real time (Senior, 1999). Integrating on-line banking with a back-end computerized systems and Internet-ready databases are necessary cutting-edge investments in the technology of the future for the banking industry. Therefore, given the desire to stay competitive and to more effectively service the increasing demands of the computer-savvy banking customers, banks cannot afford the luxury of staying outside the web of electronic banking without paying the price of a declining market share

Purpose of the Study

Mergers and acquisitions in the banking industry have increased significantly in recent years perhaps due to the positive influence of interstate banking, the threat posed by thrift organizations and other quasi-financial intermediaries, and the relaxing of Regulation Q as indicated in the preceding section. Regulation Q refers to the federal regulation that sought to regulate interest rates on bank liabilities such as customers' demand deposit accounts, checking facilities, negotiated order of withdrawal accounts, and so on. The issues relating to bank mergers and acquisitions have, in recent years, attracted the attention of many scholar-practitioners, bankers, community activists, bank regulators and researchers (Allen, 1997; Eckert, 1997; Spiegel & Gart, 1996; Spiegel, Gart, & Gart, 1996). A major thrust of this research effort is to examine the impact of the anticipated, actual, and post announcements of mergers and acquisitions and the subsequent stock market responses to the stocks of the pre- and post-merger activities involving relatively large in-market commercial banks within the United States. In effect, this research isolated and examined those big bank mergers and acquisitions, that is, banks where the acquirers and the acquirees both have assets in excess of $5 billion prior to their consolidations with respect to stock market responses resulting from decisions to integrate.

Subsequent to the examination of those large in-market banks referred to in the preceding paragraph and using specific metrics, mainly the abnormal return on stock prices, a most economically successful consolidated banking entity can be identified for a further in-depth analysis. Exploiting the uses of the research paradigms advocated by Miles and Huberman (1994) and Yin (1993, 1994), a qualitative quasi-deductive analysis can further be conducted on that model of an economically successful bank. Factors such as organizational behavior and change, leadership, training, valuing, and managing diversity, corporate citizenship, and technology may be considered as part of an in-depth analysis. In essence, a case study approach can be followed for any further in-depth analysis utilizing a variety of qualitative quasi-deductive evidence such as direct observation, systematic interviewing, and the examination and interpretation of documents, accounting data, and other artifacts.

The inclusion of any aspects of a qualitative quasi-deductive paradigm is contingent upon the results of the analysis emanating from this study, which essentially is based on a quantitative paradigm. For example, assuming that it became reasonably clear that one particular megabank merger is a tremendous economic success relative to the other mergers in this study, then it may be preferable for further clarity, completeness, and the overcoming of elements of abstraction typical of quantitative methodological approaches, to examine particular activities and events (Miles & Huberman, 1994). In order to test a conjecture advanced by Allen (1997) concerning the above normal economic successes of in-market big bank mergers and acquisitions, in recent years researchers, banking professionals, and other interested parties may seek to test the proposition that in-market megabank mergers and acquisitions among commercial banks attract abnormal gains in their stock prices. This research effort in this book has accepted the challenge to test for megabanks' economic successes in mergers and acquisitions.

Flowing out of the purpose identified above, this study in this book has sought to fill a void left vacant by researchers in the area of megabank consolidations. It will be shown that some mergers and acquisitions are more successful than others within the group of large commercial banks with assets of $5 billion or more. Complementary research in the area of big bank mergers and acquisitions including the question of size between acquirers and acquirees generally have sought to compare the economic performances of equity prices for chronological dates on either side of given merger or acquisition announcements (Allen, 1997; Peristiani, 1997; Rhoades, 1993). None of these studies, however, sought to specifically examine in-market megabank mergers and acquisitions for the period 1990 to

1997, nor do any of the researchers of these studies sought to extensively examine merger or acquisition activities for given individual megabanks.

The studies that came closest in seeking to test financial relationships associated with bank mergers and acquisitions were Cheng, Gup, & Wall (1989), Eckert (1997), Rhoades (1987, 1993) and Spiegel, Gart, & Gart (1996). Gary M. Eckert studied interstate bank mergers and acquisitions that took place between 1988 and 1995 and involved only some 33 banks, where the merger transaction involved $0.1 billion or more. Cheng, Gup, and Wall concentrated heavily only on the acquirers' perspectives, while Rhoades (1987) focused on managerial and market characteristics and Rhoades (1993) looked at shareholders' value creation. Only Spiegel, Gart, and Gart qualitatively examined the actual merger and acquisition activities among selected banks. However, none of the studies on bank mergers and acquisitions, after having identified a very successful bank merger by whatever measure used, sought to do a qualitative inductive or a qualitative quasi-deductive analysis of a successful megabank merger. While there are many advantages in averaging techniques, grounded subtle qualitative details are relegated to mere obscurity. Future researchers may want to take up the observation made by Ruback (1983) which essentially suggests that the merger and acquisition literature is short on studies involving a detailed examination of stock market responses to individual mergers and acquisitions.

The work of Spiegel and Gart (1996) endeavored to predict the future trend of merger and acquisition activities among banks. These researchers merely speculated on factors that seemed to have been driving the bank merger and acquisition activities, especially during the decade of the 1990s, and predicted that most bank consolidation will take place around adjacent- and in-market mergers. None of the studies, after isolating a most successful merger, did an in-depth analysis of the factors that were most likely responsible for the success of a newly emerged entity. In other words, quantitatively identifying an economically successful bank merger and qualitatively analyzing the behavioral, organizational, and technological aspects may lend valuable qualitative inductive evidence for future research endeavors.

The quantitative design of this study, as opposed to one that is qualitative, did not specifically lend itself to a greater insight into factors that are likely to positively influence successful mergers and acquisitions among huge banks. This researcher carefully examined the idea of introducing qualitative evidence as possible explanation as to why some mergers and acquisitions among megabanks succeeded. However, this researcher took a position that the introduction of evidence of such an explanatory nature was outside the intended purpose of this study. Ruback (1983), who made the comment that the mergers and acquisitions literature is short on the case study method of inquiry, is a very instructive observation for future research initiatives. Such research initiatives could employ the techniques of a qualitative inductive or a qualitative quasi-deductive research paradigm. In any event, a case study approach will facilitate a more indepth analysis of given mergers and acquisitions employing evidence of a primary nature such as systematic observations, interviews, physical artifacts, and so on.

Future researchers may want to concentrate on the associated negative factors that militates against successful big bank mergers and acquisitions. This researcher is aware of the conceptual foundation for plausible rival explanations (Miles & Huberman, 1994) of an underlying research phenomenon that may seem antithetical, but yet can be visualized from a wider and competing dialectical framework (Kincaid, 1996). Therefore, inductively analyzing the apparent success factors of an identified successful consolidated entity is the analytical equivalence of an inductive examination of the apparent factors that may be associated with less-successful or failed bank consolidations. This researcher has sought to focus on a more positive approach, despite the fact that successful and unsuccessful factors are not dichotomous viewpoints, but symmetrical in the explanation of any underlying research question.

Given that this research assumed a theoretical proposition that the negative and positive factors are two sides of an identical phenomenon, future research endeavors may choose to gravitate towards the other end of the continuum. It follows that such an initiative will seek to examine those factors that can be associated with the failure of commercial and thrift megabank mergers and acquisitions. Both sides of a continuum of negative and positive factors, will therefore, complement each other and will positively impact the research field of bank mergers and acquisitions. In so doing, this study did not lay any claim to an explanation of why some large bank mergers and acquisitions fail and why others succeed. In any event, this study sought to focus on factors that may have positively influenced the model for economic success of commercial and thrift megabanks in merger and acquisition activities. As a result, this study has sought to identify and measure key independent variables in identifiable successful megabank mergers and acquisitions that can correlate with the dependent variable, that is, abnormal returns on equity pricing in financial markets.

The methodology and findings may be useful to other researchers, banking professionals, bank regulators, and the general public. The methodology, which is grounded in event study methodology made popular by Brown and Warner (1980) and conventional statistical correlation and regression analyses, can be replicated for reliability. This study, while adding to the existing stock of knowledge in the area of bank mergers and acquisitions, may challenge other researchers, scholar-practitioners, bankers, and others to delve deeper into this growing phenomenon of mergers and acquisitions in the banking industry.

Theoretical Framework

The fluctuating price trend for stocks in the stock market may be due to factors other than the expected or realized variations in earnings or dividend pay out (Gaughan, 1996). There is an accepted reality that at any given moment in time some stocks in a stock market may be overpriced, while simultaneously, others may be underpriced. In fact stock traders know that in a bear market certain stocks may be undervalued, while the opposite holds true in a bull market. Prudence in money management, according to Patrick A. Gaughan, suggests that a rational investor may not want to sell an undervalued stock in a bear market given that there is speculation surrounding the premium of the given stock. Similarly, an investor may not want to purchase an overpriced stock in a bull market under the assumption that there is speculation that the price of the given stock may move downwards.

The average shareholder of a corporation is likely to view dividend pay out as an important indicator for acquiring and holding a stock. The merger analyst, however, may be more interested in cash flows and earnings of a target firm and the resulting consolidation (Gaughan, 1996). The dividend flows may influence the market price of a stock and not necessarily the price that an acquirer may be willing to pay to consolidate with another company. To the acquiring firm, free cash flows may be a better indicator of firms that are likely to involve in merger activities (Damodaran, 1997). Acquirers go after businesses that show relatively high free cash flows and acquiring firms with relatively high free cash flows themselves are targets of mergers and acquisitions (Cooley & Roden 1988; Hanson, 1992). Robert Hanson found a positive correlation between high cash flows, merger, and acquisition activities and abnormal rates of return for the underlying stocks.

Based on the assumption that a merger or an acquisition is an event with speculative tendencies, speculation takes the form of certain market signals that may influence the prices for the stocks of the parties to a consolidation. These signals give information to the event itself and may involve latent information such as leaks, insider trading or speculation about the pending merger itself (Gaughan, 1996). The expected benefits to be derived from the combine operations are the incremental cash flows that may be generated from the combined operations of previously independent entities.

There are two classes of merger and acquisition theories. One is the non-value maximizing behavior, where the organizations seek to maximize growth in sales, assets or market shares. This non-value maximization theory is more frequently associated with conglomerate mergers (Halpern, 1983). Conglomerate mergers are the equivalence of what is referred to elsewhere in this study as out-market consolidations and may involve different firms in different lines of business and markets

(Gaughan, 1996). Generally the motives for growth maximization are greater market power, hubris, monopolistic tendencies, and geographic diversification.

Greater market power is a desirable and acceptable motive up to a point where the market has become so concentrated that only a few firms control a very high percentage of the entire market (Mishkin, 1995). For example, a market may be considered highly concentrated where four or less firms control at least 75% of the total market in which they operate. The announced intentions of two or more firms to form a single entity may induce objections from bank regulators, other players in the given industry, and the public at large mainly on the grounds that the market may become too anticompetitive (Gaughan, 1996).

The hubris motive or hubris hypothesis, which was popularized by Richard Roll (1986), holds that the leaders of a proposed merger and acquisition may be motivated mainly by their own personal aggrandizement. Monopolistic orientation implies that the firm may earn economic rent by having some ability to set the price of given products at above the equation of marginal revenue and marginal cost, the competitive and societal preferred equilibrium. Setting a price higher than the normal competitive situation implies that price per output is relatively higher coupled with a lower quantity supplied to the market. The end result of such monopolistic tendencies will be that there are societal losses comprising both consumer and producer surpluses (Gaughan, 1996). Geographic diversification is a popular motive for bank consolidators in that the latter seek to acquire an operating interest in another geographical area.

The other class of merger and acquisition theories falls under value-maximization and generally holds that the consolidation of two or more organizations should be measured in the same way and using the same criteria as that which are configured in other investment functions (Halpern, 1983). Value-maximization is built on theoretical constructs such as synergy, economic returns and diversification, which to the banking industry may be captured by the term "economies of scope" (Kolari & Zardkoohi, 1987, pp. 97-98). Some major motives considered under this theory are economies of scale, efficiency in management, revenue enhancement, economies of scope, and reengineering.

Economies of scale derived from mergers and acquisitions are best described by the term synergy (Gaughan, 1996; Halpern, 1983). The economies of scale motive rests upon the presupposition that as the business expands unit costs per unit of output decline. Increases in output suggest the spreading of overhead expenses, deeper specialization, and more efficient utilization of systems and equipment. Efficiency in management is built on the assumption that the acquirer's management practices are more cost effective than the acquiree's managerial expertise. The motive here will be to "buy out" the acquiree's managerial personnel (Eckert, 1997, p. 22).

The revenue enhancement motive is a vital motive for merger and acquisition activities in that there is a fundamental assumption in the opportunity for increased shareholders' wealth via higher dividend pay out and stock appreciation will be the end result (Eckert, 1997; Spiegel, Gart, & Gart, 1996). Operationally, the new entity is expected to reduce capital costs, increase revenue and stabilize the stream of cash flows. Economies of scope dictate that a bank may utilize a given set of inputs to produce a more diversified range of services thereby lowering long run average costs (Kolari & Zardkoohi, 1987). Inputs such as administration of trust agreements, loan servicing and computerization technology can be diversified to cover a broader range of services. The reengineering motive suggests that the status quo of the past needs to be critically examined in the light of a dynamic and novel social, technological and managerial environment (Allen, 1997). The reengineering initiative implies that a fundamental restructuring and redesigning of the entire process will be undertaken to attain strategically specified objectives. Most of these motives are translated into hypotheses and will be further examined in the Literature Review chapter of this study.

The theoretical justification for a merger or acquisition, in purely economic terms, is built on a probability that the economic returns emanating from two or more entities operating as a single unit are greater than the economic returns from the given two or more entities operating as separate individual undertakings (Cooley & Roden, 1988; Gaughan, 1996). Alternatively, it may be said that the theoretical impetus in value maximization is nested in the assumption of the synergistic effects. Therefore, a researcher may conclude that the net effect of a merger or acquisition is the combined present value of the new entity measured against the present values of the pre- integration partners operating as independent units. For synergy to occur, one would expect that the post integration value creation would be greater than the pre-integration sum of the individual value creations. Symbolically one may write:

$$PV_{a+b} < PV_a + PV_b + PV_s$$

where PV_{a+b} = the sum of the present values of the acquirer's the acquiree's incremental cash flows as separate entities.

PV_a = the present value of the acquier's cash flows

PV_b = the present value of the acquiree's cash flows

PV_s = the present value attributable to the synergistic effects.

Therefore, in order to gain an economic benefit the anticipated present value of $PVs > 0$ where, in such a relationship ">" is taken to imply "must be greater than."

Valuation of the acquiree's financial worth is a major activity in the process of an acquirer seeking to integrate with an acquiree. It is the prevailing intent of both parties to agree on a most reasonable value (Damodaran, 1994). There are three major factors that may be considered in the valuation process. First, there is the consideration of the combine value of the integrated entities being greater that the sum of the individual values in isolation (synergy), which will always be a crucial factor in valuing the economic worth to be derived from integration. An acquiree that appears to be undervalued in an equity market will be a target for a potential bidding war by interested acquirers, who possess the industrial intelligence to forecast such an aberration in value.

Second, the advent of restructuring the newly integrated entities will result in added value brought on by superior managerial expertise supplied by the acquirer. Thus, it is likely to have added value through the process of restructuring the integrated entities in the post acquisition period (Allen, 1997). Note, however, that economic theory postulates that any increase in value brought on by greater managerial efficiency is almost always contingent upon situations where firms are operating below optimum (Damodaran, 1994). Finally, the acquiree may display a tendency to overestimate its true worth, especially where a hostile takeover is looming. The purpose of such an overvaluation is to project to the acquiree shareholders and the potential acquirer that the bid price should be re-valued upwards. However, in friendly mergers such as in mergers of equals both acquirers and acquirees tend to project to the public at large, including their own group of shareholders respectively, that the buying and selling activities are at a fair price.

There are two major dependent variables that are most prevalent in the theoretical framework indicative of scholarly research into bank mergers and acquisitions. These are the merger premium as a relation with book value and the abnormal return resulting from movements in stock prices. Merger premium, a measure of purchase price to book value, is the banking industry's standard for evaluating the financial transaction involving mergers and acquisitions (Cheng, Gup, & Wall, 1989; Cooley & Roden, 1988; Rhoades, 1987;). However, there seems to be a controversy in the denominator. For example, Rhoades and Cheng, Gup, and Wall suggest that premium, as a ratio, is based on book value whereas Cooley and Roden indicate that market value should be the common denominator. Mainstream wisdom in the refereed finance and economics journals seems to be following the book value approach, a wisdom that is favored in this study. However, for further clarity and reliability, other approaches will be considered when testing the hypothesis related to acquisition premiums.

The other major dependent variable in the study of bank mergers and acquisitions is abnormal stock return, which measures the difference between a given stock's "*ex post* return and that which is predicted under the assumed income-generating process" (Brown & Warner, 1980, p. 207). The wealth-maximizing hypothesis suggests that, abnormal returns on particular stock prices directly related to the underlying parties in a given merger or acquisition, should be realized around the period of speculation or actual announcement of the intended banks' merger or acquisition (Pilotte, 1989). This dependent variable therefore, could be positive, negative or zero. Zero or close to zero, as one would expect, implies a level of statistical insignificance.

This study sought to follow earlier works that have examined bank mergers and acquisitions with respect to the potential value maximization on the part of the acquirer (Carow & Larsen, 1997; Eckert, 1997; Rhoades, 1983; Sirower, 1997; Spiegel & Gart, 1996;). However, Sirower conjectured that size of the acquiree relative to the size of the acquirer will have a tremendous impact on the ensuing performance of the new entity and that larger acquisitions require greater savings through synergy. Sirower added that the emergence of the synergistic effects must occur within a relatively short period of time. That researcher concluded that the relative size of the acquiree, in terms of the acquirer, might negatively impact the acquisition premium.

Mergers and acquisitions across all industries have been studied extensively (Jensen & Ruback, 1983). Studies of mergers and acquisitions among commercial banks have not been accorded a fair portion of research attention relative to other industries (Allen, 1997; Sirower, 1997). However, in recent years a good deal of attention is directed towards the study of bank mergers and acquisitions (Spiegel & Gart, 1996; Spiegel, Gart, & Gart, 1996). More particularly, the question of size of both acquirers and acquirees is resurfacing as a contentious issue in the study of bank mergers and acquisitions (Houston & Ryngaert, 1994; Sirower, 1997). In essence, some research issues pertaining to bank mergers and acquisitions are quite settled. It is fairly well established that the acquiree shareholders obtain significant abnormal returns on their stock prices (Jensen & Ruback, 1983; Trifts & Scanlon, 1987). It is also fairly well established that the relative size of the acquiree, in terms of the acquirer, must be substantially smaller thereby rendering the former as a neutral influencing force on the latter (Sirower, 1997). However, this study is postulating that the size differentials of the acquirees have attracted varying purchase price premiums.

Research Problem

What seems to be an unsettled question among researchers in the mergers and acquisitions field of study is the question of abnormal returns to the stockholders of the acquiring firms. The literature review will show the conflicting evidence on the economic performances of the stocks held by the acquiring banks' shareholders. Another issue that is unsettled is the question of large acquirers acquiring or merging with other large banks. It is more so in such situations that some bank experts refer to these megabank mergers as "merger of equals" (Spiegel, Gart, & Gart, 1996, p. 65). The problem of large banks acquiring other large banks is a contentious issue among researchers, especially in reference to economic returns on equities for both acquirees and acquirers. In other words, a final unsettled research question that this researcher is interested in, is to examine the relationship between acquisition premium paid by large banks to acquire the assets of other large banks compared to the premium paid for smaller banks.

Ruback (1982, 1983) persuasively argued that the research literature is indeed short on utilizing the qualitative research paradigm pertaining to the study of mergers and acquisitions. Depending upon the findings that emanate from employing the quantitative paradigm to this study, it may be necessary to employ some aspects of a qualitative quasi-deductive paradigm to supplement a further understanding of the factors that bring about change following the merger of an economically successful "merger of equals" megabank. It may be necessary to employ a further in-depth analysis into the merger involving two of the largest bank in the United States as a model of economic success, for the theories proposed in this study, by interviewing key players and documenting systematic observations by this researcher. To that end, this research sought to analyze whether mergers of equals are likely to produce abnormal shareholders wealth and in so doing has endeavored to generalize to the theory of in-market megabank mergers and acquisitions and abnormal returns.

Specific Research Questions

Between the years 1990 to 1997 over 3000 mergers and acquisitions have took place in the banking industry, which comprised only about 6% of all banks (Allen, 1997; U.S. Bureau of Census, 1998). Out of those involved in some form of merger and acquisition activities approximately 30% were banks involving assets of $1 billion or more. In this study, a megabank is a commercial bank or a thrift institution with assets of $5 billion or more. In addition, both acquirer and acquirees must essentially be in the same line of business to fall under the rubric of "in-market" merger. Therefore, to be considered an in-market merger both the acquirer and the acquiree must be holding assets of at least $5 billion or more.

The Questions

The study in this book pointedly addressed the following questions:

1. For the period under review and the megabanks identified in this study the question is whether there are significant abnormal returns to be realized in the stocks held by acquirer shareholders around the official announcement date of the merger or acquisition. In other words, did the mergers or acquisitions for the group of banks identified in this study increased shareholders wealth for the acquirer and if so, did the gains continue in the post merger or acquisition period following the announcement date? The purpose and relevance of this question is based on the fact that according to previous studies (Jensen & Ruback, 1983; Sirower, 1997; Trifts & Scanlon, 1987), the acquiree shareholders attract abnormal stock returns whereas, the acquirer shareholders earn zero or negative returns. However, as was stated previously, the question of abnormal returns realized by acquiree shareholders is a fairly well settled area of inquiry. Therefore, this study proposes to test the question of shareholders' value creation for acquiring firms (acquirers) that may result from a decision to merge with or acquire another megabank.

2. This study sought to address the situation that, given the presence of an overwhelming set of evidence in the mergers and acquisitions literature supporting the theory that acquirees do realize abnormal gains around the official announcement date and where acquirers are usually over three times larger than acquirees, whether and to what extent mergers of equals among megabanks result in higher returns for those mergers and acquisitions that integrate on a merger of equals basis.

   > The rationale inherent in this question is that resources allocated for a merger or acquisition has an opportunity cost that may have to be factored into the model for analysis. The implication is that the larger the acquiree, in relation to the acquirer, the greater the opportunity cost to be met through synergy. Therefore, when large banks acquire other large banks the potential for value destruction is greater. Higson and Elliott (1998), in a post acquisition study of 100 large British firms, did not find abnormal returns greater than zero for 1 to 36 months. In that study, the large acquisitions were those situations where the acquirees were at least one quarter the size of their acquirer. The question relating to merger of equals will be such that the acquiree and the acquirer will each be holding assets of at least $5 billion on the announcement date of

the given merger or acquisition. In addition, both parties will come to a tacit understanding that they will enter the integration on a more or less equal basis. Thus, irrespective of who acquired who, the intent is that the parties "will come together as partners" (Wendel, 1996, p. 258).

3. This study has also addressed a third and final question as to whether or not megabanks attract higher acquisition premiums than smaller banks for those merger and acquisitions in the period covered by this study. In other words, price trailing four quarter earnings as measured by the Last Twelve Months Earnings per share (LTM Eps) the question is, whether large banks, with their lower relative levels of increasing returns to scale, will attract higher acquisition premiums vis-a-vis the relatively smaller banks. A similar result may be obtained using price to market value at around the merger or acquisition period relative to premium payments.

The purpose of this question is to test whether there is reliable evidence to support a theory put forward by Sirower (1997) that smaller acquirees relative to the acquirers have a greater probability for the realization of an economically successful merger than mergers or acquisitions involving relatively large acquirees. The rationale here is that acquirers may be paying relatively higher premiums to induce relatively larger acquirees to sell to the highest bidder.

Hypotheses to be Tested

For purposes of this study, a stock return is abnormal over a given period of time when such a return deviates from the expected return as reflected through a comparable market indicator, which monitors the price behavior of the equities for both acquirees and acquirers. Assuming that a positive sign prefixes the calculated abnormal return, then the return is positively abnormal. On the other hand, if a negative sign prefixes the calculated value, then the return is negatively abnormal. Resulting from the questions identified and rationalized in the preceding section, this study proposed to test the following three hypotheses:

H1: The shareholders of acquiring megabanks involved in in-market mergers and acquisitions realize negative abnormal returns on their stock prices around the official announcement date of the merger or acquisition.

Rationale: Using the announcement date of the merger or acquisition as the independent variable, the movement in the prices of the stocks of both acquirers and acquirees was tracked and measured. The theoretical constructs of merger announcements, absolute stock price changes and abnormal stock returns were operationalized and quantified using the standard market model of analysis commonly used in capital asset pricing theories (Dodd, 1980). Assuming that a merger or acquisition announcement is anticipated to increase cash flows, decrease cash outflows or a combination of both for given consolidating entities, then this speculation should be reflected in positive abnormal stock returns.

H2: In megabank mergers and acquisitions acquirees' shareholders realize abnormal or excess returns significantly greater than acquirers' shareholders around the announcement date for mergers and acquisitions that signal the intention to integrate with each other on the basis of merger of equals. In other words, this hypothesis proposed to test the extent to which abnormal returns, the dependent variable was influenced by, citeris paribus, an independent variable referred to as *merger of equals*. For purposes of this hypothesis, merger of equals is an ex post facto strategy used by an organization that acquires another, where the former seeks to generate a perception of equality and inclusiveness with the latter.

Rationale: Consistent with previous studies, this hypothesis predicts that the acquirees shareholders will realize excess returns consistently over the measurement period (Eckert, 1997). Eckert found that size of acquirees in bank mergers and acquisitions consistently impacted acquisition premium over the entire measurement period, 1988 to 1995). Size of the acquirer was found to impact acquisition premium only for the years excluding 1992 to 1995. Eckert did not attempt to test relative size of acquiree to acquirer nor was an attempt made at hypothesizing "merger of equals" and "abnormal stock returns."

H3: The acquirees or target megabanks attract higher merger or acquisition premiums than relatively smaller target banks for the period covered by the study. More specifically, this hypothesis states that the larger the bank the higher the relative price that bidders are willing to pay as an inducement for the target banks to sell and be acquired.

Rationale: The premium paid in relation to book value is the modal standard against which the purchase price of acquiring the assets of a bank is measured (Cooley & Roden, 1988; Rhoades, 1987). Under the assumption that the acquirers expect growth or value enhancements in the merger or acquisition, there should be a positive relationship between the premium paid on stocks and abnormal stock market returns for the given stocks. A possible explanation for the power or hubris motive behind the merging with or acquiring another bank may rest upon whether or not the null hypothesis (H_o) can be accepted. Accepting the null hypothesis can possibly explain the hubris motive or some other nonvalue maximizing tendencies for the given consolidation of two or more banks. However, such additional explanations are beyond the scope of this study.

Significance of the Study

This study was done at a period in the development of the banking industry when the issues of merger and acquisition, especially among those huge megabanks, took on a new dimension. In the first place, the reform of the United States legal framework made it possible for bank mergers across different countries, states lines, and cities limits to merge. Secondly, a merger involving non-banking financial entities was prohibited by law prior to the 1990s. Finally, facilitated by the preceding two adjustments in the banking industry, mergers and acquisitions among the very large banks that were once viewed as accomplices of antitrust violations, were being actively pursued as ways to rapidly increase market share and growth in revenue through the synergistic components. In the light of these recent developments, bank mergers and acquisitions have attracted unparalleled attention by researchers, banking professionals, and bank regulators.

The significance of this study is to augment the increasing intellectual attention given to the current debate on bank mergers and acquisition in general and specifically, to the merging of the very large banks or the acquisition of one big bank by another. Second, this study sought to fill a void left by other researchers into the field of bank mergers and acquisitions by comparing the premium paid for large versus small acquirees. Third, this study sought to illuminate the concept of "merger of equals" and attempted to track the economic successes relating to such a concept from an operational standpoint, in the post merger or acquisition period.

Fourth, the significance of this study is to provide a basis for confirming or not supporting prior research efforts in the area of bank mergers and acquisitions in the inconclusive question pertaining to acquirers' abnormal stock returns around the official announcement dates of the mergers and acquisition involving megabanks. Consequently, other researchers may want to replicate this study which, inter alia, may bring further validity and reliability to this research effort. Fifth, since this study has seeks to address factors that are most likely associated with an economically successful in-market megabank merger, the existing stock of knowledge in the area of bank mergers and acquisitions will be enhanced. Finally, banking professionals, lawmakers, bank regulators, investors, civic associations, and consumers at large may view the findings of this study as being advantageous in solving problems in their respective situations.

Assumptions and Limitations of the Study

The results of the study were subjected to the following assumptions and limitations.

1. The conclusions derived from the various measures are valid and reliable to the extent the theoretical constructs and conceptual framework are intended to include only the within-size categories of banks within the United States for the period 1990 to 1997. The period 1990 to 1997 witnessed some major changes in bank legislation, technology, and general growth trend that have influenced the banking industry one way or the other. Therefore, this period may be unique in the historical development of the banking industry within the United States.

2. Despite this uniqueness, acceptable predictions can be made within an acceptable statistical level of confidence concerning possible future merger or acquisition activities of in-market megabanks.

3. Megabanks are those banks inclusive of thrifts, where the acquirer and the acquiree would, on the day of the official merger announcement, have had assets of $5 billion or more and would have belonged to the market category as identified by the size of their assets. An appropriate Standard Classification Code (SIC), as allocated by federal regulators in the United States, was also used to ensure that the financial institutions were within the limits of the population covered by this study.

4. The variables identified and used in the study are not the only variables that demonstrate success or failure of a decision to consolidate or not to consolidate in the banking industry. Other variables such as free cash flows, profitability ratios, and price to market value may also be used to test the value and growth motive of bank mergers and acquisitions. Other researchers in the study of bank mergers and acquisitions most frequently use the proposed variables emphasized in this study to establish their theoretical framework.

5. The results of the study are applicable only to the body of information derived from the period covered by the study and the within-group category, that is, the years 1990 to 1997 and commercial banks and thrifts with assets of $5 billion or more.

6. A qualitative quasi-deductive paradigm grounded in the social, environmental, and organizational factors that seem to be responsible for a single unit of analysis as a successful merger or acquisition could be a useful follow-up study. Such a follow-up study is particularly necessary especially in cases where two big banks signal their intentions to integrate on an equal-basis' psy-

chology. The most plausible reason being that in such situations both acquirees and acquirers realize better than average abnormal returns around the official announcement dates. In other words, very little emphasis will be placed on factors that may have given rise to unsuccessful or failed consolidated initiative vis-à-vis successful endeavors in the area of bank mergers and acquisitions. This researcher is very much aware of the probability of plausible rival explanations in a wider competing dialectical framework. It is left to other researchers to examine the other end of the analytical continuum, that is, identify and test factors that may be responsible for the economic failures and successes of megabank mergers and acquisitions.

Outline of the Study

This study sought to introduce a background to the problem showing some of the contemporary issues surrounding bank mergers and acquisitions and included questions that were addressed, research variables that were considered and theoretical constructs, hypotheses, assumptions and limitations, and significance of the study. A review of the major scholarly research in mergers and acquisitions, inclusive of their theories and postulates, was undertaken and aimed at a more critical evaluation of the studies covering contemporary bank mergers and acquisitions. Included as a subset in the review of the scholarly literature was a detailed examination of the various research methodologies, postulates and theoretical constructs, types and sources of data, and the general analytical framework exhibited by the various research approaches. This study sought to examine in-market megabank mergers and acquisitions among commercial banks and thrifts within the United States over the given period, 1990 to 1997.

In-market consolidations were chosen for two reasons. First, in-market seems to be the strategy that produces the greater synergy and hence greater economic success. Secondly, in-market seems to be the mode among banks pertaining to bank consolidation in recent years. Surfing the tides of technological innovations and current virtual banking practices have increased the scope for in-market activities to the extent that geographical diversification is a dwindling component in contemporary banking activities. Large banks were the chosen population also for two major reasons. First, mergers among these bigger banks seemed to be an increasing phenomenon within recent years. Second, these bigger banks commanded higher premiums and greater fluctuation in abnormal returns in response their respective merger or acquisition announcements.

Event study methodology has formed a basis for the deductive approach to provide possible solutions to the problems highlighted in this study. Other quantifiable measures utilized are financial ratios such as Price Offered to Book Value and Price Offered to Trailing Four-Quarter Earnings. A qualitative quasi-deductive analysis, though useful for an in-depth look at a quantitatively identified economically successful megabank's merger or acquisition, was not be employed. Based on the design and the data that surfaced for this study, an additional qualitative quasi-deductive framework would have delimited the responsiveness of the theoretical framework to the questions asked in relation to the problems identified for this research. Hence, any in-depth study such as a case study theoretical framework is best left for future research initiatives.

This study concludes with a discussion of the findings and the possible implications of the test results. Questions that arose during the course of this study or questions that have arisen directly as a result of this study are alluded to, with the profound understanding that future research resources may be expended towards a further understanding and possible solution to some of these questions. Most pointedly, further theoretical and conceptual constructs relating to the merger of equals' phenomenon will be a research priority, as more and more arch-competitors integrate on more or less friendly terms.

The question really is, how "equal" could an acquiree be when the acquirer is the party that will take on the brunt of the risk? It follows that, quite often, it is the acquiree who will be threatened with some level of insolvency and therefore, will be anxiously seeking an infusion of new capital from an acquirer. It may be useful to postulate that parties to a "merger of equals" integration will seek to dismiss a negative perception among the acquiree's personnel who may be developing a feeling of inferiority or as victims in a merger deal.

CHAPTER 3

Review of Bank Consolidations: Trends, Theories, and Hypotheses

Speeding towards an accelerated level of mergers and acquisition in the banking industry in recent years the proclaimed target by CEOs was that financial gains through decreasing cost, increased market power, and mitigation of earnings fluctuation would be realized. Evidence from mergers and acquisition in non-banking businesses do suggest that positive value outcomes do not support the assumptions of CEOs especially acquirers. Many banking CEOs have been motivated by view that cost overlap will be reduced tremendously when in-market mergers and acquisitions occur. For example, the Chemical Bank and Manufactures Hanover Trust merger in 1991, which had projected cost savings of $650 million annually, actually saved $750 million over the measurement period. However, the projected annual savings of $1.5 billion from the Chemical-Chase merger of equals did not fully materialized as the banking industry at that time was experiencing decreasing revenues towards the close of the decade of the 1990s. In this chapter, recent trends in bank mergers followed by a review of the major research relating to mergers and acquisition inclusive of theories and methodologies advanced in the research literature will be examined.

Recent Trends in Bank Mergers and Acquisitions

According to the Statistical Abstract of the United States 1996, there were some 14,434 commercial banks in the United States in 1985. Five years later the number of commercial banks dropped to 12,347, a decrease of approximately 14.5%, which amounts to about 2.5% annually. In 1995 this number had shown a decline of 19.5% or approximately 3.9% annually when the number of commercial banks dropped from 12,347 to 9,941 (U.S Bureau of the Census, 1996). The downward trend continued throughout the 1990s and into the new Millennium when the total number of banks reduced to 7,903 in 2002.the extent that the number of banks reduced to 9,528 (U.S. Bureau of the Census, 2003).

The 1990 to 1995 period declined at an average rate of 3.9% compared to an average of almost 4.0% for the period 1995 to 2000.

Clearly there seems to be a momentum of closures and consolidations at an accelerating rate from year to year for the entire period under consideration, 1990 to 1997. The speed of the decline decelerated at the end of the last and the beginning of the new century and when the reduction in the number of banks decreased at an average of 2.29%. As was shown in chapter 1 the spate of mergers and acquisitions slowed somewhat given that economic activities in the United States, as indeed other major countries around the world, entered in to a recessional period. Despite the slowdown, however, Johnson (1995) assertion, that the declining number of banks would bottom out when the number reaches approximately 5,000, still holds.

More current research findings suggest that consolidation among banks occur in spurts or waves (Hanweck & Shull, 1999). After a particular wave or shock a new steady state equilibrium in the bank's population will be attained as endogenously generated driving forces will produce further shocks followed by a short-lived equilibrium, only to be followed by another shock and so on. It follows that simple linear extrapolation should be replaced by a more cyclical and dynamic equilibrium analyses to better explain the movements in the banking population. It seems appreciatively clear that a driving force behind the declining number of banks is consolidation via mergers and acquisitions as these financial entities seek to become more cost-effective in order to boost their bottom-lines.

The merger and acquisition thrusts have move towards larger and larger deals as banks seek to capture wider markets and economies of scale (Allen, 1997; Spiegel & Gart, 1996). The competition for scale has led to the bidding up of the prices for acquiring the stocks of potential acquirees measured in value to book multiples and price/earning ratios. It would appear that some banks are being lured to sell because of the relatively lucrative bank merger market (Johnson, 1995). Historically, banks were closely monitored by responsible federal and state agencies whenever mergers and acquisitions issues surfaced. Bank regulators have shown deep concerns for anti- competitive practices and banks were more or less expected to operate within certain defined geographic areas (Eckert, 1997). In some cases the only way a bank can expand was through a multibank holding company. In such situations only bank holding companies (BHC) can legally acquire banks and limited nonbanking entities in varying markets and geographic regions.

Although the concerns for diminishing competition and monopolistic tendencies are still the concerns of bank regulators, lawmakers and students of banking (Gaughan, 1996), the Garn-St. Germain Act of 1982 (cited in Johnson, 1995) permitted hundreds of mergers and acquisitions that would have been otherwise questioned by bank regulators. Effective June 1997, a bank holding company may merge or acquire a bank in any state. Such mergers may be subject to minor restrictions such as, the acquirer must be a resident of the state for as least 5 years, the home state of the holding company must be where the cash deposits base is the strongest, and so on. Also as of June 1997 national and state banks may merge across state lines thereby facilitating interstate branches, with limitations similar to those above and subject to state-prescribed reciprocity rules (Allen, 1997).

Consolidation in the banking industry is at a record pace. In fact, some of the largest mergers took place during the year 1995 (see Table 6.1 in chapter 6). Megadeal mergers such as Chemical Bank and Chase Manhattan, First Bank Systems and First Interstate, and First Union and First Fidelity all took place in 1995 (Spiegel & Gart, 1996). Spiegel and Gart estimated that the 50 largest banks hold approximately 75% of the banking industry's assets and if this consolidating trend continues those 50 banks could fold into 15 megabanks by the early part of the 21st century. Clearly, the historical data tended to suggest that levels of greater market concentration are occurring within the banking industry at an accelerating pace and there is little doubt that this trend would continue at least over the near future.

Review of Merger-Related Theories and Hypotheses

The state of the merger and acquisition market is expected to reflect a speculation that the net present value will be positive in the post consolidation period, given that the decisions among banks to merge will drive up the gains for the underlying stock prices above normal levels (Halpern, 1983). Halpern argues that there are two major classes of merger theories. One is the growth or non-value maximizing theories and hypotheses while the other tests a number of theories and hypotheses under what is referred to as "value maximizing behavior" (p. 299). Gary M. Eckert (1997), though not classifying the hypotheses under the value or non-value maximizing orientation for mergers and acquisitions, enumerated 10 general merger theories or motives. Six of the 10 theories examined by Eckert seemed to be gravitating towards the value maximizing class of merger and acquisition theories whereas, the remaining four theories and hypotheses are within the realm of the growth or non-value maximizing class of theories.

The growth maximization class of theories attempts to increase market share, maximize sales or increase power relative to other competitors. Hypotheses such as management self-interest, hubris, monopoly orientation and geographic diversification are under the rubric of the growth-maximization theories. Growth maximization therefore, assumes non-value maximizing behavior for leaders of acquiring banks with a relatively stronger desire for increases in sales or assets or greater market control in a given industry (Halpern, 1983). Hypotheses such as economies of scale, efficiency in management, revenue improvement and reengineering initiatives are under the umbrella of the value maximization theory. Theories that fall under the value-maximization behavior hold that the objective of two or more firms combining to form a single entity is essentially to maximize economic returns to the shareholders. The two classes of theories are enumerated, analyzed and explained below.

Growth Maximization Group of Theories

Growth maximization assumes a non-value-maximizing behavior for leaders of acquiring banks who possess relatively stronger desires for increases in sales, assets or wider geographic control. The following are some of the major theories and hypotheses that previous researchers have advanced under the growth maximization motive for mergers and acquisitions.

Management self-interest hypothesis. The management self-interest hypothesis proposes that if management's compensation are positively correlated with increasing size of their firm, then the value creation merits may not be the dominant reason for the merger or acquisition (Varaiya, 1986). The underlying assumption of this hypothesis is that management may not preclude themselves from undertaking mergers and acquisition projects that have a projected net present value to the acquirer. Varaiya selected a sample of 97 acquirers over the period 1975 to 1983 with approximately 50% comprising tender offers and mergers respectively. That researcher found support for the management self-interest hypothesis among bidding firms or "acquirers," as conceptualized in this study.

In a comprehensive examination of the scientific literature on mergers and acquisitions Jensen and Ruback (1983) articulated the view that managers seek their own self-interest when they anticipate that their replacements are being brought on by a pending merger or acquisition. Managers, these researchers argue, may have an incentive to reduce the probability of a takeover even though there is speculation for positive shareholders wealth for either, or both, the acquirer and the acquiree. Jensen and Ruback evaluated 13 major studies on mergers and acquisitions and arrived at a general conclusion that managerial groups compete for the rights to manage greater and greater amounts of resources. These 13 studies are, even up to this day, regarded as some of the major works undertaken by researchers in the field of mergers, acquisitions and proxy contests.

The hubris hypothesis. The hubris hypothesis suggests that the average increase in the acquirees market should be more than offset by an average decline in the value of the acquirer's market. According to this hypothesis, made popular by

Richard Roll (1986), there is no economic gain to be realized from the merger and at best may be a wash. Roll endeavored to explain why managers might want to pay a premium for a stock over and above what the market has correctly valued. Hubris hypothesis is based on the assumptions that the market for banking products and the related derived factor markets are indeed competitive and efficient.

A number of research efforts were directed towards the testing of the hubris hypothesis. Jensen and Ruback (1983), while reviewing the major research works in the area of mergers, acquisitions, and proxy contests, found that acquirers generally do not show abnormal returns. In many cases the acquirers earn zero or negative abnormal returns. Jensen and Ruback reviewed much of the scientific evidence up the time of their study in 1983. Varaiya (1986, 1988) found evidence to support the hubris hypothesis. In Varaiya (1988), the researcher found that the hubris hypothesis is a special case of the winner's curse from auction theory. The highest bidder will have the highest negative value in the merger or acquisition and may win the bid at the expense of losing the prize. In Varaiya (1986), the researcher tested the hypothesis that there is no gain to be obtained from corporate takeovers. In the sample involving some 97 acquiring' firms, the researcher found that stock returns over the period 1975 to 1983 were not positive generally greater than 0.

Monopolistic orientation. The aim of the monopolistic orientation hypothesis is to deal with a conception that there are too many banks in the United States and some concentration of monopolistic power may be an effective approach to compete with huge foreign financial entities (Allen, 1997). Freixas and Rochet (1997) articulated the viewpoint that oligopoly, a model of imperfect competition where there are very few dominant firms, can better characterize market behavior in the banking industry. Parenthetically, this hypothesis is inclined to suggest that some level of efficiency may be realized in the internal dynamics of the new entity unimpeded by barriers to entry for competitors.

Combinations of firms that result in increased market power may have a significant impact on a firm's ability to have greater control over the scope of market operations. Whether market power positively correlates with mergers and acquisition is subject to the size of the merged entity vis-à-vis other players in the given industry coupled with the intensity of competition within a given market. Market power derived from a monopolistic orientation suggests that the business enterprise can establish and maintain product price above the comparatively lower competitive price level. According to prevailing economic theories, market power bestows on the business organization the capability to dictate a price greater than marginal cost (Gaughan, 1996). An index developed by Abba Lerner (cited in Gaughan, 1996, p. 26) sought to measure the deviation of the monopolist's product price from marginal cost in relation to the product price itself.

The Lerner Index, which is given below and is adjusted to reflect pricing of single commodity, establishes a numerical value to the monopolistic orientation of a business entity as follows:

$$\text{Lerner Index} = [(Pa - MC_a)(1/P_a)]$$
$$= [(1 - MC_a/P_a)]$$

where P_a = price of product a

and MCa = marginal cost of product a

Monopolistic power may be generated from three major sources. These sources are product differentiation, barriers to entry into the given market and market share. The monopolistic intent of merging firms was not tested per se, but Eckbo (1983) tested a related hypothesis on collusion.

Under the collusion hypothesis, according to Eckbo (1983), the competitors of merging firms gain from mergers in a large competitive environment, given that a successful collusion attempts to increase prices, cut back production and drive profits upward. The collusion hypothesis was tested using a sample of 126 firms mainly in the manufacturing and mining industries matched by a corresponding average of 15 rival firms in each of the industrial categories. The researcher concluded that if even scale economies are involved, then these seem to be on average to be insufficient to make the rival worst off" (p. 272). Thus, the evidence of that researcher does not support a monopolistic (predatory) price tendency even after the consummation of a merger or an acquisition. Pilotte (1989) also arrived at a similar conclusion in her empirical examination of horizontal mergers and antitrust policies. That study, which covered a period of 61 years (1925 to 1986) and includes hundreds of challenged and unchallenged mergers, did not significantly support neither collusion nor predatory/competition advantage hypotheses. The predation/competitive advantage hypothesis, according to Pilotte, drives the speculation concerning economic rent, which essentially can be derived from a monopolistic situation.

Geographic diversification. With interstate and intrastate branch banking, the turnaround time for servicing products that are linked to a checking account may be shortened as "on us" checks will now cover a greater number of bank branches an a wider geographic area. For non-bankers an "on us" check is a check drawn on one of the branches of a given bank and the clearing period is shorter than that of a check drawn on a competitor's branch. The new entity may now be able to efficiently and effectively cover a more diverse and wider geographic spread of actual and potential customers (Spiegel & Gart, 1996). Spiegel and Gart hold the view that there is a major impetus for banks to continue with merger and acquisition activities, as these banks will no longer be constrained by interstate banking laws. Under this hypothesis, the buyer is zealous of having a stake in another geographic area and will acquire, horizontally or vertically, any other entity (Gaughan, 1996). The 1987 acquisition of Texas Commerce Bank by Chemical Banking Corporation is an example of geographic diversification. Gaughan argues that the acquisition of one regional bank by a bank from another region within the United States gives rise to a novel type of bank known as "the superregional bank" (Gaughan, 1996, p. 107).

In a study to test the effects of geographic deregulation in the banking industry Adkisson and Fraser (1990) argue that states within the United States that permit interstate banking (geographic expansion) positively influence the premium paid by acquirers to acquirees. In a methodology which combined qualitative and quantitative analyses of the variance (ANOVA) and regression analysis respectively and involving 174 holding company acquisitions and at least 37 different states, these authors, like so many researchers in other studies, found that acquirer shareholders do not realize abnormal returns. However, with geographic expansion based on the repeal of certain interstates' restrictions, a decrease in barriers to entry brings about a comparable downward movement in a given merger or acquisition premium.

Value Maximization Group of Theories

Theories that fall under the value-maximization behavior hold that the objective of two or more firms combining to form a single entity is to maximize economic returns to the shareholders (Halpern, 1983). Halpern further argues that the value maximization group of theories gravitate towards the view that a merger event should be measured in the same way and by utilizing the same criteria that are configured in other investment initiatives. Some of the major hypotheses that are tested under this group of theories are economies of scale, efficiency in management, revenue improvement, and reengineering.

<u>Economies of scale.</u> Economies of scale derived from the consolidation of different banks are best captured by the term *synergy*. The economies of scale hypothesis postulates that economies of scale can be realized most efficiently where banks integrate horizontally and utilize excess capacities in addition to the leveraging additional resources and in so doing set in motion the process of

decreasing average cost. The debate concerning the advantages of scale in banking is an unresolved issue. For example, Hughes and Mester (cited in Freixas & Rochet, 1997, p. 81) argue that large banks suffer some diseconomies of scale. Diseconomies of scale, in this situation, are the antithesis to economies of scale. Allen (1997) argues that in an effort to increase size and search for scale, large banks command higher acquisition premiums as oppose to smaller banks. Allen supported his conjecture by producing data, which show that large banks (assets between $1 billion to $5 billion) in mergers and acquisitions sold for an average price/earnings ratio of 1.8 times, whereas smaller banks (assets under $100 million) sold for a comparable ratio of only 1.4 times.

When a firm utilizes a set of inputs to produce a wider range of goods and services the end result, especially in the banking industry, is economies of scope (Gaughan, 1996). The new entity, as successor by merger or acquisition to any previous individual entity, may now share inputs such as systems and technology, trust department, equipment and so on, to offer a broader range of services to a wider and deeper market. Couched in the concept of synergy are the economies of scale (scope) hypothesis. Sirower (1997) conjectured that mergers as a whole do not create value and do not necessarily reduce unit cost. Sirower based his study on 168 acquirers drawn from a sample frame between the years 1979 to 1990.

Consistent with the free cash flow conjecture formulated by Hanson (1992), Sirower concluded that acquirers, armed with excess cash reserves, engage in low-benefit or value-destroying mergers and acquisition. Sirower finally made the observation that under the ill-founded hope in the economies of scale scenario is hidden the so-called "trap" of synergy (Sirower, 1997, p. 16).

<u>Efficiency in management.</u> The assertion from this hypothesis is that the acquirer's management practices are more efficient than those of the target bank hence the need to "buy out" the acquired bank's managerial personnel (Eckert, 1997). Allen (1997), however, submits a competing opinion with respect to efficiency in management hypothesis. Allen conjectured that both banks; that is, the acquirees and the acquirers should be subjected to a "stand alone" reengineering scrutiny. Walter Shipley Chairman and CEO of The Chase Manhattan (quoted in Wendel, 1996, p. 247), articulates the view that banks, irrespective of who acquired whom, "merger of equals" is the more positive approach in management of the new entity. This controversy will continue to attract the attention of academicians, bankers, investors, bank regulators, and so on.

A related hypothesis to the efficiency in management hypothesis is the improved management hypothesis (Gaughan, 1996). The improved management hypothesis, which states that the value of the acquiree's business unit can be enhanced by a superior quality acquirer's management, is built on the assumption that the acquiring firm's management can better manage the acquiree's resources. Gaughan concluded that the managerial resources are assets that the usually much larger acquirer can offer the typically much smaller acquiree. In an examination of some 4,900 transaction concerning mergers and acquisitions covering a period of 1980 to 1990, Peristiani (1997) found that acquirers fail to improve x-efficiency after the merger has taken place. Consistent with other studies, that researcher concluded that acquiring banks do achieve moderate gains in efficiency. Conclusive evidence in support of the improved managerial efficiency hypothesis is not yet deterministic, as envisaged by Peristiani, mainly because of the level of difficulty in quantifying measures of success or failure attributable to an improved management theory.

Revenue enhancement. This is a major hypothesis in the study of organizational integration, which states that an ultimate aim of the merging entity is to improve earnings per share and boost the stockholders' value creation (Spiegel & Gart, 1996). Spiegel and Gart articulated the view that, as large banks move to consolidate through in-market mergers and acquisition, there will be greater operating efficiency resulting in a higher stream of income for the new entity. These researchers did not test their conjectured relationship, but speculated that shareholders revenue will be expected to increase followed by greater dividend pay out and stock appreciation for the new consolidated entity. In a British study of mergers and acquisitions, Higson and Elliott (1998) measured post-takeover returns for 1 to 12, 1 to 24, and 1 to 36 month intervals comprising 814, 776 and 722 samples, respectively. These researchers concluded that the abnormal returns realized by large takeovers were not significantly different from zero and seem conclusively negative for the first year.

Loughran and Vijh (1997) examined 947 acquisitions between 1970 and 1989 and evaluated a 5-year post acquisition performance of each of these acquisitions. These researchers concluded that stock swaps earned lower returns than stocks paid for in cash in the majority of the acquisitions examined (Loughran & Vijh, 1997). Consistent with Loughran and Vijh, Rau and Vermaelen (1996) in a post-merger analysis of acquirers compared the mergers with tender offers and ended up with conclusions similar to Loughran and Vijh. However, Rau and Vermaelen went a step further and postulated that the long term underperformance of acquiring firms in mergers is due to low book-to-market ratios. Those researchers also tested a means of payment hypothesis and found that in mergers, where payment is typically made through the allocation of shares, underperform tender offers.

In tender offers, payments by acquirers to acquirees are usually in the form of cash transactions. Rau and Vermaelen (1996) entire study was based on a sample of 2,823 mergers and 316 tender offers spanning a period of 12 years, January 1980 to December 1991. Contrast these findings with, though a somewhat different class of acquirees Cheng (1998). Cheng found that acquirers offering common stocks to acquire privately held firms earn positive abnormal returns, whereas acquirers offering cash experience zero abnormal returns. That researcher utilized the standard market model typical of event study methodology with the parameters of the given model estimated for the periods, -210 to -11 days and -1 to 0 day. In his study, Cheng analyzed a total sample of 536 with privately held mergers amounting to 281 merger proposals whereas 255 were of publicly held acquirees' type drawn over an eleven-year period, 1981 to 1992.

Mueller (1995) surveyed the theories and evidence concerning mergers across industries and across countries and found that for the United States, as indeed many other countries, anticipated profitability from mergers generally did not materialize. Mueller examined six major scientific studies relating to mergers and acquisitions that occurred between the years 1974 to 1987 within the United States. One of Mueller's main conclusion was, even though serendipitous, that in a bull market bidders who are usually enjoying above average stock returns will seek to enter a merger that will result in value destruction to their own stockholdings. Mueller suggested that, perhaps in a bull market all market participants might be victims of their own haughtiness. In an effort to test the efficiency effects among banks that participate in horizontal mergers, Rhoades (1993) conducted an ordinary least squares and logit study of mergers and acquisitions involving 898 banks over a period of 5 years, 1981 to 1986. That researcher concluded that these merged entities did not yield gains in efficiency. Rhoades findings were astounding given that the acquirers, the much larger banks in the mergers or acquisition undertakings, were generally more efficient than the relatively much smaller acquirees, and that the mergers involved tremendous overlapping markets. The implication here is that one would expect tremendous cost savings, as these market overlaps are opportunities to enhance efficiency. The evidence, according to Rhoades, does not lend support to such an implication.

<u>Reengineering initiatives.</u> The reengineering hypothesis holds that the way things were done in the past must be critically examined in the light of a dynamic and new operating technological and social environment (Allen, 1997). Allen conjectured that drastic changes would have to be made to ensure long term survival of the business undertaking. The researcher further argues that reengineering is not simply cost cutting and shadowing behind euphemisms such as downsizing, restructuring, total quality control, and horizontal management but a complete redesign of the operations. Consistent with other hypotheses examined in this study, the reengineering motive covered by the value maximizing group of theories is applicable to both the target and acquiring banks.

In an effort to reduce costs, the newly merged entity seeks to reengineer the organization by undertaking some form of restructuring. Gaughan (1996) used data on restructuring to show a regular and consistent pattern by companies seeking to downsize with the aim of boosting productivity. Using data on corporation layoffs, Patrick A. Gaughan showed a pattern of persistent layoffs by some of America's largest corporations during this current decade. Gaughan concluded that the irony of the reengineering effort is, that such an effort occurred at a time when companies were expanding through mergers and acquisitions with the main objective, of course being, to increase production per unit of input.

A final observation was encountered as the literature review for this study was undertaken. The observation was that there is a doctrine known as "too big to fail," which suggests that the Fed will bail out a failing large bank fearing that such a failure may set in motion a domino effect (Rochet & Tirole, 1996). The doctrine, in essence, assumes that a large bank may take more risks (moral hazard) under the notion that it will be rescued if bank performance fail to meet expectations. However, the regulatory agency for banks would not want to appear willing to bail out any bank.

The Federal Reserve Bank may prefer to follow a process of constructive ambiguity (Freixas & Rochet, 1997). Constructive ambiguity is implied as a process of non-committal to any "too big to fail" doctrine and as such, peer monitoring may be a favored option for bank regulators in the light of such moral hazards.

Concluding Comments on Hypotheses and Theories Reviewed

Mergers and acquisition theories and hypotheses reviewed in this section suggest that gains to a given business entity can accrue through cost reduction, increased marker share narrower earnings volatility and perhaps economies in scale and scope. Apparently the economic gains anticipated couldn't be statistically verified and yet mergers and acquisitions continues unabated. Traditionally one expects value to increase for the total shareholding clientele as the consolidating firms under a combine pool of resources is expected to accrue shareholders' value in excess of the simple sum of value independently created by each firm. However, equally important is the non-value maximizing motive for merger and acquisition where the ex ante expectations of value creation on the part of power-driven managerial personnel have systematically and quite regularly exceeded ex post economic performance.

Most of the hypotheses reviewed in this section can be a reasonable explanation for merger and acquisition activities. Most of these theories and hypotheses have overlapping implications for merger and acquisition activities. Thus it may be difficult, if not impossible, to identify which of the competing postulates or how many of the competing conjectured relationships are, in fact, the true explanation for reasons behind each merger or acquisition. In these circumstances, and for a given set of mergers and acquisitions or for a single merger event, it may be preferable to examine whether the value maximizing or the growth maximizing behavior can be the dominant explanation.

Review of Research Methodologies in Mergers and Acquisitions

The majority of studies on mergers and acquisitions measure abnormal returns previous to, but mostly after the actual merger or acquisition announcement date. Franks, Harris, and Titman (1991) found no evidence of abnormal returns in a three-year post merger span. These researchers used various multifactor benchmark portfolios covering a period of three years in the post merger or acquisition dates. Franks, Harris, and Titman's reviewed the merger and acquisition period, 1975 to 1984. Many researchers sought to measure returns prior to, during and after the merger or acquisition process (Carow & Larsen, Jr., 1997; Loughran & Vijh, 1997) by employing standard event study methodology.

Carow and Larsen, Jr. (1997) drew a sample of 56 bank holding companies (BHC) from a sample frame found in the Standard and Poor's Compustat Database files and track the daily stock returns. These researchers tested the null hypothesis (H_0), that bank size and risk are not factors on the effectiveness of FDICIA on bank returns. FDICIA, which stands for Federal Deposit Insurance Corporation Improvement Act of 1991, is a far-reaching banking legislation demanding, among other stipulations, that banks curtail their appetites for excessive risk taking. The authors tested an additional null hypothesis, that the adoption of a new financial regulation will not have any a significant effect on the common stocks of banks being traded in the stock market. Carow and Larsen (1997) tested the levels of abnormal return among significant event dates pertaining to the introduction of the FDICIA and through to the final passage in the United States Congress. These authors tested five events starting with the introduction of the Bill in the Senate and passage of the final Act in Congress and spanned a period of 13 months.

Carow and Larsen (1997) sought to generate abnormal stock returns by computing daily returns for security j in time t in the market model. These researchers concluded that the FDICIA had a negative impact on shareholders wealth and rejected all null hypotheses. Similar to Carow and Larsen's effective use of event-study methodology, Yermack (1997) studied the correlation between CEOs of various companies awarding themselves stock options and abnormal stock returns. The author measured the movement of stock prices between the events plus and minus 6 to 10 days, 2 to 5 days, and 1 day around the announcement of stock option awards and discovered that prices do increase after CEOs award themselves such options.

In a research design exploiting the tremendous potential of event study methodology in explaining mergers and acquisitions, Ruback (1983), pursuing a qualitative quasi-deductive research paradigm, highlighted the uses of prior empirical research that may assist the researcher in forecasting market reactions to takeover announcements. More importantly, that researcher detracted from the usual averaging techniques that characterize previous event-study models of research. That researcher reasoned that the large sample sizes, common in previous studies, prohibited the uses of in-depth examinations of the stock market responses to a variety of events that precede a merger.

The examination of the behavior of stock prices associated with pre-merger announcements of a single unit of analysis, that is, the merger between Cities Services and Occidental Petroleum and other bidders, Ruback (1983) complemented previous empirical studies while demonstrating the predictive ability of existing empirical evidence. It is the single unit of analysis, a case study, which facilitated the in-depth analysis and the predictive domain in empirical social science research. Consequently, and as a supplement to the quantitative design of this study, this researcher will not follow any further indepth analyses using aspects of the qualitative quasi-deductive paradigm. Such a complementary research effort may better be served by future research initiatives and hence is beyond the scope of the research.

Jensen and Ruback (1983), who reviewed the major research initiatives up to that point in time in the area of mergers, acquisitions and proxy contests, found that acquirers generally do not realize abnormal returns in shareholders' value. In many cases the acquirers earn zero or negative abnormal returns. Jensen and Ruback reviewed much of the scientific evidence up the time of their study in 1983 and concluded that the origins of takeover gains are quite elusive phenomena. Jensen and Ruback based their findings on the examination of 13 major studies covering the years 1977 to 1983.

Brown and Warner (1980), in one of the earlier studies surrounding the evaluation of the value creation in mergers and acquisitions, helped popularized the uses of event-study methodology (Brown & Warner, 1980; 1985). Abnormal security price performance was introduced by these researchers to address the probability that different methodologies may lead to Type I or Type II errors. A performance measure for abnormal security prices can be categorized by market performance measures such as, Mean Adjusted Returns, Market Adjusted Returns and Market and Risk Adjusted Returns. These researchers argue that before an abnormal return can be measured a normal return must be first agreed upon as a benchmark. To this end, given versions of the Capital Asset Pricing Model are fundamental to the event study methodology.

The daily market reaction to the first public announcement and the ensuing acceptance or rejection of the intended merger are very noticeable, especially where, the market reaction is much more greater (or lesser) than a comparable market norm (Dodd, 1980). Dodd argues further, that going forward from the first public announcement date, there is a positive reaction when the given merger is finally approved or a negative reaction assuming a rejection by the responsible governmental agency or the responsible stockholders. The researcher's sample consisted of 151 merger proposals of firms traded in the New York Stock exchange. In the sample the author identified 71 mergers that were completed, that is, final approval by all relevant groups and the remaining 80 mergers that were eventually cancelled. Armed with data on daily stock price changes obtained from the tapes of the Center for Research in Security Prices (CRSP) and exploiting the uses of the basic market model, Dodd proceeded to analyze the "disturbance" measured as the residual in his model (p. 108):

$$R_{jt} = a_j + B_j R_{mt} + e_{jt}.$$

In the above equation Dodd (1980) identified the disturbance as being reflected in the term e_{jt}. More specifically, Dodd interpreted the term, e_{jt} as a measure of the abnormal return to the stockholders of firm j for a given period t and represents a deviation of an actual from the expected. The expected return is the return reflected in a relevant market index for the period surrounding the merger events. The other terms in the equation are the generally accepted market model terms.

In one of the few major studies, that concluded that acquirers gain positive abnormal returns, Asquith, Bruner, and Mullins (1983) faulted all those researchers who failed to consider the endogenous merger plans of the acquirers. Assuming that acquirers do make protracted bids as part of a planned merger program of activities, then those groups of mergers, relative to a given acquirer, should be considered in toto. These researchers argued that by identifying single merger events and by pooling such individual events would dismiss the "program effects" on acquirers (p. 124). The methodology employed was basically event study methodology and the sample consisted of firms that had 156 first bids, 113 second bids, 88 third bids, and 71 fourth bids all together stretched over a period of a quarter of a century, 1955 to 1979. As a possible explanation for the difference in these researchers' findings, compared to other studies, they argue that their tests control for factors such as size, successes of merger bids, and the time period over which the relevant bids occurred. Using a different methodology from the seemingly popular event study methodology, Rhoades (1983) pursued an alternative approach to the study of mergers and acquisition. Rhoades sought to investigate bank mergers and acquisitions from a stock premium basis since it is the premium paid, according to Rhoades, that will point to the maximizing behavior which will motivate the acceptance or rejection of the merger or acquisition. Rhoades pointed out that a major advantage in this approach is that such a behavior is not dependent on judicious pronouncements of outside investors and speculators, but on internally generated ratios that can guide premium payment in the merger or acquisition process. That researcher argued that by studying mergers and acquisitions from a stock premium perspective will inform whether the acquirer' managers have a high/low growth or value maximizing motive.

In his review of the popular event study methodology, Halpern (1983) concluded that a preferably technique to study acquisition is to integrate the residual (event study) analysis with micro economic analysis prevalent in industrial organization studies. By studying the deviation of the security prices from the norms of the market, enhanced by specific information such as concentration ratios, integration relationships, methods of payments and so on, will better explain abnormal performances. Halpern concluded that perhaps the overwhelming evidence uncovered concerning positive abnormal returns realized, on the part of acquirees, might not help very much in explaining the underlying motivation behind mergers and acquisitions. This line of reasoning suggests that the behavior of acquirers can better explain the motives that drive merger and acquisition activities.

In a 1987 study that examined the value maximization effects of interstate bank mergers and acquisitions for both the acquirers and the acquirees, Trifts and Scanlon (1987) found that acquirees earn positive abnormal returns vis-à-vis acquirers, the latter of whom, more or less, broke even. Banks involved in relatively large mergers and acquisitions, these researchers found, earn significantly positive abnormal returns at a rate significantly higher than those of mergers and acquisitions involving relatively smaller banks. The methodology employed was basically the market model with α_i and β_i being the estimated parameters and e_i being the random error. Measured over a 61 week period around the announcement date and a total sample of 21 bank mergers, these researchers employed the cumulative abnormal returns (CAR) coupled with the measures of variance that were consistent with the method employed by, the previously cited, Brown and Warner (1980).

For a greater indepth revaluation of banks involved in mergers and acquisitions, Houston and Ryngaert (1994) measured the combined value of acquirees and acquirers in a major study comprising some 153 mergers 22 of which were cancelled prior to their actual merger dates. The measurement of abnormal returns for the newly merged entities were tested over a 152-day post announcement period using data drawn mainly from the Center for Research in Security Prices (CRSP). These researchers concluded that the combined revaluation of both acquirers and acquirees is not significantly different from zero. Houston and Ryngaert reasoned that the positive and negative returns of acquirees and acquirers respectively, might have cancelled each other out. These researchers defined merger of equals as, when the smaller firm is at least 45% of the combined assets of the merging firms and the new board of directors will comprise 50% each from the two merging entities.

Following some of the techniques advanced by Brown and Warner (1980) and utilizing many aspects of their return models, Sirower (1997) followed a method of utilizing seven event windows juxtaposed with four different return model measurements. Apparently building on the Brown and Warner study, Sirower added a fourth return model, which was referred to as "raw returns" (Sirower, 1997, p. 104). In total, there were seven event windows spanning a period of -1 day prior the official announcement date of the merger or acquisition to +4 years after the given announcement date. To complete one part of his theoretical framework, Sirower added four models of measurements making a total of twenty-eight measures of performance for the dependent variable. The independent variable included measures such as acquisition premium, relatedness, payment methods (cash), contested acquisitions, relevant size and other measures making a total of thirteen measures inclusive of the control variables. Sirower used standardized statistical techniques that are common in the study of mergers and acquisitions to test his seven major postulates.

In his D.B.A. dissertation, which investigated the factors affecting the probability of bank mergers and acquisitions, Eckert, while using a relatively small number of 33 acquired banks each with a transaction value of above $100 million, tested six hypotheses built around his six independent variable (Eckert, 1997). Eckert's study covered the period 1988 to 1995 and utilized the stepwise statistical regression method to test the relationships between acquisition premium paid, the dependent variable, and the five independent variables, namely profit, credit quality, leverage, diversification, and size. Based upon his stepwise regression analysis, that researcher developed a matrix to elucidate further, the factors influencing the probability of bank mergers and acquisitions. Eckert model also used a bivariate and multivariate approach in testing his six independent variables relationship with the corresponding dependent variables. In his sub-analysis size, measured in terms of total assets, was separated in two variables, that is, the size of acquirer and size of the acquiree thereby making a total of six variables instead of five as was stated in his original theoretical framework.

CHAPTER 4

Research Methodology for the Study

A sound research process will be conducted systematically and objectively as possible using as many controls as are feasible and necessary within constraints such as cost, time, and availability of reliable data. A systematic research activity will necessarily involve *a priori* specific pre-planned procedure grounded in an appropriate research design to answer identifiable research questions. To be objective, the research procedure, findings, and interpretation of results must not be influenced by the researcher's beliefs, values, or any other subjectively preconceived human biases after the research has began. In a research process, where the researcher states the intention to test hypotheses to answer the postulated statements about the parameters of a given population, he or she may conclude that the dependent variable or variables did not influence the status quo.

The theoretical foundation of hypothesis testing dictates that the null hypothesis be considered true until the data assembled indicate otherwise. Where the null hypothesis is considered false then something else must be true. The something else would be an alternate hypothesis. Thus the alternate hypothesis is essentially the opposite of the null hypothesis and represents the conclusion that would be reached after it has been proven that the latter hypothesis is unlikely to be true. Assuming that a researcher fails to reject the null hypothesis then he or she can only conclude that there is insufficient data to warrant its rejection.

Crucial to this entire study is the question of identifying what is the goal or goals of the business. More specifically, one may want to identify the true goal or goals of the banking business. Throughout this study emphasis is placed on tracking shareholders value. The movement of shareholders value in response to a certain consolidating event such as a merger or an acquisition is a major theoretical construct used for testing the first hypothesis of acquirers' shareholders value. Before the actual research methodology for this study is laid out and discussed, a detailed discussion of the goals of a business undertaking with special emphasis on financial intermediaries and business market and the business valuation processes will be undertaken.

Goals of a Public Business Organization

The goals of a public business undertaking are, by and large, the end results by which the organization wishes to achieve over a relatively long period of time such as between one and ten years. Some major goals of a business organization are profit maximization, sales maximization, stakeholders value maximization, and shareholders value maximization.

1. <u>Profit Maximization</u>: The goal of profit maximization stresses the efficient use of capital resources and assumes away many of the complexities of the real world and for this reason, this is an unacceptable goal given that:

a Profit maximization goal assumes away uncertainty of returns. That is, projects are compared by examining their expected values or weighted average profit, which is merely a percentage of sales after all expenses are met over a given period.

b Profit maximization also assumes away timing and differences of returns. That is, such a goal does not indicate over what interval of time that the inflows of cash will take place.

c Profit Maximization also ignores the cost for using shareholders funds given that, there is an opportunity cost for shareholders common equity.

d Profit Maximization ignores the risk-return dichotomy in that there is an expected return for delaying consumption combined with an additional expected return for taking on additional risks.

2. <u>Shareholders' Value Maximization</u>: The goal of shareholder wealth maximization is tremendously important in the sense that the effects of all financial decisions are reflected in this goal. The *raison d' etre* for such a goal is grounded in:

a The consequences of a financial decision in the business operations are interpreted through fluctuating events surrounding the behavior of the given business's stock prices.

b The focus of management therefore, is to factor in the effects that their decision will have on the stock price, all other things being held constant.

c All decisions about the organization manifest themselves into the volatility of the stock as individual investors and hence, the market reacts to inherent fundamentals of the business organization.

d Efficiency of the market facilitates the fair value of a given stock as all decisions about a corporation are, intentionally or unintentionally, fed into the market on a timely basis.

3. <u>Stakeholders' Value Maximization</u>: Given that the corporation exists for the purpose of meeting the wants and needs of society, then it is possible that the satisfaction of all those needs of stakeholders are worthwhile distributive goals.

Thus, stakeholders such as customers, employees, management, shareholders, community organizations, and pressure groups must be able to have the maximum of their interests met. However, as one attempts to implement such a goal there are some drawbacks such as:

a zero-sum game, which suggests that one person's or a group's value maximization may be at the expense of some other person or group of stakeholders in the given corporation. For example, giving the customer a quality product at a cheaper price may be at the expense of reduced dividends paid on common stocks. Thus, the goal of stakeholders value maximization, though socially desirable, may increase the incidence of conflict and may also involve deeply subjective allocation processes.

b Unless some form of rigid rules are supported within a legally mandated framework this goal of stakeholders value maximization may be difficult to be realized, or if achieved, cannot be maintained over any considerable period of time.

4 <u>Sales Maximization</u>: Sales maximization suggests that the corporation is seeking to expand sales irrespective of underlying constraints that inhibit efficiency measures related to such a growth in sales. Some problems associated with sales maximization are:

a Hubris: the self-motivated need to expand market share to satisfy one's own ego. Thus, seeking to take over or acquire competitors without first doing sound cost-benefit analysis is an example of hubris.

b Sales expansion may not have anything to do with the profit motive nor stakeholders' interest, but the whims and caprices of an adventurous CEO.

c Sales maximization must be considered in the light of capacity, fixed and variable costs, and reliable forecasting of financial indicators.

Goals in Managing the Banking Business

A variety of goals also exist for banks as intermediaries. One goal is to service the needs of the community where a bank or its branch is located. Another goal may be assets and loan growth so as to become a dominant player in the banking business thereby assuming a greater influence over the bank's marketing area. A major goal of the bank's management is to maximize the long-term return on the capital invested by bank owners namely, the shareholders. Since many banks are privately owned, the goal of shareholders value maximization using intrinsic valuation models is also applicable. Given that, cash flow models factor in riskiness associated with variability and timing of cash flows, such models are also useful in measuring return on capital invested in privately held corporations.

The goal of shareholder value maximization also applies to the management of commercial banks, where the public holds the stocks of these banks. As would be expected, a vast number of commercial banks are held by private shareholders (Johnson & Johnson, 1989). Many of these shareholders have genealogical roots within limited liability business structures. In addition, many banks are subsidiaries of holding companies, where the parents may be involved in nonfinancial industrial activities. Thus, for these privately held and parent-controlled banks maximization of shareholders' value may not be a meaningful operational goal.

The Optimum Goal

For our purpose *Stockholders' Value Maximization* will be the preferred goal. The reasons for relying on such a goal are:

a Shareholders' wealth maximization goal deals with all the complexities of the operating environment, whereas the other goals do not.
b Shareholders' value maximization is a long-run goal and the public image of the corporation may be of deep concern to shareholders including the wealth effect.
c The effects of all financial decisions are reflected in the total equity value of the corporation.
d The complexities and uncertainties in the external environment are all absorbed in the value of the stock. Thus, over a longer period of time the prices of stockholdings to stockholders reflect effective and efficient valuation.

Conclusion

The above analysis does make it quite clear that shareholders' value maximization is a more sound and reliable financial goal of a corporation. Therefore, as we proceed to understand and apply the models and concepts to the study of banking and finance we must keep this goal in mind. In this book, all the banks referred to and being in the category of megabanks were public companies and hence, their equities were traded in one of the stock exchanges. Samples of banks that made up the small bank category were not isolated in terms of publicly traded and non-publicly traded entities. In fact, such a demarcation was not a part of the theoretical constructs of this research undertaking and hence, banks were not differentiated along the lines of publicly traded or private corporations.

Value and Market Efficiency

The value of an asset, namely a stock, is the intrinsic or economic value of the asset derived by discounting the expected future cash flows. These cash flows are discounted back to the present using an appropriate investor's required rate of return. The underlying principle here is that a dollar today is worth less than one dollar anytime in the future given the fact that there is inflationary trends that depress buying power and that the future earnings of the dollar will necessarily involve some risk.

The Basic Valuation Process

The basic valuation of an asset will involve three components:

a   The quantity and timing of the asset's future cash flows
b   The riskiness of these cash flows
c   An appropriate investor's required rate of return for investing in the asset, which is the minimum rate necessary for the investor to acquire or hold such an asset in the light of the opportunity cost of funds.

Thus, the basic valuation process will involve the following:

$$V = CF_1[1/(1+k)^1 + CF_2[1/(1+k)^2 + ... + CF_n[(1/1+k)^n \quad (4.1)$$

$$V = \sum_{t=1}^{n} CF_t (1/(1+k)^t$$

where V = intrinsic or present value of the cash to be received from the asset starting from period 1 through n

CF_t = the cash flow to be received in time t

k = the appropriate investor's required return

Because of the intrinsic assumption involved in estimating k, the investor's required rate of return, financial experts had much difficulty in arriving at an appropriate estimation of k in equation 4.1. Since an investor's required rate of return will comprise a risk free rate, the rate that rewards postponement of consumption, plus a risk premium for assuming additional risk, we may write:

$$k = k_{rf} + k_{rp} \quad (4.2)$$

where k = required rate

k_{rf} = risk-free rate

k_{rp} = risk premium

Finding an appropriate estimate of k_{rp} has proven to be quite elusive in the finance profession. For example, if the returns on a Microsoft stock and Treasury bill are the same a rational investor would not want to give up the safety of his government security for an asset such as Microsoft stocks, even though the latter is currently one of the most financially sound company in the world. Adapting for postponement of consumption and enduring additional risk, the market risk premium is adjusted by Beta, the measure of the market's riskiness. The equation for estimating an investor's required rate of return has come to be known in the finance literature as the Capital Asset Pricing Model (CAPM). Based on the previous work of noble prize winner, Harry Markowitz, who in a pioneering study introduced the paradigm of portfolio theory which sought to explore how risk-averse investors build portfolios in order to optimize <u>expected</u> <u>returns</u> for a given level of <u>market risk</u>. Markowitz (1991), which was rooted in this author's earlier article on portfolio selection, examined the benefits of <u>diversification</u> of asset holdings.

Building on the previous work of Harry Markowitz and pushed further by Sharp (1964) and others, the capital asset pricing model became the standard bearer for the measurement of investor's return on stocks for financial analysts. The model is written mathematically as follows:

$$k_j = k_{rf} + \beta_j (k_m - k_{rf}) \qquad (4.3)$$

where k_j = investor's required rate of return for asset j

k_{rf} = risk-free rate

β_j = beta for associated with asset j

k_m = return derived from an appropriate market index

An examination of equation 4.3 will suggest that the required return on a risky asset j is comprised of the return one would earn from a riskless asset plus an additional premium for additional risk undertaken for such an investment. Since the CAPM is based on a fully diversified portfolio, the only risk that matter is market risk. Hence, the market risk premium (k_m) is adjusted by beta (b), the metric for market risk of an underlying asset.

Market Efficiency

An efficient market is said to exist where market prices are true estimates of the value of given investments and hence the market adequately reflects, an a timely basis, all available and relevant information about such investments. Thus, in an efficient market the price of an asset, as determined by demand and supply, will equate the investor's intrinsic valuation on the given asset. Essentially therefore, in an efficient market, prices swiftly and scrupulously adjust to reflect a precise intrinsic value of a given asset. The net effect is that, the market prices of high risk versus low risk assets will adjust to mirror the levels of risk associated with such investments. It follows that market participants will be willing and ready to react as new information about a particular investment is factored into the buy, sell, or hold decision-making process.

If the market is indeed efficient then market price should reflect true value, that is, intrinsic value will always equal market value and hence, no gains or loss can occur by preferring to trade one asset instead of another. It follows that, whenever an asset's intrinsic value differs from the current market value the rational investor will go after profit-making opportunities and in so doing drive prices in the direction to finally equate market value with intrinsic value. Since an efficient market suggests that all the current information is already factored into the asset price, then what could cause the market price of a given asset to deviate from intrinsic value? The answer is, new or unanticipated information relative to a given asset. Faced with new or unanticipated information, traders would take positions so as to maximize their gains (or minimize losses) thereby causing prices to adjust in tandem with a new piece of information. However, the market will not always react to new information. Figure 4.1 demonstrates this point.

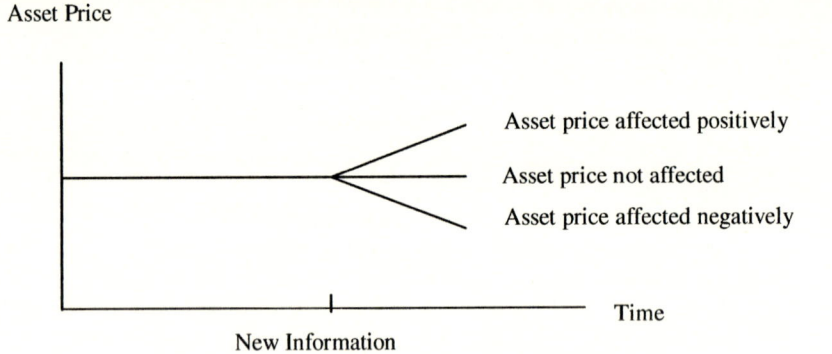

Figure 4.1. Asset price adjustments to new information

An examination of Figure 4.1 reveals that asset price will likely move with wider deviations over the given timeframe. However, a new convergence of price levels will occur when market price and intrinsic value coincide once more perhaps at a lower, same, or higher price level compared to the pre new information continuum. Note that, more often than not, upon rumors or actual information released about a given asset, the deviation may simply be a slight "bump on the road" lasting no more than a day or two or just for a few days around a given day. The given day being, when the information actually became knowledge to investors. The testing of hypothesis I in this book relates specifically to asset prices responding to a major announcement such or a merger or an acquisition.

Basic Event Study Methodology

The search for expanding markets and increasing returns to scale are reflected in the premium paid to acquire relatively large banks (SNL Securities LC, 1998). For example, acquiring banks in the $100 million asset category commanded an acquisition price of 140% of book value and a price ratio of 12.8 to earnings. On the other hand, the $1 billion asset category commanded a price to book ratio of 180% and a price to earning ratio of 14.7 (Allen, 1997). Scholars and practitioners have raised doubts about the economic benefits likely to be derived from bank consolidations. For example, while dealing with mergers in general and with particular reference to shareholders' benefit, Loughran and Vijh (1997) argue that a merger is an important event. These authors examined delistings found in tapes kept by the Center for Research in Security Prices (CRSP) and found that a good deal of acquisitions involved one publicly traded company acquiring another publicly traded company.

Employing standard event-study methodology, Carow and Larsen (1997) drew a sample of 56 bank holding companies (BHC) from a sampling frame found in the Standard and Poor's Compustat Database files. These researchers tracked and tested the null hypothesis, (H_0), that bank size and risk are not factors in the effectiveness of FDICIA on bank returns. FDICIA, which stands for Federal Deposit Insurance Corporation Improvement Act of 1991, is a far-reaching banking legislation which, among other stipulations, demands that banks restrict their appetites for excessive and unreasonable leveraging of customers' deposits. The researchers tested an additional null hypothesis, that the adoption of a new financial regulation will not have any significant effect on the common stocks of banks being traded in the stock market.

These authors then tested the levels of abnormal return among significant event dates, pertaining to the introduction of the FDICIA and through to the final passage in the Senate of the United States, by computing daily returns for security j in time t for the market model represented by the following equation:

$$R_{jt} = \alpha_j + \beta_j R_{mt} + E_{jt} \qquad (4.4)$$

where t = time, running from -30 days to +5, in days surrounding the event; the day of the event is $t = 0$.

α_j and β_j are parameters in the market model, estimated using regression.

R_{jt} = return on security j for day t

R_{mt} = return extracted from CRSP equally weighted market index.

E_{jt} = unsystematic part of return for security j on day t

The error term E_{jt} can be obtained from the total risk less the systematic risk; that is, $(1-R^2)\, v$. Risk and return analysis arising out of the Capital Asset Pricing Model suggests that the beta (β) of a stock is represented by the conventional slope of the regression (b). The firm-specific or unsystematic risk is that portion of the total risk or variance where R^2 represents the systematic portion of the risk (Damodaran, 1996). Total risk, therefore, assumes a value of unity as the following equations further elucidate:

$$\text{Total Risk or Variance }(v) = \text{Systematic Risk }(R^2) + \text{Unsystematic Risk}$$

$$\text{And Unsystematic Risk} = 1 - \underline{R}^2 = (1 - \underline{R}^2)\, v. \qquad (4.5)$$

The estimates of the market model parameters α_j and β_j are derived from daily returns on day t and an equally weighted market index m on day t. Carow and Larsen used the following equation to calculate ex-post abnormal returns (AR) for firm j in tth period, as represented by Ar_{jt} (Carow & Larsen, 1997):

$$Ar_{jt} = R_{jt} - (\alpha_j + \beta_j \underline{R}_{mt}) \qquad (4.6)$$

Equations (1) and (3) above are the basic market model measures for daily and average abnormal returns on stocks traded in the stock market (Carow & Larsen, 1997). From these two identity statements written in algebraic form, a measure such as average abnormal return on any given day can be calculated, assuming that the sample size $\underline{n}$ is known. Also the standardized cumulative average abnormal return can be estimated following which a test for significance may be applied. For the subsequent determination of forecast errors and using a cross-statistical regression model, Carow and Larsen concluded that banks with higher capital ratios responded less negatively to the new legislation than banks with low capital ratios. These authors interpreted their results to mean that large banks attribute their negative responses to the additional regulatory requirements, higher insurance premium and an indirect minimization of a too-big-to-fail policy.

Theoretical Constructs

Mergers and acquisitions across all industries have been studied extensively (Jensen & Ruback, 1983; Mueller, 1995; Rhoades, 1993). Jensen and Ruback reviewed some of the major scientific evidence in the field of mergers and acquisitions and concluded that the studies reviewed, generally concluded that acquirers realize zero or negative returns as opposed to acquirees, who experienced positive excess returns. Consistent with the general summation made by the Jensen and Ruback's study were the observations made by Rhoades (1993) and Mueller (1995). Rhoades concluded that gains in efficiency generally eluded the newly integrated organization despite the pre-merger efficiency experiences of acquirers, whereas Mueller observed that the anticipated profitability from merger and acquisition activities did not materialized.

Studies of mergers and acquisitions among commercial banks have not been accorded an equitable portion of research attention relative to other industries (Allen, 1997; Sirower, 1997). However, in recent years a good deal of attention has been directed towards the study of bank mergers and acquisitions (Spiegel & Gart, 1996; Spiegel, Gart, & Gart, 1996). More specifically, the question of size for both acquirers and acquirees is resurfacing as a contentious issue in the study of bank mergers and acquisitions (Sirower, 1997). An earlier work by Trifts and Scanlon (1987) has also examined the question of size of acquirees in mergers and acquisitions. Trifts and Scanlon pointed out that their data suggest that large acquirers acquiring small banks do not generally realize excess returns > 0.

In essence, therefore, some research issues pertaining to bank mergers and acquisitions are quite settled. It is fairly well established that acquiree shareholders obtain significant abnormal returns on the stock prices (Houston & Ryngaert, 1994; Jensen & Ruback, 1983). It is also fairly well established that the relative size of the acquiree, in terms of the acquirer, must be substantially smaller thereby rendering the former as a neutral influencing force on the latter (Sirower, 1997). However, this study has as one of its conjectured relationships, the premonition that relative size of acquirees will be positively associated with the size of the premium paid by acquirers to acquire the assets of the former.

What seems to be unsettled questions among merger and acquisition researchers are first, the question of abnormal returns to the stockholders of the acquiring firm. The literature review, in the preceding chapter, has shown some conflicting evidence on the economic performances of the stocks held by shareholders in acquiring banks. For example, Varaiya (1986) did not find positive economic gains for acquirers, whereas Asquith, Bruner, and Mullins (1983) found positive excess returns for the given group. A second question that seems inconclusive is the question of large banks acquiring or merging with other large banks. It is more so that, in such situations, some bank experts refer to these megabank mergers as "merger of equals" (Spiegel, Gart, & Gart, 1996, p. 65). The problem of large banks acquiring other large banks is a contentious issue among researchers, especially in relation to economic returns on equities for both acquirees and acquirers. A third and final unsettled research question, and one that this researcher is interested in similar to the other two questions identified in this section, is to examine the relationships between the acquisition premium paid by the very large banks to acquire the assets of other very large banks. Extending this question further, the question of premium being paid to acquire the very large banks against the premium paid to acquire the relatively smaller banks is essentially an open one. The questions formulated in this study are not only contentious within the scholarly and banking community, but are relatively novel research questions particularly in situations where the very large banks are acquiring or merging with other large banks.

The population for this study comprised all those banks in the $5 billion or above assets category that were involved in mergers or acquisitions within the United States over the period 1990 to 1997, and were considered as in-market mergers and acquisitions. In-market bank mergers and acquisitions are those commercial banks that are competitors to each other and, therefore, rival one another as they trade more or less along very similar product lines. Given the sharp rise in Internet banking activities, especially among megabanks and given the relaxing of legal framework that once prohibited interstate banking, all megabanks in this study are considered direct or potential competitors to one another. To assist in the mechanics of calculating the various operationalized constructs and to test the various conjectured relationships, Microsoft Excel, SAS, and SPSS software packages proved invaluable quantitative aids in the analysis and interpretation of the data and findings for this study.

The Independent Variable.

Merger announcements. Chen, Lin, and Sauer (1997) found that an official announcement by a corporation could affect the changes in stock prices. Also important, these researchers argued, were the quality and quantity of information disseminated at the time of the earnings' announcement dates by a large number of firms that influence changes in stock prices (Chen, Lin, & Sauer, 1997). Merger announcement dates for the mergers and acquisitions in this study as publicized in the public media, were identified and tracked as the independent variable for each of the megabanks' mergers and acquisitions identified. The daily changes in stock prices, were the basis for a comparative analysis denoted by period t_0, while the other periods are represented by $t_{\pm i}$. The actual announcement date is represented by t_0 and the other days around t_0 are represented by t_{-i} and t_i. These dates are by themselves considered essentially as independent variables, where t_{-i} and t_i are pre- and post merger announcement dates respectively. The symbols t_{-i} and t_i are integers representing single-day units on either side of the official announcement date, t_0.

The Dependent Variable

Abnormal returns. The dependent variable, abnormal or excess returns, was measured for megabanks involved in in-market mergers or acquisitions with assets of $5 billion and above for the acquiring and target banks. The data were obtained from SNL Securities electronic storage facility, Compustat, and Center for Research in Security Prices (CRSP) databases and Mergerstat Reviews. There were no more than 43 such deals in the period under review and hence, the number of banking units involved was ≤ 86. Based on the assumption that the population does not comprise a large number of banks and the required data are essentially to be found in software packages and statistical publications, an attempt was made to collect data on all megabanks mergers and acquisitions for the total population in the period under review. This researcher is aware, however, that in situations where the sample size $\underline{n}$ is close to the population size $\underline{N}$, an effective use of statistical probability and inferential techniques may be necessary to enhance reliability of the findings given that one is interested in the population parameters.

The population consisted of very much close to 43 mergers and acquisitions over the period under review. Reliable data were obtained for 34 or 79.1% of those mergers and acquisitions that constitute the population. The fact that the reliable data were found for only a part, albeit a huge part, and not all the data points of the total population some form of inference is to be made. Moreover, since generalization is sought in relation to the total population and since only 79.1% of the data of the targeted population were obtained, it follows that some level of inferential statistics was appropriate (Freund, Williams, & Perles, 1993). Freund, Williams, and Perles held the view that a population "consists of all conceivably possible (or hypothetically possible) observations of a certain phenomenon; if a set of data contains only a part of these observations, we call it a sample" (p. 45).

Given that the data were not possible for 20.9% of the population and following Freund, Williams, and Perles (1993), this study has sought to make generalization about the total population. However, this researcher is cautious about the fact that, despite the available data that constitute a very large proportion of the total population, the absence of a predetermined scientific selection of a sample may raise questions about generalization to the population. Hence, one may question the reliability of the findings. In the final analysis, there is no reason to suggest that the missing 20.9% of the missing population data will not conform a normal distribution consistent with the other 79.1% of the population distribution. The underlying official announcement dates for the relevant proposed mergers and acquisitions, the independent variable, were tracked, analyzed and fitted into applicable event study equations. In order to compensate for possible information leakage concerning the merger or acquisition event, other units measured in days around the announcement date ($t = 0$) were also analyzed and tested for significance.

Various statistical tests were applied to this study as this researcher sets about the tasks of testing the three postulates identified previously in the form of hypotheses. The three hypotheses identified earlier, in the first chapter of this study, are now reiterated for further clarity and methodological relevance where μ_M and μ_S represent the means of the population for megabanks and small banks respectively.

1. The first hypothesis posits that the shareholders of acquiring megabanks (acquirers) of in-market mergers and acquisitions realize negative abnormal returns around the official announcement dates of such mergers and acquisitions. Symbolically, the null hypothesis (H_0) and the alternate hypothesis (H_1) are stated as follows:

$$H_0 : \mu_M \geq 0$$

$$H_1 : \mu_M < 0$$

where μ_M = mean abnormal returns for megabanks

For statistical purposes, the number of observations related to this hypothesis was considered to be large ($\underline{N} = 34$) and tended to be a normally distributed set of data points. It follows that parametric tests were to be the appropriate approach to evaluate the hypothesized relationship.

2. For in-market megabank mergers and acquisitions, the acquiree shareholders will realize excess or abnormal returns significantly greater than acquirers' shareholders around the announcement date for those mergers and acquisitions that signal their intentions to integrate on the basis of mergers of equals. Symbolically, the null hypothesis (H0) and the alternate hypothesis (H_1) are stated as follows:

$$H_0 : ER_2 = ER_1$$

$$H_1 : ER_2 > ER_1$$

where ER_2 = excess returns calculated for acquirees

and ER_1 = excess returns calculated for acquirers.

For this hypothesis, the number of observations are relatively small ($\underline{N} = 7$) and this researcher did not wish to make the rigorous assumption that the relevant data tended towards normalcy, therefore, nonparametric techniques were the preferred choice of analysis leading to a test of the null hypothesis (H_0).

3. The premium paid for the stocks of the acquirees in in-market megabank mergers and acquisitions are relatively higher than the premium paid to acquire the banks that belong in the small bank category. Symbolically, the null hypothesis (H_0) and the alternate hypothesis (H_1) are stated as follows:

$$H_0 : \mu_M \leq \mu_S$$

$$H_1 : \mu_M > \mu_S$$

where μ_M = the mean merger or acquisition premium for banks in the megabank category.

and μ_S = the mean merger or acquisition premium for banks in the small bank category.

Similar to the assumptions made for the first hypothesis, the third hypothesis of this study has also follow techniques of parametric testing. The justification for such a test is rooted in the condition that $\underline{N}$ is large and is tending towards a normally distributed set of observations.

CHAPTER 5

Research Design

The design of this research will follow the logic of a quantitative paradigm that links the data to be collected and the conclusions drawn relative to the questions asked and related hypotheses formulated. Parts of the design were therefore presented earlier in this study. Drawing upon the Capital Asset Pricing Model (CAPM), a popular risk and return technique prevalent in the finance literature, and the event study method, which is technically the modality of a methodological paradigm associated with mergers and acquisitions in the refereed business and economics journals, this study has quantitatively analyzed the economic returns of in-market megabank mergers and acquisitions at various events in the merger and acquisition processes. To meet the criteria of banks to be included in this study, the business entities would have had to possess the following set of characteristics.

1. Be headquartered in the United States.
2. Operate within converging markets.
3. Have assets $\geq$ $5billion in the megabank category and $\leq$ $100 million for banks in small bank category.
4. Have identical United States federally stipulated Standard Classification Codes (SICs). Industry Group numbers 602 and 603, which include commercial banks and savings institutions respectively, together with Bank Holding Companies under SIC 671 constitute the population for this study.
5. The merger or acquisition must have been officially announced in a major newspaper or some other official publication within the United States.
6. Only mergers and acquisitions that took place between the period 1990 to 1997 did qualify to be included in the sampling frame.

Sample Selection

The sources used to compile the samples for this study were found in SNL Securities, L.C. databases, Mergerstat Reviews for the years 1990 to 1997, Center for Research in Security Prices (CRSP) tapes, and the Wall Street Journal Indexes. The sampling frame consisted of the stocks of the acquirees and acquirers of megabanks that hold assets $\geq$ \$5 billion and small bank acquirees with assets of $\leq$ \$0.1 billion on the date of the given merger or acquisition official announcement. The stocks of the megabanks were traded in either the New York Stock Exchange (NYSE) or the American Stock Exchange (AMEX) on the date of the announcement over the given period, 1990 through 1997. The total population is restricted to those mergers and acquisitions involving banks covered under Industry Group Numbers 602 and 603 of the Federal SIC that grouped banks as either, "Commercial Banks" or "Savings Institutions," respectively. Bank Holding Companies (BHC) bearing SIC code 671 were also included in the population.

The data for the period referenced in this study pointed to the fact that there were no more than 43 mergers and acquisitions involving megabanks and thousands of mergers involving small banks. An attempt was made to collect data for all of the banks in the megabank category. However, given that for reasons such as incomplete data, unavailability of data to estimate given parameters of the population in the small population that characterizes the megabank category, it was statistically prudent to consider the total megabank mergers and acquisitions as the entire sampling frame for the megabank category. Therefore, the data on megabank mergers and acquisitions that will be close to, but less than the total population and hence for all intent and purposes, will be theoretically treated as a statistical sample. For the small bank category of mergers and acquisitions and given the relatively large sampling frame $\underline{N}$, the sample $\underline{n}$ will be drawn using a computer-generated table of random numbers. The size of $\underline{n}$ will be determined statistically to yield a confidence interval set tentatively at 95% (Levine, Berenson, & Stephan, 1998).

Thousands of banks that comprised the small bank category were involved in over 2,000 merger and acquisition activities for the period under review. To scientifically determine the sample size $\underline{n}$ from a finite sampling frame represented by $\underline{N}$, it is assumed that a sample error will lie as close as possible to the given population parameter. It follows therefore, that a researcher will seek to have the sample mean ($\bar{x}$) to lie as close as possible or to have as short a distance (d) as possible to the population mean (μ) with a probability of $(1 - \alpha)$. Thus, the sample size will be directly influenced by the confidence interval we are willing to facilitate and the level of confidence $P(1 - \alpha)$ that a researcher seeks to establish (Sincich, 1996). The term $P(1 - \alpha)$ represents the probability that $\bar{x}$ will lie within $\pm Z_{\alpha/2}$ standard deviation of μ and is commonly referred to as the confidence coefficient. Mathematically, one may write:

$$d = Z(\sigma/\sqrt{\underline{n}}) \quad (5.1)$$

where Z = the statistical measure representing how many standard errors $\overline{x}$ is from

σ = standard deviation of the population

$\underline{n}$ = size of the sample

To obtain the sample size, one needed to solve for "$\underline{n}$." Therefore,

$$\underline{n} = [(Z)^2 (\sigma)^2](d^2)^{-1} \quad (5.2)$$

Calculating the value for $\underline{n}$, this researcher assumed a confidence level of $Z_{0.05}$, which is equal to two standard deviation (2σ) from the population mean. For a 95% confidence level the Z value is approximated at 1.96. Thus equation (5.2) becomes:

$$\underline{n} = [(1.96)^2 (\sigma)^2](d^2)^{-1} \quad (5.3)$$

A Z-score of 1.96 suggests that 95% of the observations will lie a distance of 1.96 on either side of the mean where the Z-score measures the number of standard deviations that a point $\underline{x}$ lies from the population mean μ.

The data for this study covered a number of years where each year realized varying amounts of merger and acquisition activities. Hence, it was necessary to devise a strategy whereby data can be proportionately stratified according to annual aggregation. The objective of such aggregation is to assemble the data into strata so that there is greater homogeneity within data than the overall total. In other words, there is likely to be less variability within strata than between strata for the entire population. In order to facilitate size of samples for a randomized selection of proportions for a given population, the entire population of size $\underline{N}$ is divided into k strata of sizes $\underline{N}_1, \underline{N}_2, \ldots$ and $\underline{N}_k$. In general a sample size of $\underline{n}_1$ may be drawn from a population $\underline{N}_1$, a sample size $\underline{n}_2$ drawn from population $\underline{N}_2$ … and a sample size $\underline{n}_k$ drawn from population $\underline{N}_k$. The allocation of samples in such a manner will be proportional to the extent that, $\underline{n}_1/\underline{N}_1 = \underline{n}_2/\underline{N}_2 = \ldots \underline{n}_k/\underline{N}_k$. Thus, letting:

$\underline{n}_i$ = the sample size for each stratum

and $\underline{n}$ = the overall sample total

$\underline{n}_i = \underline{N}_i/\underline{N}(\underline{n})$

$$\therefore \underline{n} = \sum_{i=1}^{k} \underline{n}_i \qquad (5.4)$$

The data obtained for the area of this study which will seek to test the comparative relationship of premiums paid to acquire or merge with large banks versus smaller ones are partitioned into nonoverlapping annual subsets comprising the overall 8-year period. Sincich (1996) proposed that samples should be drawn from each stratum in relation to that stratum's quantifiable relationship to the total population that is being studied. The following equation was adapted from Sincich (p. 445), in order to approximate the total sample size $\underline{n}$ for a stratified population mean μ based on a 95% confidence interval:

$$\underline{n} = \frac{(\sum \underline{N}_i^2 \sigma_i^2 / w_i)}{\underline{N}^2(d^2/4) + \sum(\underline{N}_i \sigma_i^2)} \qquad (5.5)$$

where $\underline{N}_i$ = number of elements in population strata i

σ_i = standard deviation of the elements in population strata i

d^2 = desired half-width of the confidence interval and can be approximated using equation (5.1)

w_i = proportion of the total elements found in stratum i

Equation (5.5) suggests that the sample n_i is to be allocated to each stratum proportional to the ratio of the given population stratum N_i to the overall population as was explained in the paragraph leading to, and including, equation (5.4) above. The sample size n for the small bank category in the merger and acquisition will be drawn from a finite sampling frame N consisting of 2,236 mergers and acquisition spread disproportionately over the period 1990 to 1997. The actual size of n and proportionately stratified random samples drawn from N_i in relation to N was analyzed and approximated in the following chapter.

Historical data identified in printed and computerized databases were extracted, compiled and analyzed with the aim of providing answers to the questions posed in this study. Apart from this major source of secondary data, which also included megabanks' published records, primary data such as structured interviews and systematic observations were also sought. Such primary data may be necessary under the assumption that it may become necessary to supplement the results of this essentially quantitative paradigm with qualitative inductive data. In the final analysis, the data collected, analyzed and summarized focused firstly, on a series of quantitative ratios and then to systematically apply these ratios to make statistical and logical sense in response to the theoretical constructs and postulates formulated in this study.

Hypothesis 1: Megabank Acquirers and Abnormal Return on Equities

This hypothesis sought to test economic value creation for acquirer shareholders among megabanks over the period 1990 -1997. Excess or abnormal returns, the dependent variable, were theoretically constructed as explained earlier in this chapter and followed the works of Carow & Larsen (1997), Sirower (1997), and Brown & Warner (1983, 1985). The independent variable is represented by the official announcement date of the underlying mergers and acquisitions and all days considered in a well-defined event window.

The Dependent Variable: Abnormal returns.

The dependent variable, abnormal or excess returns, was measured for megabanks involved in in-market mergers or acquisitions with assets of $5 billion and above for the acquiring and target banks. This data were obtained from SNL Securities Bank M&A DataSource electronic storage facility, Compustat, and Center for Research in Security Prices (CRSP) databases and Mergerstat Reviews. Duplicating the parameters and the relevant elements stated in equation (1) above and following the techniques adopted by Carow and Larsen (1997) and

Ruback (1983) the regression equation applicable to this study for the returns on stock prices (R_{jt}) were calculated using:

$$R_{jt} = \alpha_j + \beta_j R_{mt} + E_{jt}$$

Following the ordinary least squares techniques (OLS), the parameters a_j and B_j of the market model were estimated and relevant data points were tested at 95% confidence level, and where appropriate, at a 99% or 75% levels generally applying one-tailed statistical tests. The results of these tests sought to demonstrate whether, and to what extent, abnormal returns were realized for each of these consolidations and whether generalizations can be made within a degree of confidence about future mergers for the category of banks identified. In addition, some of the findings related to this hypothesis have formed a subset of the data that were used to test the merger-of-equal hypothesis formulated in another area of this study.

The ex-post abnormal returns for *j*th firm in *t*th period (AR_{jt}) is obtained as follows.

$$AR_{jt} = R_{jt} - (a'_j + \beta'_j R_{mt}) \quad (5.6)$$

a' and β' = parameters of an individual firm, *j*, in the *t*th period.

The components in equation (5.6) are very similar to equation (4.1) except that the data points are representing measurements only for an individual unit in the sample. For a sample of n securities the average abnormal return (AAR) on day *t* is:

$$AAR_t = (\sum_{j=1}^{n} AR_{jt}) \, 1/\underline{n} \quad (5.7)$$

To estimate the cumulative average abnormal returns (CAAR) as close to the official announcement date (-1 to 0 day/week) was taken to be:

$$CAAR = \sum_{t=-1}^{0'} AAR_t \quad (5.8)$$

To test the abnormal returns for significance each abnormal return (AR_{jt}) was standardized as applicable to test for significance using the standard deviation of its forecast's error (S_{jt}) as follows:

$$SAR_{jt} = (AR_{jt})\, 1/S_{jt} \qquad (5.9)$$

To calculate the standardized average daily abnormal returns for all banks in the sample (SCARj) and to arrive at the standardized cumulative abnormal return the following equation is derived:

$$SCARj = \sum_{t=-1}^{n} SAR_{jt} \qquad (5.10)$$

To arrive at the standardized cumulative average abnormal return for the -1 to 0 period, where 0 = the announcement day or week, the following equation is arrived at:

$$SCAAR = \sum_{j=1}^{n} SCARj\,(1/\underline{n}) \qquad (5.11)$$

The final equation, following Carow and Larsen (1997), to calculate the t statistic of the standardized cumulative abnormal return for the sample of $\underline{n}$ banks is:

$$SCAAR_{t\text{-statistic}} = \sum_{j=1}^{n} SCARj\,[\,1/(\,2^{1/2} \times \underline{n}^{1/2}\,)\,] \qquad (5.12)$$

The $\underline{t}$ statistic for this study has follow the Brown & Warner (1985) study, which was more or less reiterated in the Carow and Larsen (1997) FDICIA Regulatory events-study test and effectively recaptured in equation (12) above. Since this study does not assume a 100% knowledge of the true population standard deviation and given that the sample, which is relatively large ($\underline{n} > 30$) and assumed to be normally distributed except for Hypothesis II, the degrees of freedom is assumed to be ($\underline{n} - 1$), where $\underline{n}$ = the number of elements in the distribution. The tests for this study generally focused at a 95% confidence level. However, analyses at 90 and 75 percent levels were presented merely as statistical reference points and not in any way exclusively related to the drawing of conclusions about the relevant hypothesis being tested.

The Independent Variable: Event window period.

Merger announcement dates for the mergers and acquisitions in this study as publicized in the public media, were identified and tracked as the independent variable for each of the merger or acquisition identified for the megabanks. The daily changes in stock prices, were the basis for a comparative analysis at the date of official announcement of a given merger or acquisition denoted by period t_0, while the other periods are represented by $t_{\pm i}$. These dates are by themselves essentially considered as independent variables, where t_{-i} and t_i are pre- and post merger announcement dates respectively.

The symbols t_{-i} and t_i are integers representing single-day units on either side of the official announcement date, t_0. In actuality, the event window considered in this study will cover a period 20 days on either side of t_0 and can be symbolized by day $t(t = n...0...+n)$. More specifically day $= (t\ -20,...,0,...,+20)$, which is consistent with the suggestion of Dodd (1980), simply implies that the event period being considered is 20 days on either side of the announcement day which tallies to a 41-day observation period.

Hypothesis 2: Mergers of Equals In-market Megabanks

To test the merger of equal hypothesis a subanalysis was conducted, after identifying those banks that lay claim to integrating with one another on a merger-of-equal basis, from the larger sample of the megabank category. There were no more than 18 such banks involved in the mergers and acquisitions identified for this study, comprising a total of 9 mergers or acquisitions. Given that this hypothesis stipulates that the difference between the excess returns of the acquirers and the acquirees are significantly different, appropriate small sample distribution test statistics were formulated to ascertain whether or not the null hypothesis can be rejected.

The nature of the small size of the data points compounded with the notion that a researcher does not wish to rely on a stringent assumption that the data represent a normally distributed population, a nonparametric test is an appropriate procedure for testing the merger of equals' hypothesis (Keller, Warrack &, Bartel, 1994). Therefore, rather than asking to test variances about the mean of a population or calculating a mean value for a sampling distribution representing a given population, a nonparametric test is a preferred procedure for testing the differences between measures of location between two or more sets of data. Despite the fact that the data may be of a quantitative type, the conditions necessary for testing $\mu_2 - \mu_1$ may not have been satisfied in the light of a given situation where the normality requirements necessary for conducting such a parametric test have been violated.

The popularly used Wilcoxon signed rank sum test for matched pairs data is the chosen nonparametric test for the merger of equal hypothesis in this study. The Wilcoxon signed rank sum test determines whether one population's location is the same, or significantly different from another and seeks to detect movements in the relative frequency distribution of the given population (Keller, Warrack, & Bartel, 1994). More specifically, such a ranked test takes into consideration the magnitude of the differences between one population and another. The Wilcoxon signed rank test for matched pairs is the chosen nonparametric test for two major reasons. Firstly, that the number of units in the population or the sample is small, that is, less than 15 (Freund, Williams, & Perles, 1993) and is suspect of being nonnormal in its distribution. Secondly, the observations that comprised the data are paired, in that each of the observations is matched against another in the given set of data.

The Wilcoxon signed rank sum test for matched pairs sought to rank differences between matched pairs of data ignoring the prefixes of signs to such differences. A ranked value of 1 is assigned to the smallest numerical difference in absolute value $|\mu_2 - \mu_1|$ terms. A rank of 2 is assigned to the second smallest absolute value difference and so on, to a rank of n, the highest integer which is assigned to the largest numerical difference in absolute value terms. In the given situation of $|\mu_2 - \mu_1|$ the implication is that the alternative hypothesis is that $\mu_2 > \mu_1$.

There were no zero differences in the values resulting from value T^-; neither were there any numerically equal differences. Therefore, for all the tests, the observations remained constant at $\underline{n} = 7$. The procedure for performing the Wilcoxon signed rank test for matched pairs is based on a comparison of the ranked sums of the negative and positive differences between the underlying pairs of observations. The symbol T^- is used to represent the total assigned values for differences < 0, whereas T^+ is used to represent those assigned values > 0. According to the Wilcoxon signed rank test for matched pairs the value of T^- and T^+ are determined as follows:

$$T^- = \sum_{i=1}^{\underline{n}} |\mu_2 - \mu_1|_t \text{ with negative signs reallocated for all}$$

$$\mu_{2t} < \mu_{1t} \qquad\qquad (5.13)$$

$$T^+ = \sum_{t=1}^{n} |\mu_2 - \mu|_t \text{ with positive sign reallocated for all}$$

$$\mu_{2t} > \mu_{1t}. \tag{5.14}$$

The merger of equals' hypothesis in this study states that acquirees realize excess returns significantly greater than acquirers for those mergers and acquisitions among megabanks that integrate on a merger of equals basis. Consistent with the consensus among major researchers in the field of studies relating to mergers and acquisition, acquirees generally do realize positive value creation on their stockholdings (Houston & Ryngaert, 1994; Jensen & Ruback, 1983; Peristiani, 1997). The research interest in this part of the study is to test whether the positive gains to acquiree shareholders around the official announcement date holds true in situations where megabanks integrate on a merger of equals basis.

Since $\underline{n}$, the data representing the population distribution, is small ($\underline{n} < 15$), the appropriate test statistic for the merger of equals hypothesis is:

H_1 : ER_2 = ER_1

H_0 : ER_2 ≤ ER_1

where ER_2 = excess returns for megabank acquirees

and ER_1 = excess returns for megabank acquirers

Excess or abnormal returns for each of the 7 observations in the merger of equals' hypothesis were calculated for a shortened 11-day event period using equations (5.13) and (5.14). In such a situation excess return averaging was not necessary in the analytical framework for this hypothesis. Freund, Williams, and Perles (1993) identified a one-tail directional test, which utilizes the Wilcoxon signed rank test with a test statistic represented by T. Those authors hold that when the alternative hypothesis is one-directional and positive ($\mu_1 > \mu_0$), T^- will tend to be small. In the setting for this research and following Freund, Wiliams and Perles, the test statistic is represented by the T^- given that the merger of equal hypothesis is a one-directional positive test ($ER_2 > ER_1$). In other words, given that this researcher has the hunch that acquiree shareholders value creation significantly exceeds that of the acquirer shareholders, the assigned values will be negative and tend to be small. It follows, therefore, that the values for T^- will be the test statistic for the merger of equal hypothesis for the excess returns of acquirees (ER_2).

The decision rule is to reject H_0 where the calculated numerically ranked total with negative values is equal to, or is less than the critical value T_α ($\alpha = 0.05$) as given in the Wilcoxon signed ranks sum test statistics for paired differences. Essentially, letting T^- = the test statistic, H_0 will be rejected for all $T_t^- \leq T_\alpha$ where T_t^- = negative values for each of the period in the 11-day event window.

Excess returns were calculated for each of the days in an 11-day event window which included 5 days on either side of the official announcement date with the announcement date being $t = 0$. The terms $ER_{2(-t, t)}$ and $ER_{1(-t, t)}$ represent calculated excess returns for acquirees and acquirers respectively, where the $(-t, t)$ symbol represents the period (-5, 5) days around the official announcement date. The decision of whether $ER_{2(-t, t)} > ER_{1(-t, t)}$ is significant on any given $\pm t$ day is determined by a calculated T statistic and an applicable critical value of the Wilcoxon signed rank statistic for matched pairs. Thus the Wilcoxon signed rank sum test for matched pairs will help determine whether on any given day in the event window one distribution shifted to the right of the other.

The preceding theoretical relationship tended to suggest a one-tailed statistical test for small samples. Taking up from equation (1), the residual error or disturbance term E_{jt}, which represented the abnormal returns to stockholders of firm j for period t, was further analyzed and this differential gave an indication of the true value for the abnormal returns in mergers and acquisitions. The ex-post abnormal returns for the jth firm in tth period (ER_{jt}) for the banks identified in the sample "merger of equals" were calculated using equation (4.6), which was discussed in chapter 4. Since the sample size for this hypothesis is statistically small, then the assumption that the population data are normally distributed, may have been violated. To compensate for such a possible violation of normalcy in the populations considered and the data may be considered as paired for statistical purposes, a nonparametric test utilizing the Wilcoxon signed rank sum test for matched pairs was formulated to test for significance.

Hypothesis 3: Acquisition Premium and Megabanks

As a consequence of a merger or an acquisition the combined operations of the integrated entities are expected to increase revenue over time. Contingent upon the relative size of acquiree vis-à-vis the acquirer, a small growth in revenue from operations of the integrated entities can justify a premium payment. For example, assuming that Bank A acquires Bank B, the latter of which has a total number of outstanding ordinary shares amounting to 7 million at the onset of the agreement to integrate as a single unit. In addition, it is projected that at the end of 5 years revenues from each individually operated entity will amount to $60 and $640.5 million discounted, respectively. Also, it is further projected that revenue from the combined operations will amount to $750 million discounted at the end of the measurement period. It can be shown mathematically that a premium of up to 82.5% (net value from synergy minus net revenue projected from independently operated Bank B per ordinary share) may be justified.

One intuitive lesson to be learnt from the preceding example is that a small change in the synergistic effects may bring about a much larger change in the acquiree's economic value. Based on this abstraction, it not a surprise that Sirower (1997) found premium payments to be value destroying in relatively large acquisitions. Another intuitive lesson to be learnt from this example is that by expanding the measurement interval further into the post announcement period revenue growth is likely to occur under the assumption of decreasing long run average costs over time.

To test the hypothesis that large megabanks are attracting higher premium payments than relatively smaller banks, three measures are identified. These are: purchase price offered to book value, market price to trailing-four-quarter earnings per share abbreviated in the finance literature as LTM Eps(x) (SNL Securities LC, 1998) and acquisition premium as a percentage.

Purchase price to book value.

Despite the shortcomings in a measure using book value instead of market value this ratio was used nevertheless, given that such a measure represented the modality of the research activities in the area of mergers and acquisitions. The justification for the popularity of using price to book value rather than price to market value is perhaps due to the historical nature of costing to financial entities. Assuming that during the analytical stage of this study and given the cross-sectional nature of the data proposed for this study, any possible idiosyncrasies that may arise due to the problem of heteroscedasticity was addressed by introducing scaling to relative size. The implication, therefore, is that bank size will be introduced only as a control variable in this part of the study.

Market price to trailing-four-quarters earnings per share.

Purchase price to book value was used to measure the market-determined value of the stock in relation to the acquiree's internally assessed book value at the time of the merger announcement. LTM Eps(x) was obtained by dividing the agreed merger or prevailing acquisition price per share by the trailing-four-quarter earnings per unit of equity. Symbolically, this ratio can be derived from:

$$P_A \left[\sum_{i=1}^{4} (Y_i / S_A) \right]^{-1} \quad (5.15)$$

Where P_A = the agreed purchase price per share for security A

$\sum_{i=1}^{4}$ = the total of the four quarters preceding the actual announcement date

Y_i/S_A = earnings per book value share with Y_i being the income per ith period and S_A representing the book value of security A.

The measurement constructed in equation (5.15) was used to calculate all the samples in the megabank and small bank categories and the testing of the differences between their means were conducted. This study hypothesized that ($\mu_2 - \mu_1$) > 0 and, therefore, megabanks are indeed attracting a higher premium, assuming that the data point to a significant difference between the centers of location population parameters.

Acquisition premium as a percentage of book value.

Acquisition premium, as a percentage, is defined as the difference between the market price of the acquiree's stock and the price to be paid for acquiring the acquiree's bank stocks (Eckert, 1997). Measured as a percentage change of the merger or acquisition premium the calculations become:

$$P = [V_j (1/V_b)] \, 100 \qquad (5.16)$$

where P = acquisition premium ratio

V_j = the premium actually paid to acquire the stocks, and

V_b = the book value of the acquiree's stocks.

This study has utilized one or more of the financial, measures or ratios as enumerated in above to test the third and final hypothesis formulated in this study. The decision to utilize one measure over the other hinges on the availability of reliable data.

The works of Cheng, Gup, and Wall (1989) and Rhoades (1987) used statistical correlation tests to assess whether a relationship exists between acquisition premium and abnormal stock returns. The strength of the correlation at $\alpha = 0.05$ was conducted with the aim of also testing the strength of the relationship between acquisition premiums and abnormal returns at the week of merger announcement (Chen, Gup, & Wall, 1989). An absence of a positive correlation between these two variables in a merger or acquisition may suggest that the motivation for power or hubris motive may be a plausible explanation behind a decision to consolidate (Rhoades, 1987). To reiterate a previously stated limitation, the testing of the hubris motive in bank mergers and acquisitions is beyond the scope of this study.

Threats to Validity

This study sought to maximize the internal validity of its design by placing confidence in the conjectured relationships that the independent variables influenced or covaried with the dependent variables. Based on the construct validity assumption, that the independent and dependent are associated, a postulation that has been validated by previous researchers, this study has been constantly vigilant for creeping threats to internal validity of the model being tested. More specifically, validity threats to this study that may be associated with normality of the sample distribution and homoscedasticity, sequencing of variables, reverse causation, rival explanations, and creeping mortality were constantly and systematically monitored. These possible threats to validity are further examined below.

Normality in sample and homoscedasticity.

The general linear model of regression and correlation assumes normality of the sample distribution and homoscedasticity. Statistical tests such as the t-distribution and the analysis of variance's (ANOVA) F tests are very robust against departures from the normality assumption. Homoscedasticity implies that the variations around the line of the regression will remain constant (Levine, Berenson, & Stephan, 1998). To control for threat to homoscedasticity, this study has sought to apply data transformations and appropriately weighted least square method.

Sequencing of variables.

Sequencing of variables implies that when a group of firms experience the same phenomenon, such as a merger or an acquisition event, a measure of central tendency can be seen as capturing the impact of the event. The theoretical constructs make the assumption that, in the light of the correlative nature of the variables, the independent variable precedes the dependent variable. Previous studies have validated that merger or acquisition announcements, the independent variable, precedes the effects of shareholders' value creation, the dependent variable.

Reverse causation.

Reverse causation as an internal validity threat suggests that the dependent variable caused the independent variable (Campbell & Stanley, cited in Sproull, 1995, pp. 138-140). This presumed cause coming before the effect does not pose much of a threat to validity in this study given that the conjectured relationships do not, per se, sought to show causality. Rather, this study sought to test associationships and possible covariances among variables. Moreover, previous studies testing the relationships between announcement of mergers and acquisitions and stock price changes have shown, by and large, that the independent variable precedes the dependent variable and will most likely influence the latter within specified event windows.

Rival explanation.

Given the conjectured relationship established in this study between mergers and acquisitions and value creation for shareholders, this researcher is aware that other factors such as radical shift in a company policy, earnings announcement, or massive trading in one's own equity can also explain the dependent variable. Generally, business organizations do not simultaneously announce a major shift in company policies or earnings announcements with an important event such as a merger or an acquisition. However, in the rare event that another variable can effectively intervene to explain the dependent variable, one possible solution is to exclude that merger or acquisition from the sample. This researcher was, nevertheless, constantly vigilant for possible rival explanations.

Creeping mortality

Creeping mortality suggests that over time, the sample may fade away prior to the end of the study due to attrition or some other creeping mortality. To counter this threat, an upward allowance in the sample size was effected in the small bank category. Therefore, instead of proportionately selecting stratified sample groups from the target finite population that comprised a theoretically safe and mathematically determined "d," as was earlier demonstrated in this chapter. Thus, to derive the largest possible sample size the calculated value of d must be at a minimum (see Tables 8.3 and 9.1 in chapters 8 and 9 respectively).

In addition to a large sample size as technically possible, the event window is short, such as only days on either side of each event announcement and thus will lead to reducing the probability of creeping rival events. Moreover, delistings of parties to a merger or acquisition can be tracked by examining the records of trading for the various New York stock exchanges. In any event, the complete delisting of one of the parties to a merger, or in less frequent cases, the delistings of both parties to a merger or acquisition to the listing of a new entity, does not occur within days or even weeks. The modal period for the birth of a newly integrated legal entity occurs over several months into the post merger or acquisition period.

Threats to Validity: A Summary

The scientific basis for concluding that there is a relationship between the independent variable and the dependent variable rests intricately upon the ability of the researcher to measure what was intended to be measured and to generalized the results, where applicable, to the target population. This study has examined some of the major threats of validity that could detract from the reliability of the findings. Within the errors anticipated, the tests developed in this study and the resulting conclusions are significantly consistent with the methodology and findings generated by other researchers in the merger and acquisition field of inquiry.

Market Reaction

Substantial benefits can be achieved by consolidating and unifying the managerial and financial practices among megabanks (Houston & Ryngaert, 1994), thereby leading to increased profits and customer service quality. Beyond any immediate economic benefits realized around the time of the merger or acquisition, the combined banks might be viewed as having tremendous speculative prospects for achieve operating cost savings and service improvements as a result of an underlying integration (Spiegel & Gart, 1996). These added savings are perceived to be sometimes much greater than that, for which the merging megabanks could have achieved independently. Such perceptions by investors are indeed compelling economic reasons why banks should continue to consolidate. In some cases integration between merging entities generate economic benefits for shareholders only for a few days or months in the post announcement period, a situation described by Damodaran (1996) as an "over-reacting market" (p. 168). In an overreacting market, the security price for either of the merging parties was more or less a "knee-jerk" reaction to the news of the underlying merger or acquisition announcement. The synthesis in such a situation, therefore, is that investors may have initially overvalued the common stocks of the integrating parties in a merger or an acquisition. The end result is that these investors sought to reverse their decisions by selling off the underlying securities in the immediate post-announcement period.

The main focus of this study sought to examine megabank mergers and acquisitions with particular reference to in-market consolidations, over the period 1990 to 1997. In-market bank mergers and acquisitions are those consolidations between banks in converging product lines and markets. With the steep rise in Internet banking activities and the relaxing of the legal barriers to interstate banking, all the megabanks considered in this study are direct or potential competitors to one another. Technically and strategically, megabanks within the United States are essentially in-market players.

The promotion of greater competition is more readily apparent in recent times given the relaxing of the legal framework surrounding financial intermediaries and the advent of a broad-base application of information technology. An interesting phenomenon surrounding market behavior concerns new-market bank deals, as financial service entities configure their propensities to integrate with one another. New-market bank mergers and acquisition are those consolidations consisting of banks in different geographical locations such as within states, within and outside regions and internationally.

CHAPTER 6

Results and Discussion of Value Creation for Acquirers Hypothesis

The explicit purpose of the study as evidenced in this book thus far was to isolate and examine those banks and thrifts that were involved in merger and acquisition activities within the United States of America over the period 1990 to 1997, and held assets of at least $5 billion at the time of their respective merger or acquisition announcements. In addition, this study sought to examine value creation for shareholders in situations where these very large banks and thrifts acquired or merged with other very large banks and thrifts. These underlying banks have grown to be very huge financial powerhouses within a relatively short period of time to the point where they are referred to as "megabanks," the concept used throughout this study in reference to these huge financial entities

The value creation emphasis is mainly directed towards acquirers in the integration process by tracking the dynamics of equity pricing behavior and the underlying excess returns resulting from abnormal stock price swings. This study focused on the acquirer banks involved in the integration process, given the reality that the debate over economic gains for acquiree shareholders are predominantly a settled issue among academicians and banking professionals. What is very much in contention, however, is the question of value creation for the acquiring shareholders (acquirers) within the dynamics of merger and acquisition activities among the financial entities.

This study also sought to examine the shareholders' value creation among those megabanks that signify their intentions to integrate on the basis of merger of equals. On this question, the research effort in this study also examined value creation for both the acquiring (acquirers) and acquired (acquirees) shareholders among those megabanks identified in this study. For purposes of this study and as previously stated in chapter 2, "merger of equals" is an ex post facto strategy usually introduced during the pre-announcement phase. In this phase, it is expected that such a concept will usher in a philosophy of diversity and inclusiveness for purposes of guiding the organizational and operational activities of the newly integrated entity. Thus, the operational dynamics going forward in the post integration period will be guided by a philosophy of equality, irrespective of who acquired whom. Note that, the results of the merger of equals' hypothesis are discussed in chapter 7.

In order to achieve the above stated goals, this chapter will test Hypothesis 1 using the data compiled, while chapters 7 through 9 will discuss the results of hypotheses 2 and 3. The first part of this chapter will show the results of the test conducted to assess the dynamics of value creation for acquiring shareholders using the data compiled from several sources. This chapter will also seek to demonstrate the results of the various quantitative tests applicable to the underlying hypothesis formulated for this research activity. Thus, the first part will seek to answer the question posed in Hypothesis 1 concerning the dynamics of value creation for shareholders among acquiring megabanks (acquirers). The second part will seek to address the issue of threats to internal validity while the final part will summarize and synthesize the results of the analysis of data extracted to test validity and reliability of the findings.

Test Results of Value Creation for Acquirers

This part of the data analysis will seek to discuss the data collected, analyzed, and interpreted in terms of the first hypothesis stated in this study, which sought to address, the question of shareholders value creation for acquiring shareholders referred to in this study as "acquirers." Hypothesis 1 states that "the shareholders of acquiring megabanks involved in in-market megabank mergers and acquisitions realize negative abnormal returns on their stock prices around the official announcement date of the merger or acquisition." Symbolically, the null hypothesis (H_0) and the alternate hypothesis (H_1) are stated as follows:

$$H_0: \mu_M \geq 0$$
$$H_1: \mu_M < 0$$

where μ_M = average excess returns for the targeted population of megabank acquirers

In the context of the hypothesis formulated above one may deduce and test the null hypothesis that in-market megabank acquirers, on the average and for the period under study, do not realize positive abnormal returns where μ, the population mean, is suggested to be ≥ 0. Identifying and extracting the data on bank mergers and acquisitions were rooted in three data sources. These data sources were the Wall Street Journal Index, Megerstat Review, and SNL Securities LC's DataSource on bank mergers and acquisitions. The announcement dates for the megabanks that fit the criteria for this study were cross-referenced with the three different data sources and these dates were found to be fairly consistent. Figures on daily stock returns and market price movements were identified and extracted from the Center for Research in Security Prices (CRSP) database. The S&P 500 stock data were referenced as the basis for determining excess (abnormal) returns. Thirty-four mergers and acquisitions out of a total of 43 that fit the criteria as specified in the Research Design of this study and occurred over the referenced period 1990-1997 were identified. Table 6.1 gives the number of banks in the population per year over the referenced period for which reliable data were obtained.

There were 43 megabank mergers and acquisitions involving banks and thrifts over the period 1990 to 1997, according to data compiled electronically by SNL Securities LC. These data were cross-referenced with annual Mergerstat Reviews and the Wall Street Journal, and the number that comprised the target population were found to be consistent across all databases. From this number of mergers and acquisitions, 9, or 20.9%, were eliminated from the data compiled for the total population based on reasons such as insufficiency of information, unreliability of data on stock price movements, or competing explanation for abnormal equity price movements over the 41-day period. Hence, as can be seen in Table 6.1, a total of 34 or 79.1% of mergers and acquisitions involving some 68 banks made up the proportion of the population identified as megabanks for the acquirer shareholders' value creation test.

Table 6.1
Mergers and Acquisitions Involving Megabanks in the United States for Period 1990 to 1997

Year	No. of Megabanks
1990	02
1991	12
1992	06
1993	04
1994	02
1995	22
1996	06
1997	14
TOTAL	68

Note. Compiled from Mergerstat Review. (1990-1998). Los Angeles, CA: Houlihan Lokey Howard & Zukin; SNL Securities LC. (1999). Bank M & A DataSource. Electronic database Version 2.1, June. Charlottesville, VA.

Table 6.1 gives the number of mergers and acquisitions (34) involving some 68 banks, where both acquirers and acquirees, at the time of the official announcement to integrate, would each have had assets of $5.0 billion or more. Table 6.1 shows that the latter half of the period under review realized 64.7 % of the merger and acquisition activities indicating an acceleration in the integration among this category of banks.

Excess returns were calculated over an event period consisting of 20 days on either side of the official announcement date for each of the 34 acquirers. The parameter estimates are based on the pre-event window (-T, -t) days, which extends over a period of 240 days (-260, -21) by using the ordinary least square estimates of the market model regression. The parameter estimates for the average excess returns (A_{jt}) were calculated as follows:

$$A_{jt} = R_{jt} - a_{jt} - \beta_{jt}(R_{mt}),$$

where a_{jt} = ordinary least square values from the estimation period

(T-260, t -21)

R_{jt} = Return on the CRSP value weighted index for jth stock

in the ith period

R_{mt} = return on the CRSP equally weighted market index m for

β_{jt} = ordinary least square values from the estimation period

(T-260, t -21)

$$\beta_{jt} = \frac{n \Sigma R_{mt}(R_{jt}) - \Sigma R_{mt} \Sigma R_{jt}}{n \Sigma R_{mt}^2 - n(\Sigma R_{mt})^2}, \text{ over the estimation period}$$

The estimation period for β_{jt} and a_{jt} extends over 240 days prior to the identified event window period of (-20, 20) days around the announcement date (t = 0). The excess or abnormal return for each acquirer was then aggregated and an average was calculated to arrive at the average excess returns (AER) for each of the days in the 41-day event window. The cumulated average excess return (CAER) was also calculated starting from -20 days through to +20 days, on either side of the official announcement date for each of the acquirers identified in the megabank category. A t statistic was then calculated for each of the 41 days within the event window. The t statistic for this study has follow the Brown and Warner (1985) study, which was more or less reiterated in the Carow and Larsen (1997) FDICIA Regulatory events-study test and effectively recaptured in equation (9) of Chapter 3. Since this study assumes no 100% knowledge of the true population's standard deviation (σ) and given that the distribution is relatively large ($n > 30$) with a tendency to be normally distributed, the t-statistic is an appropriate test to be employed (Keller, Warrack, & Bartel, 1994). The shape of the sampling distribution is essentially influenced by ($n - 1$) degrees of freedom.

The dependent variable t test assumes normalcy in the distribution of the data points with unequal variances between the estimation or reference period and the comparison or event-window period. The tests focus at the 5% level of significance. However, analyses at 10 and 25 percent levels of significance are presented merely as statistical reference points or supporting analytical information and not strictly as a basis for conclusions surrounding the hypothesis being tested. The critical value for the one tail test critical value limit = $t_{\alpha = 0.05}$, with ($n - 1$) degrees of freedom (d.f.).

The question of whether excess returns around and including the announcement date are non-negative is answered by estimating the t statistic for each of the days over the event window using:

$$(\text{AER}_{t(t=-n\ldots0\ldots+n)}) \times (\text{S.E. }t(t=n\ldots0\ldots+n))^{-1}$$

where $\text{AER}_{t(t=-n\ldots0\ldots+n)}$ = Average excess returns over the event window (-20 to 0 to +20) days

and $\text{S.E. }t(t=-n\ldots0\ldots+n)^{-1}$ = Standard error for each of the period included in the event window

A mathematical formula for the standard error (SE) in relation to the applicable t statistic is given in Appendix B. Table 6.2 captures the average excess returns (AER) and cumulative average excess returns (CAER) over the 41-day event window with the corresponding calculated t statistic.

Table 6.2
Average and Cumulative Average Excess Returns Calculated Over the 41-day Event Window with Applicable *t* Statistic

Days(t)	Average Excess Returns (AER)	Cumulative Average Excess Returns (CAER)	*t* Statistic (AER)
-20	-0.34399%	-0.34399%	-0.8285 ***
-19	0.34682%	0.00283%	0.8327
-18	0.31863%	0.32146%	0.7651
-17	0.15193%	0.47339%	0.3648
-16	-0.32963%	0.14376%	-0.7913***
-15	-0.15937%	-0.01561%	-0.3826
-14	0.25691%	0.24130%	0.6182
-13	-0.16848%	0.07282%	-0.4045
-12	0.14119%	0.21401%	0.3391
-11	-0.01687%	0.19714%	-0.0405
-10	0.27790%	0.47506%	0.6672
-9	-0.32881%	-0.14325%	-0.7894***
-8	-0.15030%	-0.00405%	-0.3608
-7	-0.10467%	-0.10872%	0.2512
-6	0.23951%	0.13079%	0.5152
-5	0.36314%	0.49393%	0.8718
-4	0.26130%	0.75523%	0.6273
-3	0.04435%	0.79958%	0.1065
-2	0.08621%	0.88579%	0.2073
-1	-0.31811%	0.56768%	-0.7637***
0	-1.93599%	-1.36831%	-4.6481*
1	-0.83411%	-2.20242%	-2.0028*
2	-0.03608%	-2.23850%	-0.0866
3	-0.01955%	-2.25805%	-0.0469
4	0.11568%	-2.14237%	0.2777
5	-0.05684%	-2.19921%	-0.1364

(table continues)

Days(t)	Average Excess Returns (AER)	Cumulative Average Excess Returns (CAER)	t Statistic (AER)
6	0.64996%	-1.54925%	1.5691
7	0.17187%	-1.37738%	0.4126
8	0.12155%	-1.25583%	0.2918
9	-0.35834%	-1.61417%	-0.8603***
10	0.07260%	-1.54157%	0.1743
11	-0.30125%	-1.84282%	-0.7232***
12	-0.13666%	-1.97948%	-0.3281
13	0.37258%	-1.60690%	0.8945
14	-0.13938%	-1.74628%	-0.3346
15	-0.03364%	-1.77992%	-0.0808
16	-0.02079%	-1.80071%	-0.0499
17	0.05975%	-1.74090%	0.1435
18	-0.59638%	-2.33464%	-1.4318**
19	-0.00544%	-2.34008%	-0.0131
20	0.14517%	-2.19491%	0.3485

*, **, ***. Indicates 5, 10, and 25% levels of significance, respectively.

There is considerable evidence that megabank' acquirers do realize negative abnormal returns around the official announcement date, as can be seen by the frequency of negative abnormal returns shown in Table 6.2. Wherever the t statistics are essentially significant at the 5% level, the event affects returns. The sign of the excess returns indicates whether the event' effect for each day in the event window is positive or negative. Around the official announcement dates of -1, 0, and 1, excess negative returns averaged around -0.31811% (-0.7637) with 25% level of significance, -1.93599% (-4.6480) and -0.83411% (-2.0028) both with a 5% level of significance. T statistics are given in the accompanying brackets. In addition, Average CAER around (-1,0, 1) = -1.02951 with a t statistic = -2.47140. Clearly, and consistent with other research findings in the banking and finance literature, acquirers on the average do not realize positive abnormal return and instead, as this study has shown, may even realize negative abnormal returns.

Figure 6.1 gives a pictorial representation of the AER and CAER over the 41-day event window with a graph of the data showing movements in average excess returns and cumulative average excess returns over the 41-day event window. A cursory look at Figure 6.1 reveals a swift downward shift in the average and cumulative average Excess Returns over the event's measurement period suggesting that the market did not reward the acquirer shareholders in mergers and acquisition involving megabanks. Such a sharp downward trend is especially indicative around the announcement day as represented in this study by (t = 0).

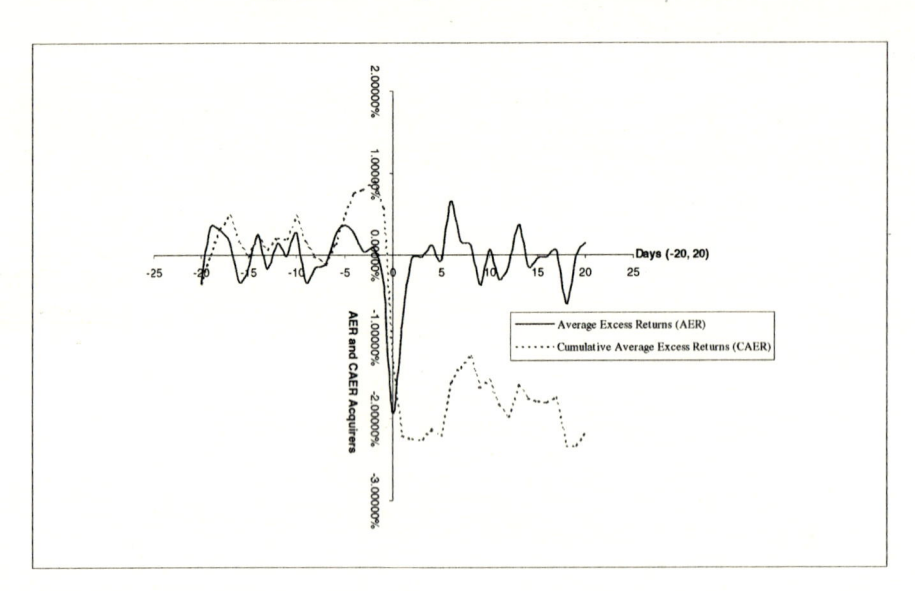

Figure 6.1: Graph of AER and CAER

Figure 6.1 shows a sharp downward shift in the average and cumulative average excess returns around the announcement date (Days = 0 on the horizontal line). The market reactions to acquirers reflected over the 41-day measurement period suggest that the decision to integrate did not reward the acquirer shareholders in those mergers and acquisition involving megabanks. In reality, acquirers as a group lost economic value as demonstrated by the CAER in Figure 6.1. CAER on day (-20) was negative and took on negative values for only 4 other days prior the announcement day (t_0). The other 15 days prior day (t_0) CAERs took on positive values. For day (t_{-1}) the $\underline{t}$ statistic was significant at the 25% level and negative, whereas for days (t_0) and (t_1) the $\underline{t}$ statistics were significant and negative at the 5% level.

Average excess returns (AER), which fluctuated prior to days $(t_{-1}$ to $t_1)$, continued to fluctuate in post $(t_{-1}$ to $t_1)$ period with deep negative swings one day prior and post announcement day $(t = 0)$. Therefore, Figure 6.1 does give a clear indication that acquirers do realize significant negative abnormal returns around the official announcement date. Table 6.3 shows that 64.7% of the megabank acquirers realize negative or zero abnormal returns. The remaining 35.3% experienced abnormal returns greater than 0, suggesting that a great majority of acquirers do not gain economically when their respective large financial corporation seeks to integrate with another huge financial organization.

Table 6.3
<u>Acquirers Grouped by Classes of Excess Returns, Frequency, and Cumulative Percentages (%) Over the Event Window</u>

Classes of Excess Returns (ER)	Frequency	Frequency %	Cumulative Frequency	Cumulative %
$(-0.4 < ER \leq -0.3)$	4	11.8	4	11.8
$(-0.3 < ER \leq -0.2)$	4	11.8	8	23.6
$(-0.2 < ER \leq -0.1)$	6	17.6	14	41.2
$(-0.1 < ER \leq 0.0)$	8	23.5	22	64.7
$(0.0 < ER \leq 0.1)$	2	5.9	24	70.6
$(0.1 < ER \leq 0.2)$	4	11.8	28	82.4
$(0.2 < ER \leq 0.3)$	3	8.8	31	91.2
$(0.3 < ER \leq 0.4)$	3	8.8	34	100.0

Table 6.3 reveals that 64.7% of megabanks realized 0 or negative returns over the 41-day event window for the period 1990 to 1997, whereas 35.3% experienced positive returns. A subanalysis undertaken for a shorter period around the

announcement date of -1, 0 and 1, revealed an average excess return of -1.12941% with a t-statistic of -2.4714. Clearly, the data and the analyses emanating from such data indicate that a null hypothesis, in which the acquirers of in-market megabank mergers and acquisition realize excess returns > 0, cannot be supported. The results of this study are consistent with the relatively recent findings of other researchers who studied mainly non-banking mergers and acquisition. Table 6.4 compares the findings of this study with particular reference to acquirers' excess returns to some of the more recent research findings.

Table 6.4
<u>Results of Recent Studies on Stock Market Reaction to Acquirers in Mergers and Acquisitions Covering the Period 1978 to 1997</u>

(1) Study	(2) Period Covered	(3) Sample Size	(4) Announcement Date Period	(5) Acquirers CAER	(6) % with CAER > 0
Maharaj (2001)	1990-1997	34	(-1, +1)	-1.13 (t = -2.47)	35.3 (Z = -3.59)
Sirower (1994)	1979-1990	168	(-1, +1)	-2.30 (t = -5.01)	35.0 (Z = -4.02)
Banerjee and Owers (1992)	1978-1987	57	(-1, 0)	-3.31 (Z = -11.75)	21.0 (Z = -5.36)
Byrd and Hickman (1992)	1980-1987	128	(-1, 0)	-1.23 (Z = -6.78)	33.0 (Z = -4.14)

The findings of this study clearly indicate that the acquirer shareholders of large banks who acquire other large banks, similar to the findings in mergers and acquisitions among non-bank entities (Benerjee & Owers, 1992), generally do not realize excess returns on their stock holdings > 0. Table6.4 lists the results of recent major empirical studies documenting the value-destructive consequence on acquiring shareholders' value creation. Column 6 of Table 6.4 gives the Cumulative Average Excess Returns (CAER) as a percentage of the sample that realized positive abnormal returns compared against those that attracted negative returns. The <u>t</u> and <u>Z</u> statistics listed in Column 5 of Table 4 are the results of the statistical tests reported by various researchers emanating from their respective studies. The <u>Z</u> statistics in Column 6 depict the magnitude of the differences between the number of acquirers with positive CAERs versus those with negative CAERs. A further examination of Table 4 indicates that between 64.7 and 79.0% of all acquirer-shareholders in the group of studies mentioned realized negative or zero returns from their merger and acquisition endeavors.

Threats to Internal Validity Analysis

This researcher was invariably vigilant for creeping threats to internal validity of the model being tested in this hypothesis and indeed the other hypotheses. Four threats that could detract from the internal validity of the model and findings were specifically examined. These are the nonnormalcy condition, homoscedasticity assumption, sequencing of variables, and rival explanation. In addition, statistical techniques were employed to ensure that errors were kept to a minimum.

<u>Non-normalcy condition.</u> Non-normalcy condition suggests that the distribution of a set of data points tends not to cluster in a symmetrical fashion around a central value and may not give rise to the typical bell-shaped distribution curve. Figures 6.2 and 6.3 present a graphical representation of the scatter and shape of the data points for the megabank acquirers in the sample.

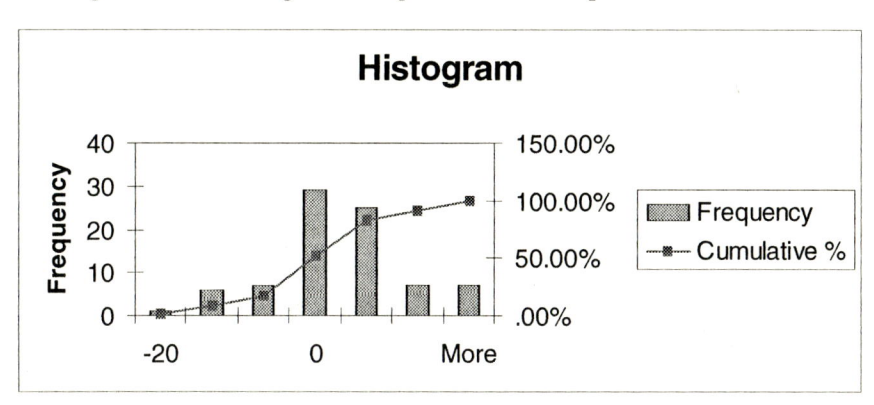

<u>Figure 6.2.</u> Graph of cumulative frequency distribution of the average excess returns in the acquirers' megabank category.

The cumulative frequency distribution plots the frequencies in a progressive fashion for the number of occurrences of given values in the data set. The cumulative frequency distribution captures the percentage of scores between the lowest bound and the given bound being examined. The cumulative frequency curve plotted in Figure 6.2 approximates that of a normally distributed set of data points. Figure 6.3 depicts the set of data points representing Average Excess Returns (AER) for acquirers extended over the entire 41-day event window.

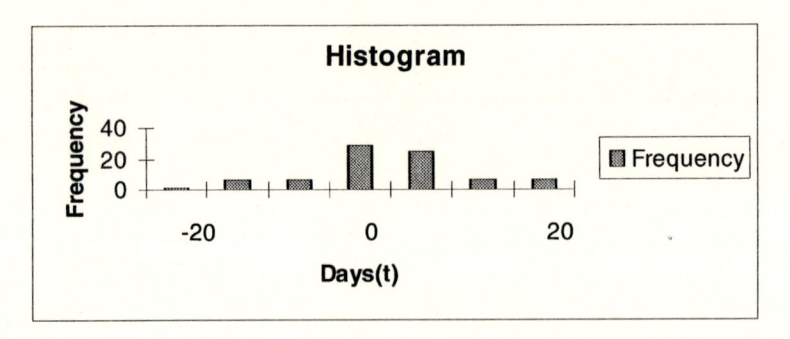

Figure 6.3. Graph showing frequency distribution of the data points representing Average Excess Returns (AER) in the megabank category.

Figure 6.3 plots the frequency distribution of the data points representing Average Excess Returns (AER) for acquirers in the megabank category. The histogram drawn in Figure 6.3 represents the number of occurrences for given demarcated values for the given sample distribution. The coordinates plotted in Figure 4 tended towards a fairly symmetrical and seemingly normally distributed set of data points for acquirers in the megabank category examined over the 41-day event window.

Sequencing of variables. This study hypothesized that the official announcement of an event such as a merger or an acquisition triggers a stock market response to the stock prices of the merging entities resulting in returns that are positively or negatively above normal. Such a hypothesized relationship posits that the event, the relevant official announcement date, is directly associated with (Granger-cause) the dependent variable, abnormal stock return. Granger (1969) posits that the future is influenced (Granger-caused) by the present or the past. From a Granger's causality viewpoint, and as this study has postulated, that since the event (a merger or acquisition announcement) occurred prior to the abnormal stock return, it stands to reason that the dependent variable could not cause the independent variable. It is more realistic to posit, as this study has done, that the independent variable influenced (caused) the dependant variable.

Rival explanation. In event study methodology, as indeed other research approaches, this researcher was vigilant for the presence of competing explanations for the hypotheses being tested. Complicating the preceding analysis for Hypothesis 1 is the fact that the occurrences of other megabank events may significantly affect excess returns. Events such as end-of-quarter announcements, major reshuffle in the ranks of top executives or any major restructuring activities among megabanks in the sample can be significant enough to rival the merger or acquisition activities identified in this study. For the 34 banks that comprised the distribution of megabanks for this study, none of the elements in the set of data points recorded an event significant enough to rival the merger or acquisition event. The remaining nine mergers and acquisitions, though part of the population, were excluded in the analysis for reasons such as the information was unavailable or unreliable. Thus, sound data were obtained for 79.1% of the units in the population.

The indexes of Wall Street Journal and the New York Times were meticulously and systematically examined for activities involving any of the 34 megabank acquirers that could possibly rival the merger or acquisition explanation over the applicable 41-day event window. Extra precautions were taken to identify any rival explanation over the subperiod (-1,0,1) for each of the 34 merger or acquisition events given the volatile behavior of the acquirer stock price at around day 0. Factors such as an end-of -quarter earnings' announcement, where projected earnings' estimates are not realized or some other major announcement such as organizing restructuring that could result in expense-related volatility, changing of top executives and so on could cause deep swings in equity pricing behavior.

This researcher did a careful search for possible rival explanations that could have contributed, partly or in toto, for the pricing behavior of each stock in the market for all the elements that made up the set of data points. The 68 banks examined and more specifically the subset that comprised the group of acquirers did not appear to have any significant competing explanation for the stock price changes over the 41-day event window other than the related merger and acquisition announcements.

An exhaustive search was also done with the aim of identifying possible sources of rival explanation for the 68 megabanks examined in this study especially over their respective three-day period (-1, 0, 1). In effect, over the applicable 3-day period, nothing of significance was reported in the New York Times or the Wall Street Journal that could have rivaled the merger or acquisition announcement for any of the given 34 megabank acquirers that formed the group of the sample for the megabank acquirers in this study. Narrowing the observation period increased the probability of keeping the error to a minimum as possible.

In addition to the preceding specific attention and careful examination and manipulation of the data sources, a further reduction in the threats to internal validity was an integral part of the various statistical tests. For example, each test statistic, where possible and applicable, reported an associated p-value. Most of the statistical tests done in this part of the study also made reference to a related Type I error and, or a related p-value. All of these checks formed an integral part of the analytical framework of this study with the intent on ensuring greater validity of the results of the tests for each of the three hypotheses formulated.

Value Creation for Acquirer Shareholders: A Synthesis

The analysis of the data and the conclusion drawn suggest that there is considerable evidence that megabank' acquirers do realize negative abnormal returns around the official announcement date. Given that the t statistics are essentially significant at the 5% level, a consolidating event does affect stock returns. In addition, the sign of the excess returns indicates whether the event's effect for each day in the event window is positive or negative. Around the official announcement dates of -1, 0, and 1, excess returns reveal a swift downward shift in the average and cumulative average Excess Returns graph over the event's measurement period suggesting that the market did not reward the acquirer shareholders in mergers and acquisition involving megabanks. Such a sharp downward trend is especially indicative around the announcement day as represented in this study by the period, t = 0.

The results of this study are consistent with the relatively recent findings of other researchers who studied mainly non-banking mergers and acquisition. Table 6.4 above compared the findings of this study with particular reference to acquirers' excess returns to some of the more recent research findings by other researchers. The findings are consistent with the research literature, though scant for acquirer' shareholders value creation tests. The tests conducted in this chapter were done against the background of invariably creeping threats to internal validity and reliability of the model being formulated to test the hypothesis.

Threats that could detract from the internal validity of the model and findings were specifically examined. The tests done were the nonnormalcy condition test, homoscedasticity assumption, sequencing of variables, and rival explanation. In addition, statistical techniques such as non-violation of normalcy conditions, Granger's causality tests, among others had been observed so as to ensure that errors were kept to a minimum. Clearly, the data and the analyses emanating from such data indicate that the null hypothesis, in which the acquirers of in-market megabank mergers and acquisition realize excess returns > 0, could not have been supported.

CHAPTER 7

RESULTS AND DISCUSSION OF MERGER OF EQUALS HYPOTHESIS

The concept "merger of equals" can be considered as a merger or acquisition strategy with a major behavioral component rather than a strictly prudent financial management strategy. Acquirers in particular, who advocate such a basis of equality, irrespective of who acquired whom, are primarily embarking on a philosophy of inclusiveness with a major aim of maximizing the fullest human resource potential for the merging entities. Such mergers and acquisitions among the very large banks are perhaps attempts at neutralizing the traditional acquiree-acquirer relationship with a socio-psychological and human relation dimensions rooted in a "merger among equals" philosophy. Such a conceptualization of merger of equals envisages that, as was the case in the 1991 Chemical Banking Corporation-Manufacturers Hanover Trust merger, the acquiree's leadership is given the top position of the newly merged entities by the acquirer.

In a conventional sense, the acquirer assumes the domineering role and more or less dictates the future courses of action that the new organization will adopt. However, on a proclaimed merger of equals' basis, the acquiree's leadership is allowed to co-partner the future course of events and the decision making process accommodates the acquiree's modus operandi, at least over the transition phase. There is a growing consensus of opinion among the community of researchers in the area of mergers and acquisition which holds that shareholders' value declines for the acquirer banks and that value is generally created for the shareholders of the acquired banks (acquirees). With these tested propositions in mind, in this chapter an effort is made to test whether this also holds true for megabanks that integrate on the basis of merger of equals. In other words, one is interested in testing whether "merger of equals" among megabanks does support the conventionally accepted proposition that value is created for the acquirees' shareholders rather than those of the acquirers.

Following conventional wisdom therefore, hypothesis 2 states that, for in-market megabank mergers and acquisitions, acquiree shareholders realize abnormal returns significantly greater than acquirer shareholders around the announcement date for those mergers and acquisitions that signal the intentions to integrate with given partners on the merger of equals basis. The non-value maximizing behavior that is inconsistent with value maximization behavior, which may be a subset of the overall intent and purpose of a merger of equals' dilemma, is beyond the scope of this research. Thus, the enigma surrounding the decision to integrate, or not, continued throughout the 1990s. The data for this hypothesis were obtained from SNL Securities LC, M&A DataSource, The Center for Research in Security Prices (CRSP), and MergerWatch Annuals.

The Analysis

The ex-post abnormal or excess return for the jth firm in the tth period is represented by (AR_{jt}) for all banks identified in the merger of equals' sample. Over the referenced period of this study, 1990 to 1997, nine megabank mergers or acquisitions were identified as meeting these criteria:

1. Having assets of $5.0 billion or more at the time of the official announcement date for the given merger or acquisition.
2. Both acquirees and acquirers must be headquartered in the United States.
3. Both Banks can be either a commercial bank or thrift institution.
4. An announcement must be made and reported in a public medium or popular periodical concerning the proposed integration.
5. The integrating parties will integrate on a "merger of equals" basis.
6. The announced merger or acquisition must have occurred within the period 1990 to 1997.

A total of 18 banks fitted the criteria established above and comprised a set of nine mergers and acquisitions that made up the sampling frame. Attempts were made to obtain data for all the elements in the population necessary for this study, but incomplete or unreliable information were present in two of the mergers comprising a set of four megabanks. Therefore, the data points consisted of a total of 14 banks and thrifts comprising seven mergers or acquisitions, which in reality constitute 77.8% of the entire population.

Given that the number of data points for this hypothesis is small and this researcher does not wish to make the stringent assumption that the observations approximate a normally distributed population, a nonparametric test is believed to be an appropriate statistical procedure. Therefore, rather than seeking to test variances about the mean of a population or calculating a mean value for a sampling distribution representing a given population, a nonparametric test is a preferred procedure for testing the differences between measures of location between two or more sets of data. The merger of equals' hypothesis requires that

1. a comparison is made concerning two populations, that is, acquirees and acquirers
2. in the megabank category; the data, though quantitative, do not essentially possess the characteristics of a normally distributed set of data points that can adequately facilitate the rudiments of a parametric test; and
3. the sets of data points representing the two populations, for statistical purposes, are not independent of each other and therefore are considered "blocked" or "paired" (Keller, Warrack, & Bartel, 1994, pp. 562 -568).

The data for the merger of equals hypothesis consist of a population size ($\underline{N}$ = 18) for which reliable data were obtained for 14 of those units. In the light of the given situation that the sample size $\underline{n}$ is small and this researcher does not want to make the stringent assumption that the data approximate a normal distribution curve, a parametric test was not the preferred choice. Alternatively, a nonparametric test is the preferred choice over the parametric inferential technique. Thus, rather than testing the differences between two population means, it is scientifically more prudent to determine whether the population locations are significantly different from each other.

The process of ranking the data to test certain population characteristics, without referring to specific population parameters that are associated with the normally distributed very large sample size, may enhance reliability among a relatively small sample. In the specific hypothesis being tested here, one is interested in knowing whether on the part of acquiree shareholders value creation significantly exceeds that of the acquirer shareholders within an acceptable level of confidence. In other words, consistent with the modal findings that acquirees generally realize abnormal or excess returns in their equity holdings vis-à-vis acquirer shareholders (Chen, Gup, & Wall, 1989; Jensen & Ruback, 1983; Sirower, 1997; Trifts & Scanlon, 1987), this part of the study sought to test whether the same holds true for megabanks that integrate on a merger of equals basis.

The popularly used Wilcoxon signed rank sum test for paired samples was the chosen nonparametric test for the merger of equal hypothesis formulated in this study. The Wilcoxon signed rank sum test for matched pairs seeks to determine whether one population's location is the same, or significantly different from the other (Freund, Williams, & Perles, 1993). More specifically and for establishing relationship among variables, such a ranked test can ascertain whether one population's data are directional, that is, one set of population's data can be ranked as greater or less than the other. Such "greater than" or "less than" scenario may be achieved by ascertaining whether a given set of data is to the right or to the left of another set of observations on a standardized statistical continuum and whose sets of data points are essentially matched pairs (Keller, Warrack, & Bartel, 1994).

Following an analytical procedure, similar to that of qualitative data that utilized a ranking process, the data for this hypothesis were ranked according to size, with the smallest quantitative measure given a numerical value of 1 and the largest data point assigned the highest numerical value of 14. Such a numerical value is determined by the difference between acquiree and acquirer megabanks' excess or abnormal returns for each pair of the data. The absolute value of the differences are then ordered and ranked by assigning a set of numbers beginning with the natural number "1" to the smallest observation to $\underline{n}$, where n represents the largest numerical value assigned to the largest observation in the set of data that comprised the group of paired observations. There were no zero differences between the given pairs of data and hence the number of observations was constant for both the 11-day and the fully expanded 41-day event windows.

For the data obtained relative to the merger of equals hypothesis formulated in this study a ranked value of "1" is assigned to the smallest numerical difference in absolute value ($|ER_2 - ER_1|$) terms. A rank of "2" is assigned to the second smallest absolute value difference and so on. Since there was no difference that resulted in 0, the value of 14 remained the highest assigned value that any difference among the matched pairs could have commanded. In the given situation of $|ER_2 - ER_1|$, the implication for the alternative hypothesis is that the excess returns for each acquirer is subtracted from the corresponding (paired) acquiree ($ER_{2t} - ER_{1t}$) for any given day(t).

There were no zero differences in the values resulting from $ER_{2t} - ER_{1t}$; neither were there any numerically equal differences. Therefore, for all the tests, the paired observations remained constant at $\underline{n} = 7$. The procedure for performing the Wilcoxon signed rank test for matched pairs is based on a comparison of the ranked sums of the negative and positive differences between the underlying pairs of observations. The symbol T^- is used to represent the total assigned values for differences < 0, whereas T^+ is used to represent those assigned values > 0. Since this researcher is interested in determining whether the distribution of excess returns for acquirees is shifted to the right of the distribution of excess returns for acquirers, the T^- determinant will be the test statistic. Thus the approach will be to reject H_0 when $T^- \leq T_{(0.05)}$. According to the Wilcoxon signed rank sum test for matched pairs the values that will be assigned to T^- are determined as follows:

$$T_t^- = \sum_{t=1}^{n} |\mu_2 - \mu_1|_t \text{ with negative signs reallocated}$$

for all $\mu_{2t} < \mu_{1t}$ (7.1)

The sum of the rank of one set of data points of a given population is compared to the assigned rank numerical values relative to the identified "other" population's set of data points. The merger of equal hypothesis formulated in this study holds that the calculated excess returns for banks in the megabank category are significantly greater for acquirees vis-à-vis acquirers. The alternative and null hypothesis are now stated in terms of the Wilcoxon type matched pairs experiment. Thus, the test for the merger of equal hypothesis is deduced as follows:

H_1: The location of population ER_2 is to the right of the location of population ER_1
H_0: The location of population ER_2 and population ER_1 are the same

The term ER_2 represents excess returns for the megabank acquirees and ER_1 represents excess returns for the megabank acquirers.

Excess or abnormal returns for each of the 14 observations in the merger of equals hypothesis were calculated for a shortened 11-day event period using equations (16) explained in chapter 3. In such a situation, excess returns averaging were not necessary in the analytical framework for this hypothesis, given that the resulting values in ER_2–ER_1 essentially represented calculate excess return values for the 14 data points pertaining to each of the days in the narrower defined 11-day event window. Freund, Williams, and Perles (1993) identified a one-tail directional test, which utilized the Wilcoxon signed rank sum test for matched pairs with an identifiable test statistic represented by T. Those authors hold that when the alternative hypothesis is one directional and positive ($\mu_1 > \mu_0$), T^- will tend to be small. In the setting for this research and following Freund, Wiliams, and Perles, the test statistic is represented by the T^-, given that the merger of equal hypothesis is constructed as a one-directional positive test.

The decision rule is to reject H_0 if the calculated numerically ranked total value is equal to, or is less than the critical value ($\alpha = 0.05$), found in the Wilcoxon Signed Rank Sum for Paired Samples statistics. It follows therefore, that where T^-

$\leq T_\alpha$ and the number of absolute differences |d, where d ≠ 0| = n̲, the critical value ($\alpha_{0.05}$) is given as $T_{\alpha\,0.05}$ = 4, where n̲ = 7. Hence, the decision rule is to reject the null hypothesis (H$_0$) if the test statistic (T) represented by T^- is less than or equal to the critical value of 4.

The ranked values are assigned to the absolute value differences |ER$_2$–ER$_1$| in ascending order with the smallest in the combined array of calculated excess returns for both acquirees and acquirers being accorded the value of 1. The number 2 is assigned to the next highest value of the excess return difference and so on, until finally, the largest calculated excess return difference is assigned the highest numerical value. Similar to the procedure for calculating excess return represented by equation (3) in chapter 3, excess or abnormal returns (ER) for merger of equals megabanks are calculated as follows:

$$ER_{jt} = R_{jt} - (a'_j + \beta'_j R_{mt})$$

where R_{jt} = calculated returns for the *j*th firm in the *t*th period

a' and β' = parameters of an individual firm, *j*, in the *t*th period

R_{mt} = market returns for the *t*th period identified in the Center for Research in Security Prices (CRSP) daily return data file.

Excess returns are calculated for each of the days in an 11-day event window with 5 days on either side of the official announcement date The announcement date is accorded (*t* = 0) and ER$_{2(-t,\,t)}$ and ER$_{1(-t,\,t)}$ represent calculated excess returns for acquirees and acquirers respectively, where the (-t, t) symbol identifies the period (-5...0...5) days around the official announcement date. Table 5 presents ER$_{jt}$ for both acquirees (ER$_2$) and acquirers (ER$_1$) for each *j*th megabank in the *t*th period over the 11-day event window. The signed rank sum total is derived from a calculated test-statistic (T), where T^- mirrors the T values for day (D$_t$) and measures the ranked values of acquirees in the merger of equals hypothesis. Alternatively, T^+ is used to represent those assigned values > 0. According to the Wilcoxon signed rank sum test for matched pairs, the sum total of the assigned values of T^- and T^+ is the sum of the integers beginning with 1 and ending at n, where n belongs to the given set of consecutive integers. There were no zero differences, that is, there were no values in $ER_{2t} = ER_{1t}$. Thus, the assigned values of T^- and T^+ was crossed-checked using:

$$n(n + 1)/2 = T^- + T^+ \qquad (7.2)$$

where n = the largest of the assigned numbers in the set of consecutive numbers.

It can be shown mathematically that for all the ranked differences calculations the value of T^+ may be determined by:

$$[n(n + 1)/2] - T^- = T^+$$

Similarly, for all the ranked differences in calculating the value of T^+, T^- may be determined by:

$$[n(n + 1)/2] - T^+ = T^-$$

Using the value of n = 7, $T^- + T^+ = 7(8)/2 = 28$. Thus, for all the calculations over the 11-day and the 41-day event windows the totals of T^- and T^+ were crossed-checked against each other using equation (20). The alternative hypothesis (H_1), which hypothesized that $ER_2 > ER_1$, suggests that a one-tail test is an appropriate precondition to evaluate the acceptability or non-acceptability of H_0. Table 7.1 presents the results of the test of the merger of equals hypothesis over an 11-day event window with 5 days on either of the announcement day (t = 0).

Table 7.1

Excess Returns for Acquirees and Acquirers for Period t (-5, 5) with Signed Rank Values for Matched Pairs

(t)	$ER_2 - ER_1$ (D)	$\|D\|$	Rank of $\|D\|$	Signed Rank (R)	(t)	$ER_2 - ER_1$ (D)	$\|D\|$	Rank of $\|D\|$	Signed Rank(R)
(t=-5)	0.1890	0.1890	1	1	(t=-4)	-0.0042	0.0042	1	-1
	0.2353	0.2353	2	2		-0.1264	0.1264	3	-3
	0.2743	0.2743	3	3		-0.2348	0.2348	5	-5
	-2.9390	2.9390	7	-7		0.5540	0.5540	7	7
	1.8531	1.8531	6	6		0.4166	0.4166	6	6
	-0.6449	0.6449	5	-5		-0.0082	0.0082	2	-2
	-0.5955	0.5955	4	-4		-0.2219	0.2219	4	-4
		Test Statistic (T) =		16			Test Statistic (T) =		15
(t=-3)	0.0241	0.0241	2	2	(t=-2)	1.0009	1.0009	4	4
	-0.0048	0.0048	1	-1		0.0221	0.0221	1	1
	0.2773	0.2773	4	4		1.2663	1.2663	5	5
	-2.1384	2.1383	7	-7		2.0715	2.0715	7	7
	-0.5399	0.5399	5	-5		1.2726	1.2726	6	6
	-0.6369	0.6369	6	-6		0.3055	0.3055	2	2
	-0.0729	0.0729	3	-3		-0.3171	0.3171	3	-3
		Test Statistic (T) =		22			Test Statistic (T) =		3

(table continues)

(t)	$ER_2 - ER_1$ (D)	|D|	Rank of |D|	Signed Rank (R)	D(t)	$ER_2 - ER_1$ (D)	|D|	Rank of |D|	Signed Rank(R)
(t=-1)	-10.9339	10.9339	6	-6	(t=0)	-3.6243	3.6243	6	-6
	0.3681	0.3681	3	3		0.1502	0.1502	1	1
	-9.5993	9.5993	5	-5		7.1298	7.1298	7	7
	14.4085	14.4085	7	7		1.1079	1.1078	5	5
	-0.3235	0.3235	2	-2		-0.5250	-0.5250	4	-4
	0.0925	0.0926	1	1		0.2269	0.2269	2	2
	0.6074	0.6074	4	4		0.4711	0.4711	3	3
		Test Statistic (T) =		13			Test Statistic (T) =		10
(t=1)	0.3668	0.3668	5	5	(t=2)	0.8385	0.8385	6	6
	0.0064	0.0064	1	1		0.3681	0.3681	5	5
	-1.1198	1.1198	7	-7		0.1287	0.1287	4	4
	0.2489	0.2489	4	4		-0.0097	-0.0097	1	-1
	0.8218	0.8218	6	6		1.2063	1.2063	7	7
	-0.0486	0.0486	2	-2		-0.0171	-0.0171	2	-2
	0.1577	0.1577	3	3		0.0483	0.0483	3	3
		Test Statistic (T) =		9			Test Statistic (T) =		3

(table continues)

(t)	ER$_2$ − ER$_1$ (D)	|D|	Rank of |D|	Signed Rank (R)	(t)	ER$_2$ − ER$_1$ (D)	|D|	Rank of |D|	Signed Rank(R)
(t=3)	-0.1295	0.1295	3	-3	(t=4)	0.1764	0.1764	2	2
	-0.0074	0.0074	1	-1		0.0077	0.0077	1	1
	-0.8461	0.8461	7	-7		-0.5214	0.5214	5	-5
	0.3715	0.3715	6	6		-1.3982	1.3982	7	-7
	0.0322	0.0322	2	2		-0.2766	0.2766	3	-3
	-0.1312	0.1312	4	-4		-0.5404	0.5404	6	-6
	0.3936	0.3936	5	5		-0.4729	0.4729	4	-4

Test Statistic (*T*) = 15   Test Statistic (*T*) = 25

(t=5)	-0.5484	0.5484	5	-5
	-0.1085	0.1085	4	-4
	-1.0730	1.0730	7	-7
	0.8251	0.8251	6	6
	0.0457	0.0457	2	2
	0.0857	0.0857	3	3
	0.0118	0.0118	1	1

Test Statistic (*T*) = 16

An examination of Table 7.1 reveals that the rank totals for the test statistic T, which represents the negatively signed values discussed in the theoretical setting of this study as T, are in most periods larger than the critical value ($T_{0.05} = 4$). The summed ranked values for the T statistics were only significant for two of the measurement periods (t_{-2} and t_{+2}) in the 11-day event window. For all the other periods the test statistic T was not significant ($T > T_{0.05}$) and hence, it statistically prudent to conclude that there is insufficient evidence to reject the null hypothesis. Table 6 summarizes the results of the Wilcoxon signed rank sum for paired samples statistical test for each of the 11 days ($t_{-5}...0...+5$), with 0 representing the official announcement date. A test statistic for each of the 11 days is shown in column 2 with the results of the test for significance listed in column 4. For the most part, except for day (t = -2) and day (t = 2) where there were significant shifts in ER_2, all of the remaining 9 days in the 11-day observation period did not result in any significant shift of ER_2 to the right of ER_1.

Table 7.2

Summary of Wilcoxon Signed Rank Sum Test for Paired Samples Over the 11-Day Event Window for Merger of Equals' Megabanks

D(t)	Test Statistic (T) Signed Rank Total	Location Shifted Left/Right	Test Statistic Significant/Not Significant
-5	16	Left	Not Significant
-4	15	Left	Not Significant
-3	22	Left	Not Significant
-2	3	Right*	Significant
-1	13	Left	Not Significant
0	10	Left	Not Significant
1	9	Left	Not Significant
2	3	Right*	Significant
3	15	Left	Not Significant
4	25	Left	Not Significant
5	16	Left	Not Significant

* Significant at $T_{(\alpha\, 0.05)}$

Table 7.2 clearly demonstrates that the test statistic (T) is significant for only two of the 11 days captured over the entire even-window period. More importantly, as previously shown in Table 7.2 abnormal or excess returns have the widest swings around the period $t_{(-1,0,1)}$ and clearly, for this period, the location shifts were not significant enough to reject H_0. To safely conclude that there was statistical agreement between the alternate hypothesis and the data, it is required that all the location shifts for the periods covering the event window show a significant shift to the right as measured by the T statistic. Event study findings suggest that, those periods closest to the event such as t = -1, 0,1 would be where the abnormal reaction would generally appear most predominantly (Asquith, Bruner & Mullins, 1983; Benerjee & Owers, 1992;). Clearly, the period t = -1,0,1 did not show any significant shift to the right nor were there any days, other than t = -2 and t = 2, that revealed any significant shift to the right as hypothesized in this study. Therefore, the rejection of the null hypothesis H_0 cannot be significantly supported.

Consistent with findings of other studies (Benerjee & Owers, 1992; Byrd & Hickman, 1992) and the theoretical framework for event study methodology in general, the expectation is that a given event such as a merger or an acquisition will be reflected in more than normal price swings in the stock market for the stocks of either or both the acquiree and acquirer. Such an impact will be most evident for periods around the official announcement date (t = 0). Indeed, this was not the case for the merger of equals hypothesis, and hence the null hypothesis could not be rejected.

Aggregating the data and widening the test to cover the entire 41-day event window by utilizing the nonparametric median approach found in Levine, Berenson, and Stephan (1998) and Keller, Warrack, and Bartel, 1994), the Wilcoxon signed rank sum test statistic for paired samples was examined over the entire 41-day event window. To test whether the results will be any different for an expanded 41-day event window vis-à-vis, its narrower 11-day subset, the median was identified for each of the group of (n = 7). Thus the general equation for the test statistic (T) will be restated with the medians η_2 and η_1 replacing the means μ_2 and μ_1 respectively:

$$T_t^- = \sum_{t=1}^{n} |\eta_2 - \eta_1|_t \text{ with negative signs reallocated for all}$$

$\eta_{2t} < \eta_{1t}$ and where the number of data points = 41, which represents the number of periods over the entire event window.

When the distribution is large, that is, the number of elements in the distribution exceeds 15 it is assumed that the positive and negative assigned differences tend to approximate a normally distributed curve (Freund, Williams, & Perles (1993). It follows that a Wilcoxon signed rank sum test for match pairs can be based on a Z statistic. The medians were identified for both acquirers and acquirees for each of the days over the 41-day event period and given that the set of data points now being considered in the framework are larger than 15, the calculated 41-day combined rank test statistic (Z_C) will be calculated using:

$$Z_C = \frac{T - n(n+1)/4}{\sqrt{n(n+1)(2n+1)/24}} \quad (7.3)$$

where T = T^- and represents the test statistic (T_α) in the Wilcoxon signed rank sum test for paired data

n = number of data points in the distribution

Since the alternative hypothesis is formulated such that this researcher's hunch suggests that the population represented by η_2 (acquirees) is located significantly to the right of the population represented by η_1 (acquirers) the rejection region therefore, is:

$$Z_C < -Z_\alpha = -Z_{(0.05)} = -1.96$$

Replacing the appropriate values in Equation (7.1) revealed the appropriate value for Z_C as follows:

$$Z_C = \frac{442 - 41(42)/4}{\sqrt{41(42)(83)/24}}$$

$$= 0.15$$

Conclusion: *Do not reject* H_0.

Discussion of the Results

There is not enough evidence to conclude that acquirees realize significantly greater excess returns than acquirers for those megabank consolidations that integrate on the basis of merger of equals. The *p*-value or probability that the test statistic (T) my be smaller than 442, as computed above, is in essence equivalent to a test statistic Z with a distance that is even further to the center of the normal distribution than 0.15 standard deviation, is 0.4504. There is a high probability for the null hypothesis of no difference in the medians to be true. The very high probability of 0.4504, which is far above the *p*-value error ($\alpha = 0.05$), suggests that there is no difference in the medians and hence rejecting H_0 does not have significant support. Thus, the findings are quite consistent with the findings summarized in Table 7.2 above. Clearly, there is overwhelming evidence to demonstrate a lacking disagreement between the data and the null hypothesis.

Mergers of Equals: A Synthesis

Whether bank consolidations involving mergers of equals is a sound business model or whether such a practice is a takeover sham disguised in the shadow of perfunctory friendliness will continue to be a contentious issue. For it is possible, that to circumvent the seemingly negative consequences, where the acquirer is perceived by all parties as the vanquisher over the vanquished cloaked in a seemingly impassioned relationship between usually former arch-rivals in an in-market consolidation, the merger of equals neutralizes endemic hostility. Hostility and competition between hardened arch-rivals may be on both sides, but when it is known that there is an acquiree and an acquirer, intrinsic arrogance may tag along with the acquirer. Even though acquirers do not pay a relatively large premium for the right to integrate with the acquirees vis-à-vis in a traditional consolidation situation, merger of equals does involve a limited transfer of shareholders value from acquirer to acquiree. Thus, there is a constant reminder of a reality that one company (the acquirer) did "bought over" another (the acquiree) which could produce levels of superior-inferior complexes.

Typically, negotiations between top executives of the consolidating entities and jockeying for position in the hierarchy of the prospective integrated entity could prove unsettling. For example, John Reed of Citigroup resigned in a little over one year and a half. Rumor has it that Mr. Reed left because of an internal struggle in the post-merger Citi-Travelers integration. However, the mergers involving Chemical Bank with Manufacturers Hanover Trust and Chase Manhattan Bank in 1991 and 1995 respectively, were design specifically (among other strategic advantages) to negate bickering and infighting among top executives. In the merger among equals between these three organizations, Mr. Walter Shipley, the CEO of the acquirer (Chemical Bank), was reported to have said "[W]e will come together as partners and make the best decisions on people, systems, and products. To be the best, we need the best from both organizations" (Wendel, 1996, p. 258). Mr. Shipley further emphasized in the merger of equals between Chemical Bank and Manufacturers Hanover Trust Company, that the CEOs of these two companies must be prepared "to give more than 50%—all the time," for the merger to be successful (p. 246). Clearly, in the consolidations involving these three New York based megabanks, a new culture had to be nurtured in order to avoid a sham of merging on a basis of equality. It is instructive to note that, it was Chemical Bank that was in effect the acquirer in the mergers of equals involving firstly, Manufacturers Hanover Trust Company followed by the integration with Chase Manhattan Bank some four years later.

The findings detailed in this chapter suggest that acquiree shareholders do not realize abnormal returns when megabanks integrate on the basis of merger of equals. Perhaps the best reason for such a finding rests on the fact that, by and large, stockholders of the merging entities swap their current equities for equities in the new entity at a predetermined exchange ratio. Manipulating the data presented earlier in this chapter and from an analytical perspective value creation for acquirer shareholders will lead to the same conclusion, that is, that these shareholders (acquirers) do not attract abnormal returns on their shareholdings. What is in it for shareholders is a promised long-term shareholders' value-added, which could result in additional financial rewards for assuming additional post-merger risks and cost savings derived from synergy.

This author's own experiences with the Chemical Bank-Manufacturers Hanover Trust Company integration revealed that, while this merger was a relatively financial successful experiment the new entity suffered from the consequences of a human "brain drain." This situation was rooted in the fact that the severance package offered to employees was quite attractive especially to the qualified and experienced professional class of employees. Noticeably, many professionally competent and company-trained employees left only to be employed by rival commercial banks within the geographic area. Being the learning organization as it was and being led by Walter Shipley, the industry's visionary banker, Chemical Bank quickly learnt from that seemingly tactical blunder. And so, when the merger of equals with itself and Chase Manhattan Bank did come along some four years later, the optional severance package was not generous enough to lure the middle-aged and well-qualified human resources to grab the severance package and moved on to the welcoming arms of competing entities.

In advancing the merger of equals as a viable model one must not lose sight of the fact that financial and operational synergies can only come about in the short term. For over the long term these synergies can only be realized when short-term gains are translated into more concrete and human relation terms. The "we" and "they" of doing things are not only divisive, but could also lead to lower employee morale, lower productivity, and higher employee turnover. Given that cultures do not "merge," a new direction must be charted. Indeed, such was the case with the Chemical-Chase merger of equals in 1995, when the framing of a new culture began with corporate tone setting by leaders of the newly merged entity.

Tone setting in the Chemical and Chase's merger of equals manifested itself in a vision statement that was circulated to each member of the new entity. Such a document was written and hand-distributed by top management early in the so-called honeymoon period. A profoundly articulated statement with concrete aims and goals was circulated to the rank and file followed by an intense and well-integrated system of diversity training. A key component of such training was valuing the differences not only based on gender, race, and other visible biological factors, but the unconditional valuation of competing ideas and opinions. It was this ability of the "new" Chase (Chemical-Chase consolidation) to value and invest in diversity among the rank and file and to set the tone at the top, which laid the groundwork for the financial successes that followed in the years after the consolidation.

Credit Tom Labrecque of the "old" Chase and Walter Shipley of Chemical Bank for not only preparing and presenting eye-catching consolidated pro forma financial statements, but also translating financial and operating synergistic components into humanistic terms. These CEOs proposed that in the post-merger period cost-savings and revenue-enhancements were to be the major focus and in the process, the retained rank and file employees would lose friends and co-workers due to employee redundancies. In addition, closing down of departments or voluntary separation that would result when operating units integrate into a single entity, career services departments made every attempt to assist the severed employees. The leaders in the Chemical-Manufacturers and Chemical-Chase mergers of equals were prepared to view the anticipated huge financial progress for the merger of equals' experiment in both human and non-human terms and perhaps herein lies the secret to a successful merger of equals. When the dust is cleared, the retained employees in the post merger period were rewarded with relatively hefty stock options with management undoubtedly anticipating that these retained employees would have had to do the total workload with a lesser number of their colleagues.

CHAPTER 8

RESULTS AND DISCUSSION OF PREMIUM PAID TO INTEGRATE WITH MEGABANKS: PRICE OFFERED TO BOOK VALUE APPROACH

Price offered to book value is derived from the popular investment relationship "price to book" in considering whether or not an asset in under- or over-valued. The market value of an asset reflects the potential power of that asset to create value to the holder of such an asset. The foundation of the price to book relationship rests on two values, that is, market and book values. Similarly the price offered to book value rests on the price offered by the acquirer for the right to integrate with the acquiree to the price listed on the acquiree's books. In this chapter, therefore, the result and discussion will include the test conducted for examining the proposition that based on the price offered to book value technique the very large banks are attracting higher premiums than the smaller banks for the right to integrate with acquirers.

The general measure for book value of equities as listed on the balance sheet is on a historical cost basis plus any adjustments made for dividends, stock buybacks, or any losses that may impact book value. Price offered to book value supposedly reflects the true intrinsic valuation in that the return form the proposed new consolidated entity will outweigh the risk associated with such an entity. The postulation of the third hypothesis identified in Chapter 2 is restated here. Hypothesis number 3 states that "the acquirees in megabank mergers and acquisitions attract higher premiums than do acquirees in relatively smaller banks over the period covered by this study." Symbolically, the null hypothesis (H_0) and the alternate hypothesis (H_1) are reiterated as follows:

$H_0: \mu_M \leq \mu_S$

$H_1: \mu_M > \mu_S$

where μ_M = the mean merger or acquisition premium for banks in the megabank category.

and μ_S = the mean merger or acquisition premium for banks in the small bank category

Acquisition premium, which is the offered price per stock in excess of the prevailing price per stock at book value, was evaluated using two measures. These two measures of stock price offered as a ratio to stock price at book value and price offered in relation to earnings per share are the two measures commonly used in evaluating merger and acquisition premiums (SNL Securities LC, 1998).

The analysis in this part of the study to test the hypothesized relationship on merger and acquisition premiums with respect to banks in the megabank and small bank categories has adopted two approaches. One approach sought to measure the variable, price to book value whereas the other will proceed along the lines of, price offered to last 12 months earnings per share (LTM Eps). The price offered was essentially the price per share that the acquirer was willing to pay in an endeavor to take over or merge with an acquiree. The book value represented the actual monetary value per divisible unit of stockholders' equity listed in the official records of the acquiree, for the fiscal year immediately preceding the date of the official announcement of a given merger or acquisition. While either one of these ratios may give a reliable measure of premium paid in the merger or acquisition of an acquiree, this study has employed both approaches merely to guarantee greater reliability of the test results. The results of the price to book approach will be discussed in this chapter while chapter 9 will examine the results of the price to LTM Eps approach.

Price Offered to Book Value Approach: The Basis

Price offered to acquire the stocks of another company is compared with the prevailing book price per equity. The book price is usually quoted as the price prevailing in period t_{-1}, where t_0, the ensuing period, is the year in which the offering was actually made. The price offered to book value ratio is usually quoted on a percentage basis. Algebraically, price offered to book value is calculated as follows:

$$\text{Premium (\%)} = \text{Price Offered/Book Value (\%)}$$
$$= [P_{t_0} (P_{t_{-1}})^{-1} - 1](100)$$

where P_{t_0} = price offered in the current period

and $P_{t_{-1}}$ = price in the preceding period

By way of an example, assuming that a certain security has a book value of $28.00 at the end of last year and an acquirer has offered $35.00 for the right to own that security in the current year, then the premium translated in percentage (%) terms will be:

$$[P_{t_0} (P_{t_{-1}})^{-1} - 1](100) = [(35.00 \times 1/28) - 1](100)$$
$$= 25\%$$

The ratio of price offered to book value is the purchase price paid by the acquirer divided by the price per stock quoted in the acquirees record at the end of the preceding fiscal year. In this study the price offered to book value ratio is quoted in multiples of one hundred.

The Data

The information needed for this hypothesis was obtained from SNL Securities, M&ADataSource, Mergerstat Review, and MergerWatch Annual. For the period under review, there were 43 mergers and acquisitions involving 86 banks and thrifts whose assets were at least $5 billion at the time of their respective merger or acquisition announcements. All the information necessary for calculating price offered to book value were available and appear reliable. Table 8.1 lists the number of banks involved in merger or acquisition for each year in the period 1990 to 1997. The announcement dates were cross-referenced with the Wall Street Journal or the New York Times and these dates were found to be generally consistent across all published media.

Table 8.1
Number of Megabank Mergers and Acquisitions with Percentage Spread for Period 1990–1997

Year	Number of Mergers/Acquisitions	% of Total
1990	1	2.3
1991	4	9.3
1992	4	9.3
1993	1	2.3
1994	3	7.0
1995	13	30.2
1996	6	14.0
1997	11	25.6
TOTAL	43	100.0

Note: Data extracted from: SNL Securities LC. (1999). Bank M&A DataSource. Electronic database Version 2.1, June. Charlottesville, NC: June 1998. MergerstatReview (various issues). Los Angeles, CA: Houlihan Lokey Howard & Zukin.

An examination of Table 8.1 reveals that 69.8% of megabank mergers and acquisitions took place in the last 3 years of the period under review, whereas the remaining 30.2% of the megabanks' mergers and acquisitions occurred over the earlier 5-year period. Clearly, the megabank merger and acquisition activities heightened as the decade of the 1990s proceeded. Data on small bank and thrift acquirees involved in mergers and acquisitions with assets of ≤ $ 100 million numbered 2,236 for the period under study. From this total, 1, 010 acquirees were eliminated for reasons such as, that the information necessary for facilitating the calculations to arrive at the dependent variables were not available or, where such data were available, they were not meaningful. The remaining 1,226 acquirees constitute the actual sampling frame from which appropriate proportionate simple random samples were drawn. Table 8.2 captures the population and the corresponding proportionately weighted sample randomly drawn for each of the years in the study period.

Table 8.2
Data Showing Number of Small Banks Per Year in the Small Bank Category for which Reliable Data Were Available with Appropriate w_i

Year	Population N_i	w_i^*	Year	Population N_i	w_i
1990	74	0.060	1994	227	0.185
1991	124	0.101	1995	173	0.141
1992	148	0.121	1996	162	0.132
1993	164	0.134	1997	154	0.126

Note. Population statistic extracted from SNL Securities LC. (1999). DataSource. Version 2.9, June. Charlottesville NC. *The sum of all w_i = 1, where w_i = proportion of the population in stratum i.

Proportionate Stratified Random Sample

The objective of stratification is to assemble data to form strata, thereby facilitating greater homogeneity within strata than would have been possible in the aggregated data. In other words, there is likely to be less variability within strata than between strata for a population that comprises subgroups or strata (Sincich, 1996). Generally, if one divides the population of size N into k strata of sizes N_1, $N_2...N_k$ and take a sample of size n_1 from N_1, n_2 from N_2...and n_k from N_k the allocation is proportional when:

$$\underline{n}_1/\underline{N}_1 \;=\; \underline{n}_2/\underline{N}_2 \;=\; \cdots \;=\; \underline{n}_k/\underline{N}_k$$

To determine the sample size $\underline{n}$ from a finite sampling frame represented by $\underline{N}$, it is assumed that a sample error will lie as close as possible to the given population parameter.

A researcher will seek to have the sample mean ($\bar{x}$) lie as close as possible or to have the shortest distance (d) between such a sample mean and its population mean (μ) with a probability of $(1-\alpha)$. Thus, the sample size will be directly influenced by the confidence interval one is willing to facilitate and the level of confidence $P(1-\alpha)$ that a researcher is seeking to establish (Sincich, 1996). The term $P(1-\alpha)$ represents the probability that x will lie within $\pm \underline{Z}$ standard deviation of μ and is commonly referred to as the confidence coefficient. In chapter 3, it was shown that the value of d may be approximated using:

$$d \;=\; \underline{Z}(\sigma/\sqrt{\underline{n}})$$

Given that one may wish to have the value of d to be as small as possible, the problem therefore, is to approximate the value of the unknown population standard deviation (σ). One simple way to approximate the population standard deviation (σ) is to use the range. By using the range, it is assumed that for any given population or a derived sample of the underlying population where the total data points are considered statistically large and hence approximates a normally distributed set of observations, the range is estimated to be 6σ. The basis for this approximation rests on the assumption that for an assumed normally distributed set of observations, almost all of the data points will lie within $\mu \pm 3\sigma$ of a given distribution (Levine, Berenson, & Stephan, 1998).

Price Offered to Book Value Approach: The Results

The results. For the price offered to book value approach, the calculated values of d together with the range and stratum population for each of the periods in the small bank category are given in Table 8.3

Table 8.3
The Estimated Values of *d* Over the Period 1990–1997 for Price Offered to Book Value

Year	N_i	Range	σ = Range/6	$d = Z(\sigma/\sqrt{N_i})$
1990	74	281.4	46.9	10.7
1991	124	187.8	31.3	5.5
1992	148	307.2	51.2	8.2
1993	164	286.8	47.8	7.3
1994	227	274.2	45.7	5.9
1995	173	243.0	40.5	6.1
1996	162	262.2	43.7	6.7
1997	154	395.4	65.9	10.4

==

Table 8.3 demonstrates that the "*d*" which will result in the smallest differential between x̄ and μ is the calculated value of 5.5. Therefore, the sample size n, which will comprise the sample size for each stratum n_i, will be a most conservative when *d* is at a minimum (*d* = 5.5). Therefore, *d*, sometimes referred to as "half-width confidence interval" (Sincich, 1996, p. 445) will be used to approximate n, in equation (5.05) of chapter 5, which is replicated below for relevance and clarity:

$$n = \frac{(\sum N_i^2 \sigma_i^2 / w_i)}{N^2(d^2/4) + \sum(N_i \sigma_i^2)}$$

where N_i = number of elements in population for stratum *i*

σ_i = standard deviation of the elements in population stratum *i*

d^2 = desired half-width of the confidence interval.

w_i = proportion of the total elements found in stratum *i*

Substituting values in the above equation for the Price Offered to Book Value approach in the small bank category will produce the following results:

$$\underline{n} = \frac{\frac{(74)^2(46.9)^2}{0.06} + \frac{(124)^2(31.3)^2}{0.101} + \frac{(148)^2(51.2)^2}{0.121} + \frac{(164)^2(47.8)^2}{0.124} + \frac{(227)^2(45.7)^2}{0.185} + \frac{(173)^2(40.5)^2}{0.141} + \frac{(162)^2(43.7)^2}{0.132} + \frac{(154)^2(65.9)^2}{0.126}}{\frac{(1228)^2(5.5)^2}{4} + 74(46.9)^2 + 124(31.3)^2 + 148(51.2)^2 + 164(47.8)^2 + 227(45.7)^2 + 173(40.5)^2 + 162(43.7)^2 + 154(65.9)^2}$$

$\underline{n}$ = 244.06, which when rounded up
$\phantom{\underline{n}}\cong$ 245

Applying the appropriate weighted relationship w_i to each year or stratum for the Price Offered to Book Value data, Table 8.4 gives the sample size per stratum.

Table 8.4
<u>Proportionate Sample (n_i) Allocated to Strata Based on Weight of Stratum (w_i) in Sample n for the Price Offered to Book Value Approach</u>

Year	$\underline{n}(w_i)$	= $\underline{n}_i$	Year	$\underline{n}(w_i)$	= $\underline{n}_i$
1990	245 (0.060)	15	1994	245 (0.185)	45
1991	245 (0.101)	25	1995	245 (0.141)	34
1992	245 (0.121)	30	1996	245 (0.132)	32
1993	245 (0.134)	33	1997	245 (0.126)	31

The data obtained for this area of the study, which sought to test the comparative relationship of premiums paid to acquire or merge with large banks versus smaller ones, are partitioned into nonoverlapping annual subsets comprising the overall eight-year period. Sincich (1996) proposed that samples should be drawn from each stratum in relation to that stratum's quantifiable relationship to the total population being studied. Using the above equation for $\underline{n}$, the total sample size $\underline{n}$ will be approximated for a stratified population mean μ based on a 95% confidence interval.

The proportionate random sample was determined and drawn with the assistance of SPSS Base 9.0 software package. All the subsamples within each year can generally be considered statistically large with a tendency towards the normal distribution assumption. The data assembled for this part of the study were analyzed and all the samples tended to approximate the normal distribution assumption. Figures 8.1 and 8.2 show the data points distribution for price offered to book value for banks in the megabank category. The data for these banks appear bell-shaped and somewhat symmetrical with a leaning towards a rightward or positively skewed distribution.

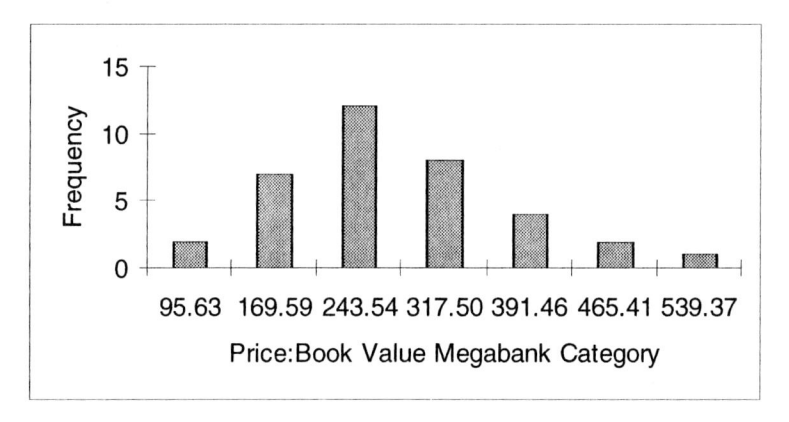

Figure 8.1. Histogram depicting price offered to book value in the megabank category.

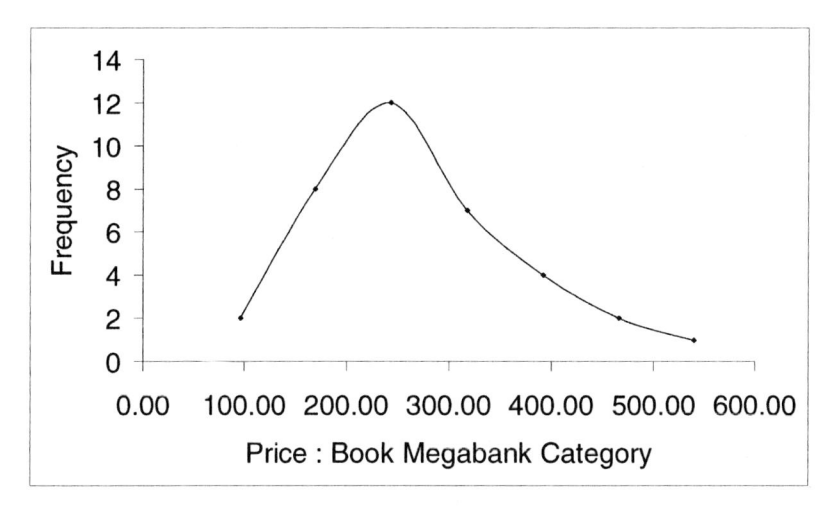

Figure 8.2. Frequency distribution curve showing price offered to book value for banks in the megabank category.

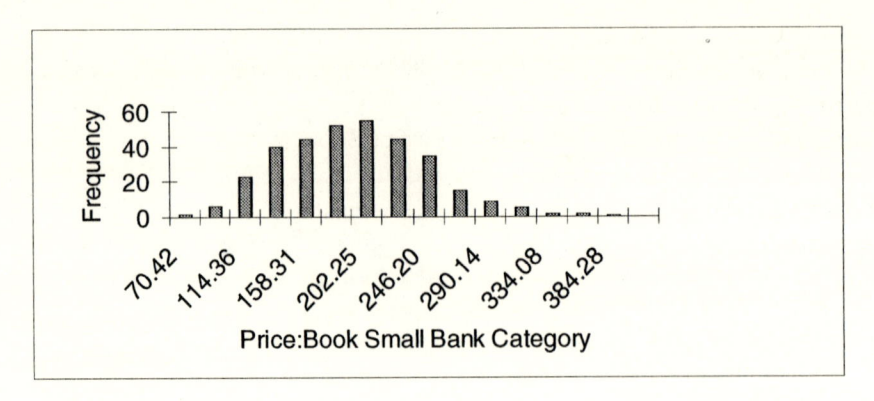

Figure 8.3 Histogram showing price offered to book value in the small bank category.

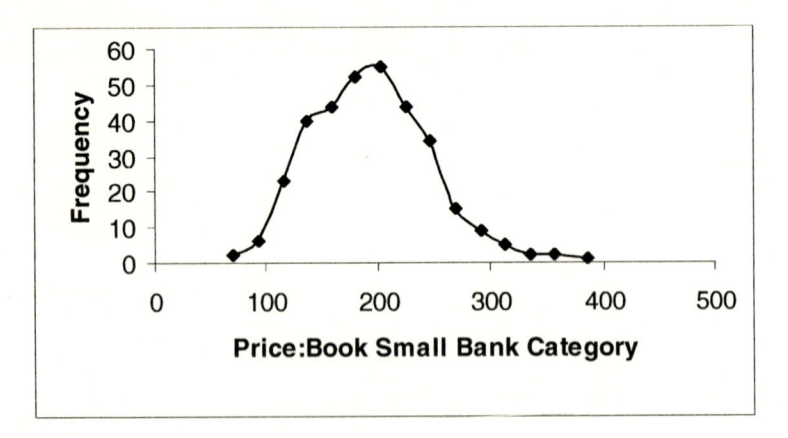

Figure 8.4 Frequency distribution curve depicting price offered to book value in the small bank category.

Figures 8.3 and 8.4, similar to Figures 8.1 and 8.2 for megabanks, depict a histogram and frequency distribution curve respectively for banks in the small bank category. Figures 8.3 and 8.4 also demonstrate that the price to book value data, like the data in the megabank category, seem bell-shaped and symmetrical. Thus, parametric tests seem to be appropriate techniques to be applied to the mergers and acquisition premium analysis employing the price offered to book value approach to test the third hypothesis identified in this study. The Single Factor ANOVA test is intended to ascertain whether two or more independent samples have equivalent measures of central tendency as represented by means or medians and thus, may be equal to one another for the given samples. Table 8.5 gives the results of the Single Factor ANOVA test for megabank acquirees.

Table 8.5
<u>Single Factor ANOVA Test for within and Between Groups for Acquirees with Asset ≥ $5.0b Price to Book Value</u>

Panel A

SUMMARY

Groups	Count	Sum	Average	Variance
1990	1	143.3100	143.3100	0.0
1991	4	686.8600	171.7150	565.4064
1992	4	761.1000	190.2750	4562.7836
1993	1	139.9400	139.9400	0.0
1994	3	373.2700	124.4233	1516.9290
1995	13	2455.1400	188.8569	1596.9758
1996	6	1303.4300	217.2383	3409.5765
1997	11	3820.2600	347.2964	7706.4819

Panel B

ANOVA

Source of Variation	SS	Df	MS	F	P-value	F crit
Between Groups	242298.3719	7	34614.05312	9.19924	2.10E-06	2.28523
Within Groups	131694.8389	35	3762.70968			
Total	373993.2107	42				

Panel A of Table 8.5 gives the summary data of central tendencies and dispersions for the respective years under review, whereas Panel B gives the between and among group variations and the accompanying statistical measures relevant to the F-test. The Single Factor ANOVA test is intended to ascertain whether two or more independent samples have equivalent measures of central tendency as represented by means or medians and thus may be equal to one another for the given samples. Panel B of Table 8.5 shows that there are significant differences among the means of the annual data presented, given that the F calculated (F cal) is greater than the F critical (F cri). Panel B gives that F calculated = 9.19924 and the $F_{(0.05)}$ critical = 2.28523. Given that F cal > $F_{(0.05)}$, the data among the different subgroups are indeed significantly different from each other with a 5% margin of error. In addition, the P-value of 0.00021% suggests that an error in the conclusion that the means between and within groups is significantly different and well within the allowable 5% margin of error.

Single factor ANOVA test for within and between groups were also calculated for the proportionate random sample in the small bank category of acquirees whose assets were no greater than $0.1 billion at the time of their respective official merger announcement dates. Table 8.6 captures the single factor ANOVA test for banks in the small bank category.

Table 8.6
Single Factor ANOVA Test for within and Between Groups in the Acquirees ≤ $0.1b Category Price to Book Value for a Proportionate Stratified Random Sample

Panel A

SUMMARY

Groups	Count	Sum	Average	Variance
1990	15	2380.24	158.6827	5306.904
1991	25	3139.67	125.5868	1118.348
1992	30	4839.03	161.3017	4630.403
1993	33	5668.85	171.7833	5104.019
1994	45	7978.84	177.3076	2828.779
1995	34	5753.89	169.2321	2647.189
1996	32	5669.76	177.1847	2057.826
1997	31	5900.59	190.3416	1429.044

Panel B

ANOVA

Source of Variation	SS	Df	MS	F	P-value	F crit
Between Groups	70093.94	7	10013.422	3.30884	0.00223	2.04835
Within Groups	717223.9	237	3026.261			
Total	787317.9	244				

Table 8.6 presents the summary and results of the F (0.05) test. Panel A of Table 8.6 summarizes the measures of central tendency and dispersion whereas, Panel B gives the F test results and related parametric measures. Again the calculated F value (F cal) was found to be 3.30884, which is much greater than the F critical value (F cri) of 2.04835 at a 5% error allowance. In addition, a calculated p-value of 0.223% indicates that the margin of error is less than 1% and therefore well within the 5% error allowed for in such a test. Hence, the between and within groups for the samples of small acquirees are significantly different from each other. Table 8.7 reports the results of the F test which sought to ascertain whether the variances for the price offered to book value between the megabank and small bank categories are indeed significantly different.

Table 8.7
F-test for Sample Variances between Acquirees in Megabank and Small Bank Categories for the Price Offered/Book Value Variable

	Price:Book Megabanks (Assets ≥ $5.0b)	Price:Book Small Banks (Assets ≤ $0.1b)
Mean	225.1932558	168.368408
Variance	8904.600256	2911.304878
Observations	43	245
Df	42	244
F	3.058629	
P(F ≤ f) one-tail	3.541E-08	
F Critical one-tail	1.434707	

Table 8.7 compares the sample variances relative to the price offered to book value approach for the megabank and small bank categories and confirms that the variance of the megabanks category is significantly different from the small bank category. This conclusion is founded on the grounds that F calculated > F critical (F_{cal} = 3.058629 and F_{cri} = 1.434707 at $F_{0.05}$). The magnitude of the variance differential is further substantiated by the fact that the P-value is close to 0 with a precise value of 0.00000541% and hence very much smaller than the 0.05 allowable error for this F-test.

Following the foregoing analysis and using the F test, it is can be assumed with a high level of certainty that the variances between the megabanks and small banks are in deed different using the price offered to book value approach. To conclude whether or not megabanks are indeed attracting higher merger or acquisition premiums using the price offered to book value measurement approach will be answered by conducting a t test. Such a test swill essentially seek to determine whether or not there is a significant difference in the means of the two categories of data obtained to test the relative premium hypothesis of this study. Table 8.8 presents the results of the t-test for significant difference in the means for banks in the megabank and small bank categories.

Table 8.8
T-test Assuming Unequal Variances on the Price Offered/Book Value Variable for Megabank and Small Bank Categories

	Megabanks (Assets ≥ $5.0b)	Small Banks (Assets ≤ $0.1b)
Mean	225.19326	168.36841
Variance	8904.60026	2911.30488
Observations	43	245
Hypothesized Mean Difference	0	
Df	47	
T Stat	3.84016	
P(T ≤ t) one-tail	0.00018	
T Critical one-tail	1.67793	
P(T ≤ t) two-tail	0.00037	
t Critical two-tail	2.01174	

Table 8.8 shows that the means and variances for the price offered to book value with the calculated t statistic (t_{calc}) is greater than the t test critical value (t_{crit}). The t calculated one-tail test (3.84016) > t critical (1.67793) indicating that in a one-way directional test the arithmetic mean of the megabanks category is significantly greater than the mean in the small banks category. The probability of committing a Type I error, that is, that the means are the same when in fact

they are different is almost 0.037% which is way below the 5% error in the level of statistical significance permissible in this study. The results of this t test suggest that the premium, as measured by price offered to book value, paid for integrating with megabanks is significantly greater than the premium paid for merging with, or acquiring smaller banks.

Clearly, using a price offered to book value approach tends to suggest that the null hypothesis (H_0), which states that premium paid as a precondition for integrating with megabanks is less than or equal to that which is paid to integrate with relatively smaller banks, cannot be supported. Therefore, the null hypothesis is rejected in favor of the alternate hypothesis (H_1), the latter of which essentially states that premiums are greater for banks in the megabank category vis-à-vis those premiums attributable to mergers or acquisitions involving banks in the small bank category.

Conclusion using the price offered to book value approach to support the conjecture that higher premiums are paid for the right to integrate with megabanks versus that paid for integrating with smaller banks:

Reject H_0.

Price to Book Value: A Synthesis

The relationship between price of an asset and book value has always been of tremendous interests to financial analysts, market watchers, and investors. Taking corporation stocks as an example, stocks selling way below their book values will be assessed as undervalued assets by the market. It follows that higher returns can be expected for assets that are trading at low price to book values when compared to those that are trading at higher price to book values. Generally, book value trends are less erratic when compared to earnings trend and hence, the former is a good basis for matching against price offered in a proposed bank consolidation.

In the context of the analysis done in this chapter, the results of the t test do suggest that the premium, as measured by price offered to book value, paid for integrating with megabanks is significantly greater than the premium paid for merging with, or acquiring smaller banks. The data assembled for the analysis had used the latest closing price for the given corporation's stock divided by the most recent book value after adjustments for recent (less than 12 months) earnings and dividend announcements were made. The findings above also revealed that big players in the financial industry are desirous of getting bigger more rapidly and to do so acquisitions of, or mergers with, smaller banks are not attractive options. Hence, the reason for bidding up the prices in merger or acquisition deals involving the other large banks.

CHAPTER 9

Results and Discussion of Premium Paid to Integrate with Megabanks: Price to LTM Eps Approach

The price offered by an acquirer for the right to integrate with another bank should be influenced by value that will accrue to shareholders. However, in order to make a comparison between two entities or trends over time the underlying metrics must be standardized. Relative value can be standardized by using price offered to book or earnings generated in relation to the acquisition of the given asset. It would seem that price/trailing four-quarter earnings multiples also known as price to Last Twelve Months Earnings per share (LTM Eps) is one of two very popular measures for comparing merger or acquisition premiums for financial intermediaries (SNL, 1998). The other measure of course is price offered to book value, which formed the basis for the analysis of merger or acquisition premium that was highlighted in the preceding chapter.

The price offered to most recent earnings per share is intended to reflect the revenue enhancement expectations about an acquiree. Theoretically, the price offered to earnings potential suggests that the consolidated financial organizations will provide a greater return than the market in general. In a more strictly financial perspective a price offered to LTM Eps gives a clue as to what acquirers are projecting about the acquiree's added value the merging entities.

Hypothesis 3 states that "the acquirees in megabank mergers and acquisitions attract higher premiums than do acquirees in relatively smaller banks over the period covered by this study." Symbolically, the null hypothesis (H_0) and the alternate hypothesis (H_1) are reiterated as follows:

$H_0: \mu_M \leq \mu_S$

$H_1: \mu_M > \mu_S$

where μ_M = the mean merger or acquisition premium for banks in the megabank category.

and μ_S = the mean merger or acquisition premium for banks in the small bank category

Acquisition premium, which is the offered price per stock in excess of the prevailing price per stock at book value, was evaluated. All the information necessary for calculating price offered to book value and price offered to LTM Eps were available and appeared quite reliable

<u>The basis for Price Offered to LTM Eps Approach:</u>

A very important pecuniary value of an asset is the stream of income the given asset can generate over a fixed period of time. Therefore, the price offered to acquire an asset can be measured as a relationship to the earnings it can generate over a given fiscal year. The last 12 months trailing earnings as a multiple of share price (LTM Eps) is used as the basis for calculating the ratio at offered price per acquiree's stock to earnings from period t_{-1}. For example, assuming that an acquirer offered a price of $35.00 to acquire each common stock in a merger or acquisition and the earnings per share in the immediate past fiscal year is $1.95, the price offered to earnings per share will be 17.9. If the price offered was $40.00 instead of $35.00 the ratio would increase to 20.5. It follows that, all other things held constant, the acquirer will prefer a lower Price to LTM Eps ratio while opposite will hold true for the acquiree.

The Results

The area of study captured by this chapter, as a further step to solidify the conclusion drawn from the price offered to book value approach as discussed in the last chapter, endeavored to follow a second business accounting ratio– price offered to LTM Eps. Using this approach, the sample size $\underline{n}$ will not necessarily be the same as that of the price offered to book value approach. Such an unequivocal situation arose for the simple reason that the d, which represent the closest distance possible between the sample mean $\bar{x}$ and the population mean μ with a probability of (1 - α), is likely to be different. Additionally, the measure of d also depends on the actual value of the population standard deviation (σ). The measures that will be identical for both the Price offered to book value and LTM Eps are the sample sizes within strata, measured by N_i and the strata weights, measured by w_i.

Similar to the analysis done under the price offered to book value approach, an appropriate d will first be identified and then will be followed by an estimation of n based on a proportionate stratified simple random sample using the sample means approach. Secondly, the total sample size will be estimated using equation (5.5) described and analyzed in chapter 5. Following Levine, Berenson, and Stephan (1998) the population standard deviation (σ) will be approximated using range/6. Table 9.1 gives the estimation of d for each stratum or years in the price offered to LTM Eps approach for banks in the small bank category.

Table 9.1
The Estimated Values of d Over the Period 1990–1997 for the Price Offered to LTM Eps Approach in the Small Bank Category

Year	N_i	Range	σ = Range/6	$d = Z(\sigma/\sqrt{N_i})$
1990	74	32.4	5.4	1.23
1991	124	47.4	7.9	1.39
1992	148	53.4	8.9	1.43
1993	164	45.0	7.5	1.15
1994	227	54.6	9.1	1.18
1995	173	46.8	7.8	1.17
1996	162	60.0	10.0	1.54
1997	154	57.6	9.6	1.52

Table 9.1 demonstrates that the "d" which will result in the small differential between $\bar{x}$ and μ is the calculated value of 1.15, the half-width interval for the period 1993. Therefore, with the half-width interval $d = 1.15$, the total sample size of n will be the largest when the value of d is the smallest suggesting that, other things being equal, a larger sample size is preferred to a smaller one. Similar to the price offered to book value approach, the following equation will again be used to calculate the size of n for a proportionate simple random sample that can best estimate the mean:

$$n = \frac{(\Sigma N_i^2 \sigma_i^2 / w_i)}{N^2(d^2/4) + \Sigma(N_i \sigma_i^2)}$$

where N_i = number of elements in population strata i

σ_i = standard deviation of the elements in population strata i

d^2 = desired half-width of the confidence interval.

w_i = proportion of the total elements found in stratum i

Substituting values in the above equation for the Price Offered to LTM Eps approach in the small bank category have produced the following results:

$$n = \frac{\frac{(74)^2(5.4)^2}{0.06} + \frac{(124)^2(7.9)^2}{0.101} + \frac{(148)^2(8.9)^2}{0.121} + \frac{(164)^2(7.3)^2}{0.124} + \frac{(227)^2(9.1)^2}{0.185} + \frac{(173)^2(7.8)^2}{0.141} + \frac{(162)^2(10.0)^2}{0.132} + \frac{(154)^2(9.6)^2}{0.126}}{\frac{(1226)^2(1.15)^2}{4} + 74(5.4)^2 + 124(7.9)^2 + 148(8.9)^2 + 164(7.3)^2 + 227(9.1)^2 + 173(7.8)^2 + 162(10.0)^2 + 154(9.6)^2}$$

n = 212.67, and by rounding up

$n \cong 213$

Applying the appropriate weighted relationship w_i to each year or stratum for the price offered to LTM Eps data Table 9.2 gives the sample size per stratum

Table 9.2
Proportionate Sample (n_i) Allocated to Strata Based on Weight of Stratum (w_i) in Sample n for the Price Offered to LTM Eps Approach for Banks in the Small Bank Category

Year	$\underline{n}(w_i)$	$=\underline{n}_i$	Year	$\underline{n}(w_i)$	$=\underline{n}_i$
1990	213 (0.060)	13	1994	213 (0.185)	39
1991	213 (0.101)	21	1995	213 (0.141)	30
1992	213 (0.121)	26	1996	213 (0.132)	28
1993	213 (0.134)	29	1997	213 (0.126)	27

Similar to the price offered to book value approach, the samples for the LTM Eps approach was drawn from each stratum in relation to that stratum's quantifiable relationship to the total population being studied as shown in Table 9.2. Using the above equation the total sample size $\underline{n}$ will be approximated for a stratified population mean μ based on a 95% confidence interval according to apportionment to each stratum.

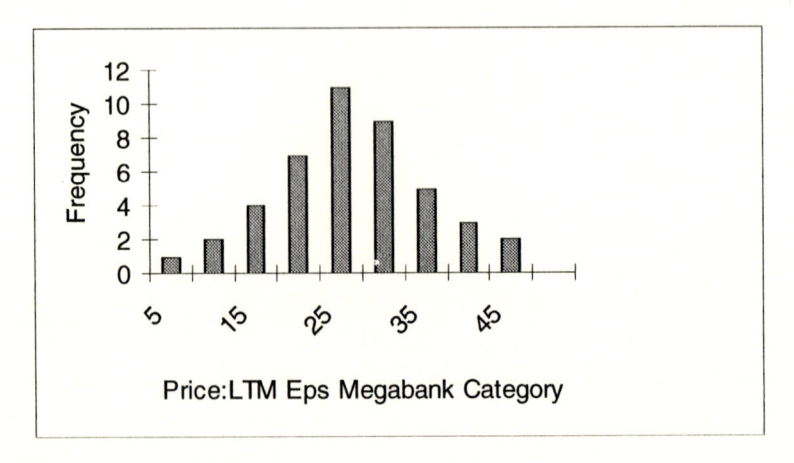

Figure 9.1. Histogram showing price offered to LTM Eps for banks in the megabank category.

The proportionate random sample was determined and drawn with the assistance of SPSS Base 9.0 software package. All the subsamples within each year can generally be considered as statistically large with a tendency towards the normal distribution assumption. The data assembled for this part of the study were analyzed and the data points tended to approximate the normal distribution assumption concerning the distribution curve. Figures 9.1 and 9.2 show the distribution of the data points in the Price Offered to LTM Eps approach for banks in the megabank category. The data for these banks appear bell-shaped and somewhat symmetrical, and hence, seem to be tending towards a normally distributed set of data points.

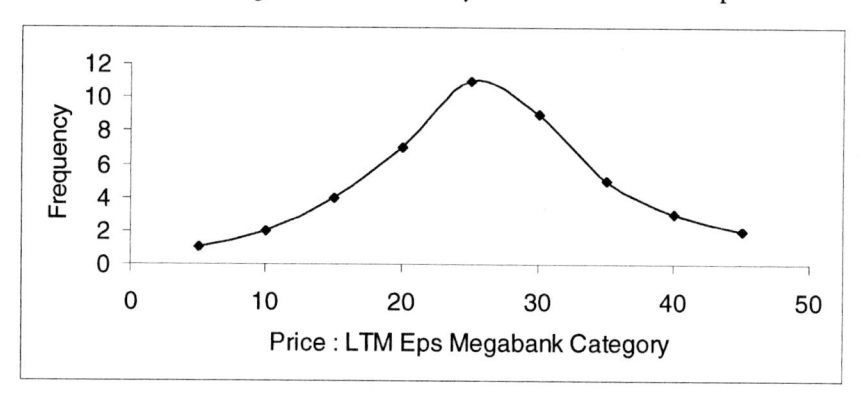

Figure 9.2. Frequency distribution curve depicting price offered to LTM Eps in the megabank category.

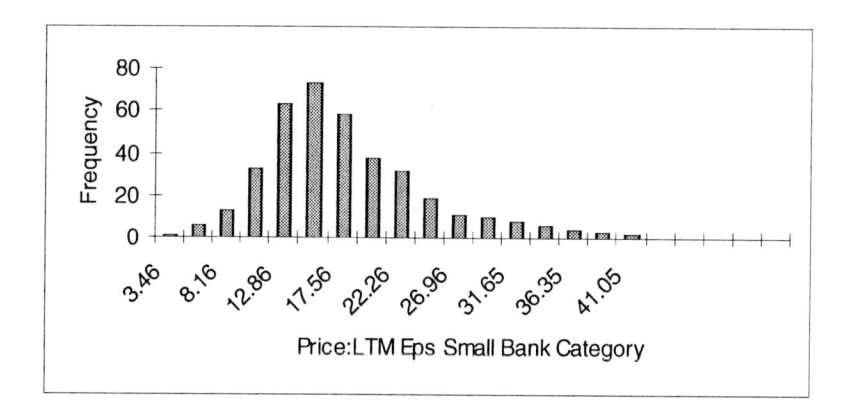

Figure 9.3. Histogram showing price offered to LTM Eps for banks in the small bank category.

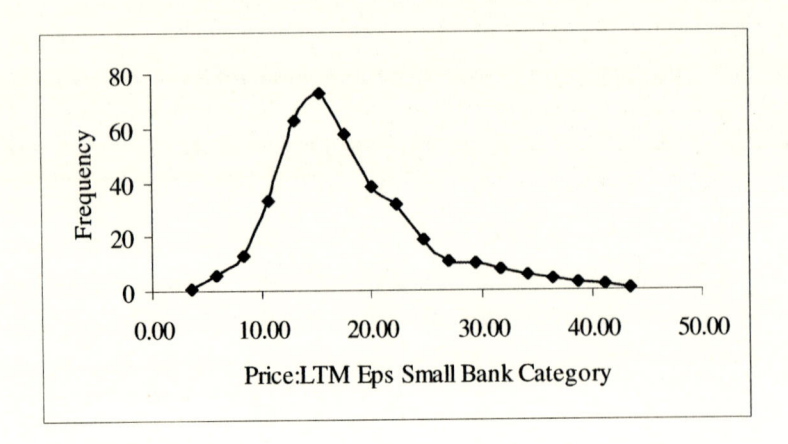

Figure 9.4. Frequency distribution curve depicting price offered to LTM Eps in the small bank category.

Figures 9.3 and 9.4 show the data points distribution for Price Offered to LTM Eps for banks in the small bank category. Similar to the megabanks' category depicted in Figures 9.1 and 9.2, Figures 9.3 and 9.4 demonstrate that the data for these smaller banks appear bell-shaped and somewhat symmetrical, and hence, may be tending towards a normally distributed set of data points.

The data summarized with the uses of charts tend to suggest that the distribution pertaining to the LTM Eps approach for testing the premium differences in mergers and acquisitions between large and small banks tended towards a normal distribution. Thus, parametric tests may be appropriately applied to test the null hypothesis that magabanks command merger or acquisition premiums as much as the relatively smaller banks.

Panel A of Table 9.3 presents a summary of the central tendency and dispersion calculations for price offered in relation to trailing four-quarter earnings multiples in the megabank category for the entire period under review. Panel B of Table 9.3 presents the F test results for the within and between groups in the price offered/LTM (Eps) variable. Given that the F calculated is greater than the F critical (F_{cal} = 3.07187 > F_{crit} = 2.28523) at $F_{0.05}$, each sub-group data means and variances are significantly different from one another. In addition, the P-value of 0.01248 suggests that the margin of error is within the allowance of α = 0.05, which formed part of the theoretical framework for this test.

Table 9.3
<u>Single Factor ANOVA Test for Within and Between Groups for Megabanks with Asset ≥ $5.0b in Price to LTM Eps Variable</u>

Groups	Count	Sum	Average	Variance
1990	1	23.200	23.200	0.0
1991	4	98.120	24.530	98.522
1992	4	89.460	22.365	58.508
1993	1	39.920	39.920	0.0
1994	3	35.080	11.693	6.693
1995	13	200.690	15.438	50.230
1996	6	131.570	21.928	105.450
1997	11	259.400	23.582	24.993

ANOVA

Source of Variation	SS	df	MS	F	P-value	F crit
Between Groups	1145.457	7	163.637	3.07187	0.01248	2.28523
Within Groups	1864.428	35	53.269			
Total	3009.884	42				

Table 9.4
ANOVA Single Factor Test for Price Offered / LTM Eps for Small Bank Acquirees with Assets ≤ $0.1b. at Announcement

Panel A

SUMMARY

Groups	Count	Sum	Average	Variance
1990	13	189.830	14.602	11.259
1991	21	323.610	15.410	55.203
1992	26	337.160	12.968	41.292
1993	29	372.910	12.859	34.668
1994	39	755.760	19.378	96.908
1995	30	610.220	20.341	180.652
1996	28	450.450	16.088	43.195
1997	27	504.780	18.696	72.369

Panel B

ANOVA

Source of Variations	SS	Df	MS	F	P-value	F crit
Between Groups	1676.917	7	239.5645	3.22847	0.00287	2.05446
Within Groups	15211.460	205	74.2022			
Total	16888.377	212				

Table 9.4 shows the single factor ANOVA test for the small bank category in relation to the price offered/LTM Eps variable. Panel A summarizes the measures of central tendency and dispersion, whereas Panel B gives the F-test results. Consistent with the preceding price offered/ LTM Eps analysis for megabanks in Table 9.3, the between and within groups variations in the small banks category in Table 9.4 are indeed significantly different given that the F calculated (F_{cal} = 3.22847) is greater than F critical (F_{cri} = 2.05446) at $F_{(0.05)}$. The calculated P-value of 0.00287 suggests that the F test be well within the allowable 5% margin of error.

Table 9.5
F-test for Sample Variances between Megabank and Small Bank Categories for the Price Offered / LTM Eps Variable

	Megabanks (Assets ≥$5)	Small Banks (Assets ≤ $0.1b)
Mean	22.28558	16.64188
Variance	117.25156	79.66216
Observations	43	213
Df	42	212
F	1.47186	
P(F ≤ f) one-tail	0.04122	
F Critical one-tail	1.44229	

Table 9.5 compared variances for the Price Offered to LTM Eps variable and confirmed that the variance of the megabanks category is significantly different to that of the small bank category. Such a difference is authenticated by the fact that F calculated > F critical (F_{calc} = 1.47186 > F_{crit} = 1.44229) at $F_{(0.05)}$. The magnitude of the variances differential is further substantiated given that the P-value = 0.04122 which is less than α = 0.05 allowable error for this F test.

From the foregoing analysis using the F test, it is can be assumed, with a high level of certainty, that the variances between the megabanks and small banks are in deed different using the LTM Eps approach. To conclude whether or not megabanks are indeed attracting higher merger or acquisition premiums using the price offered to LTM Eps approach will be answered by conducting a t test for significance in the difference between the means of the two categories of data.

Table 9.6 presents the results of the t test for significance in the differences between the means for the two groups of data.

Table 9.6
T-test Assuming Unequal Variances on the Price Offered/LTM Eps Variable for Megabank and Small Bank Categories

	Megabanks (Assets ≥ $5.0b)	Small Banks (Assets ≤ $0.1b)
Mean	22.28558	16.64188
Variance	117.25156	79.66216
Observations	43	213
Hypothesized Mean Difference	0	
Df	54	
t Stat	3.20500	
P(T ≤ t) one-tail	0.00113	
t Critical one-tail	1.67357	
P(T ≤ t) two-tail	0.00227	
t Critical two-tail	2.00488	

Similar to the t test in the price offered to book value approach, the price offered to LTM Eps variable tends to suggest the mean in the megabank category is significantly greater than the mean in the small bank category. This is evident by the fact that from Table 9.6, it can be seen that the t calculated (t_{calc} = 3.20500) is greater than the t critical (t_{cri} = 1.67357) value for the one-tail directional test. The results of this t test suggest that the premium as measured by price offered to LTM Eps paid for integrating with megabanks is significantly greater than the premium paid for merging or acquiring with the relatively smaller banks. The probability of committing a Type I error, that is, rejecting the null hypothesis when indeed it is true is calculated to be less than 0.227%, which is far below the allowable 5% error that was part of the theoretical framework for this test.

Conclusion using the price offered to LTM Eps approach to support the conjecture that higher premiums are paid for the right to integrate with megabanks versus that paid for integrating with smaller banks:

Reject H_0

A Discussion of Premium Payments to Integrate with Megabanks

The third and final hypothesis of this study holds that, in their quest to integrate with other banks, banks in the American banking industry display a propensity to pay higher premiums to integrate with megabanks than that which is paid to integrate with relatively smaller banks. This study has adopted two approaches to test the hypothesis that acquirers tend to pay higher premiums to integrate with larger banks than relatively smaller ones. The first approach, which was fully explored in chapter 8, utilized the accounting ratio of price offered to book value and measured the offering price per equity in relation to the prevailing book value per equity in the immediate preceding fiscal end-of-year. The book value represented the actual monetary value per divisible unit of stockholders equity listed in the official records of the acquiree, for the fiscal year immediately preceding the date of the official announcement of a given merger or acquisition.

The second approach, which was analyzed in this chapter, utilized the price offered to last 12 months trailing earnings as a multiple of price per stock being offered by one bank to merge with, or acquire another bank. This approach sought to test whether or not the price offered to LTM Eps ratios are greater for larger banks vis-à-vis smaller ones. In order to test that the arithmetic means for megabanks are indeed larger than the means of the relatively smaller banks utilizing a $\underline{t}$ test, three other procedures were followed with the aim of validating the test for significance in the mean differences between the underlying groups of data. First, the data were evaluated in the context for symmetry and normalcy of the distributions. The results of such an evaluation revealed that the data tended towards normalcy in the distributions and seemingly symmetrically shaped with a tendency towards positively skewed tails. To these ends, histograms and frequency distribution curves were constructed in order to demonstrate that the distributions tended toward symmetry and normalcy.

Second, the analysis of the data evaluated the means between and within groups for significant differences. The results of the single factor ANOVA $F_{(0.05)}$ test identified that the arithmetic means between and within groups are significantly different from each other. Third, a final $F_{(0.05)}$ test was carried out in order to determine, whether or not, the variances between magabank and small bank acquirees are significantly different. The $F_{(0.05)}$ test for sample variances between these two categories of banks were found to be also significant. Flowing out of the preceding analytical procedures was the need to test for significance between the means of the premiums between megabanks and small banks utilizing price offered to book value and price offered to LTM Eps approaches. To this end, t tests that actually tested the positive one-directional differences between the measured variables of price offered to book value and price offered to LTM Eps, were conducted. Table 9.7 summarized the results of the t-tests utilizing both approaches to evaluate the third and final hypothesis of this study.

Table 9.7
T-tests of Merger and Acquisition Premium Payment Hypothesis for Banks in the Megabank and Small Bank Categories: Summary Results

Approaches	t Calculated	t Critical	Reject H_0	P-value	One/Two Tail
*1. Price Offered/ Book Value	3.84016	1.67793	Yes	0.00037	One Tail
2. Price Offered/ LTM Eps	3.20500	1.67357	Yes	0.00113	One Tail

* The price offered to book value approach was analyzed and synthesized in chapter 8.

Clearly, both approaches arrive at the same conclusion, which is, to reject the null hypothesis (H_0) that banks in the megabank category do not attract premium payments as much as those banks in the small bank category. For both approaches, the calculated values exceeded the critical values which suggest that the differences in the premiums paid to acquire megabanks and small banks are indeed significant ($\alpha = 0.05$). The probability of committing a Type I error, that is, rejecting H_0 when in fact it should not have been rejected, is way below the allowable 5% error for the price offered/book value and price offered/ LTM Eps variables with a P-value of 0.00037 and 0.00113 respectively. Both approaches summarized in Table 9.7 followed the design of a one-tail probability test ($\alpha =

0.05) with the resulting p-values much lower than the five percent error built into the theoretical framework of this study.

Price Offered to LTM Eps Approach: A Synthesis

The approach in the previous chapter utilized the accounting ratio of price offered to book value, which measures the offering price per unit of common equity in relation to the prevailing book value per unit of common equity in the immediate preceding fiscal end-of-year. The book value represented the actual monetary value per divisible unit of stockholders equity listed in the official records of the acquiree. The second approach utilized the price offered to last 12 months trailing earnings as a multiple of price per stock being offered by one bank to merge with, or acquire another bank. This approach sought to test whether or not the price offered to LTM Eps ratios are greater for larger banks vis-à-vis smaller ones. In order to test that the arithmetic means for megabanks are indeed larger than the means of the relatively smaller banks utilizing a t test, three other procedures were followed with the aim of validating the test for significance in the mean differences between the underlying groups of data.

The analyses undertaken to test premium paid to integrate with megabanks were conducted under what may be referred to as relative valuation (Damodaran, 2003). Using the earnings per share that was distributed within the last twelve months as a denominator and the price offered for a given asset in the numerator presented a standardized way for a comparison between two or more assets. It is common to refer to the independent variable as price trailing four quarters earnings per share. The word "trailing," as used in the analysis, suggested that the current earnings per share was used in the independent variable rather than forward earnings per share. The word "forward" in this context meant that expected earnings per share would have replaced the current earnings per share in the independent variable used above to test premium paid for integrating with megabanks versus that which is paid to integrate with smaller banks. Clearly, banks are willing to pay relatively higher premiums for the right to integrate with larger banks, vis-à-vis that which is paid for the right to integrate with the relatively smaller banks.

CHAPTER 10

BANK CONSOLIDATIONS: IMPLICATIONS FOR THE FUTURE

The breakdown of intra- and inter-state branch banking in the United States has resulted in increased competition in the financial services industry and paved the way for deep changes among financial intermediaries. The experiment with bank holding companies has proven to be a success in growing financial organization in that interstate branching restrictions were somewhat circumvented at times by direct invention of receiving states. The failure of many financial institutions, it is believed, was the product inordinate and annihilative curses of the competitive market, high interest payment on savings, and excessive high-risk loans.

The lacking distinction and clarity of banking activities forged the basis for the enactment of the (in)famous Glass-Steagall Act of 1933, a piece of legislation which sought to prohibit the integration of the investment and commercial functions of banks. Despite repeated intimation by the U.S. Congress to repeal this act on the grounds that it was breeding unfair competition among commercial banks vis-à-vis nonbank financial entities, conformity with the Glass-Steagall's guidelines remained intact. In fact, the political establishment seemed unable to muster the collective will to amend such seemingly archaic legal business restrictions. Restrictions pertaining to the separation of commercial and investment activities including the trading in insurance products placed American banks at a disadvantage relative to those banks outside the United States. However, with the conglomerate merger in 1998 between Citicorp, a commercial bank, and Travelers Group, an insurance business, the onus to act decisively fell heavily on the political directorates.

The contents of this chapter are presented in three parts with the aim of further discussing the results within a framework of practical implications and unanswered questions that may have arisen as a result of this study. In the first part, a summary of the study is presented with the intention of further discussing the results in relation to the question raised, the theoretical framework established, and the actual findings reported. The second part will discuss the conclusions drawn and the practical implications of the issues raised in this book with particular reference to the economic and, or social impact especially within a banking environment. The final part focuses on spin-off questions that have been directly deduced from this study and some of the underlying implications for future research initiatives

Summary Results of Bank Consolidations in the U.S.

The financial services industry within the United States, as indeed around the world, is undergoing rapid structural adjustments in the midst of a vigorously evolving social and technological environment. The banking sector in the United States is strategically poised to wield significant economic power within the financial services industry by virtue of their ability to dictate the loan amortization processes, charge above-normal prices for differentiated products and services, and establish excellent franchises around customer inertia. Such a sphere of influence, however, is somewhat thwarted in the sense that there exist an increasing number of fully functional quasi-banks such as finance houses, money stores, mutual fund institutions, and credit unions that also compete for parts of the banking sector's market share. In addition, there exist parallel financing departments owned and operated by huge corporations that raise their own capital to finance the sale of their own products by way of making loans available to consumers on fairly attractive terms. General Motors Acceptance Corporation (GMAC), Toyota Motor Credit Corporation, and General Electric Small Business Solutions are examples of captive financing parallel entities that compete with commercial banks for potential debtors.

The dynamics of a competitive banking environment suggest that some banks may be forced to search for more strategic ways in order to positively impact their bottom lines and boost return on equities. One way to become more efficient is for an individual bank to increase its market share, while simultaneously holding down costs to a ratio less than the equivalent gain in market share. When banks integrate they can spread fixed costs associated with technological innovation, operating infrastructure and virtual banking services to a broader customer base. Such financial and operating synergies suggest that the consolidating entities can insulate themselves from the vagaries of an inevitably fluctuating economic and technological environment.

There are two dominant groups of theories that seek to explain the motive for business entities to integrate with each other. One is the non-value or growth maximizing motive, which suggests that businesses integrate for the purpose of increasing sales, assets or geographic and industrial control. The other is value maximization motive, which suggests that businesses integrate essentially to maximize economic returns to shareholders. Both explanations seem reasonable, as the research literature reviewed in this study indicated. However, for a single or given set of merger or acquisition events, it maybe useful to examine whether a value maximizing or growth maximizing behavior is the dominant explanation.

This study has sought to explain a set of merger events by utilizing the value maximizing motive as a dominant explanation for mergers and acquisitions among the very large United States banks, over the period 1990 to 1997. Towards this end, three hypothetico-deductive relationships were established. The first was that acquirers of megabanks realize negative excess returns on their equities. The second hypothesis sought to establish that acquiree shareholders value creation among megabanks is significantly greater than the value created for acquirers among those mergers and acquisitions that integrate on the basis merger of equals. The final hypothesized relationship holds that the premium paid to integrate with megabanks significantly exceeds that which is paid to integrate with the relatively smaller banks. Table 10.1 summarizes the results of the tests for these three hypotheses.

Table 10.1
Summary of the Results for the Hypotheses Tested in this Study

Hypothesis	H_0 Rejected/Not Rejected	n	Test Statistic
I Acquirer shareholders do not realize abnormal returns	Rejected	34	t = -2.47 (0.0026)
II Merger of equals acquirees excess returns > acquirers excess returns	Not Rejected	07	Z = 0.15 (0.4504)
III Megabanks attract higher acquisition premium	Rejected		
Approach 1			
Price Offered / Book Value			t =3.84016 (0.00018)
Megabanks		43[1]	
Small Banks		245	
Approach 2			
Price Offered / LTM (Eps)			t =3.24500 (0.00113)
Megabanks		43[1]	
Small Banks		213	

Note. P-values are given within brackets.
[1] For Hypothesis III, the population (N) in the megabank category = 43. All tests results reproduced in this table are significant at (α = 0.05).

Table 10.1 gives a summary of the results of the three hypotheses tested in this study. Consistent with the findings of many of the scholarly work attributed to the study of mergers and acquisitions, integration between megabanks realize negative abnormal returns for acquirers. This finding is evident given that the test statistic, $\underline{t}$ = -2.47 (0.0026). The hypothesis that sought to test merger of equals among megabanks, which posits that megabank acquirees realize excess returns greater than their counterpart acquirers, was not supported by the data. This study failed to reject the merger of equals' null hypothesis as evident by $\underline{Z}$ = 0.15 (0.4504). Furthermore, the nonparametric Wilcoxon signed rank sum test for matched pairs conducted for each of the narrower defined 11-day event window found no consistent significant support for the hypothesized relationship that acquirees earn excess returns significantly greater that their counterparts, the acquirers.

Considerable support, however, was found for the test relating to the hypothesis that megabanks attract higher takeover premiums than that which is paid to integrate with relatively smaller banks. Two accounting relationships—price offered to book value and price offered to LTM Eps ratios—were utilized to measure acquisition premiums. For both measures the null hypothesis was rejected as evident with $\underline{t}$ = 3.84016 (0.00018) and $\underline{t}$ = 3.24500 (0.00113) for the price offered to book value and price offered to LTM Eps ratios, respectively.

This research was conducted within an atmosphere of a persistent awareness for creeping threats to internal validity of the model being tested with particular reference to the relationship between variables. In addition to the statistical and inferential treatment of the compiled data, four possible threats to internal validity that could detract from reliability of the findings were specifically examined. These were the non- normalcy condition, homoscedasticity assumption, sequencing of variables, and rival explanations. These creeping threats to internal validity for the hypotheses being tested and the statistical techniques employed sought to ensure that errors in the theoretical construction and analytical framework were kept to a minimum. In addition, the calculated *p*-value is well under the 5% allowable limit, producing further convincing evidence that the test results are way beyond the probability of committing the Type I error of accepting the null hypothesis when indeed it is false. In this study, Type I errors may likely occur is the results emanating from the first and third hypotheses, whereas a Type II error may likely occur in the results of the second hypothesized relationship.

The findings are consistent with previous scholarly research efforts, except for the merger of equals hypothesis (Jensen & Ruback, 1983; Peristiani, 1997; Sirower, 1997). The merger of equals hypothesis is a relatively new phenomenon. The theoretical construct for such a study borders along the line of a paradigm shift in the hypothetico-deductive methodology of empirical business and financial research. The null hypothesis pertaining to the merger of equals' model could not have be rejected in this study, perhaps the major reason being the presence of a relatively small sample size. Clearly, there is a need for a more expansive research framework that can include a larger sample size, thereby promoting greater validity and reliability of the model and findings.

The findings of the merger of equals hypothesis, which pointed to a failure to reject the null hypothesis on acquirees' value creation in mergers and acquisitions, essentially deviated from the modal findings of similar studies involving shareholders' value creation surrounding mergers and acquisitions. Those other studies that are well documented in Jensen and Ruback (1983) and more recently, Houston and Ryngaert (1994) utilized larger sample sizes. However, none of these studies that was examined sought to introduce "merger of equals" as a concept, a theoretical construct or as a variable. The only explanation for this inconsistency in findings is perhaps, due to the fact that "merger-of-equals," as an explanatory variable may be working against the normally expected acquirees' value creation, which is generally found to be >0.

The ratio of price offered to book value is a major acceptable standard in the financial economics literature for measuring acquisition premium (Adkisson & Fraser, 1992; Rhoades, 1987). Price offered to last 12 months earnings per share (LTM Eps), also referred to as trailing-four-quarters Eps, is another ratio employed in the measurement of premiums in mergers and acquisitions (SNL Securities LC, 1998). While studying the freedom of banks to do business in multi-states, Adkisson and Fraser found premiums to be positively correlated with multiple-state bank mergers vis-à-vis single-state bank mergers. Rhoades, using price offered to book as one of the measures of profitability among merging firms, found that there was no evidence of profitability. The findings from the third hypothesis in this study, which hypothesized that premiums are higher for larger banks than smaller ones suggesting that acquirers will be willing to pay a higher premium to integrate with larger banks than relatively smaller ones, supported such a hunch.

Clearly, the findings in the third hypothesis ran counter to one of the rudimentary laws of economics, which is that price and quantity demanded generally move in opposites. Alternatively, higher quantity (greater assets) attracts higher prices (premiums) in mergers and acquisitions among banks. While the finding in previous studies on merger and acquisition premiums are not very conclusive, the findings of this study could help further strengthen the evidence on the side of the proponents, who believe that a measure of relative size in merger and acquisition activities does matter. The question of size and economic benefits will continue to attract the attention of banking professionals and scholars as more and more banks seek to integrate in the future.

Practical and Theoretical Implications

The theoretical thrust of this study lends support and extends the works of previous scholars and banking professionals in the area of megabank consolidations through mergers and acquisitions. For one thing, when big banks acquire or merge with other big banks the value creation results are approximately the same as when size does not matter. The practical and theoretical implications in the banks' integration debate suggest that acquiree shareholders, by and large, realize significant abnormal returns on their equities. On the other hand, the acquirer' shareholders generally do not realize positive abnormal returns on their shareholdings. Yet, as this study has shown, banks continue at an accelerating pace to seek out possible candidates for integration into their business operations. This seemingly paradoxical scenario among merging entities continues to puzzle academicians, bank regulators, and financial analysts, a situation regularly referred to in this book as a continuing enigma.

The evidence documenting the destruction of value creation for acquirer shareholders may continue to point to the other set of explanations known in this study as non-value or growth maximization motive for mergers and acquisitions. This study supplements the literature by further illuminating the convention that acquirer shareholders earn 0 or negative excess returns with the addition that, merger and acquisitions among the huge banks in the United States endure the same consequences. That is, those value creation for acquirers generally do not realize positive excess returns around the merger announcement date. Richard Roll, the finance professor, popularized the grandiloquence motive of leaders in organizations for pursuing objectives that may be non-value maximizing, using the term "hubris" to describe such ego-driven leadership (Roll, 1986, p.197). The acquirer shareholders must pay a penalty (a premium) to acquire another firm of which the market has already valued correctly. It is this payment above market value that gives rise to the concept of a "premium" to be paid by acquirers to acquirees in merger and acquisition transactions. Hence, it is the lacking equivalence between price offered and market value per acquiring unit of equity that gives rise to the presence of a merger or acquisition premium.

The jury is still out on the non-value maximizing prerogative, which suggests that managers of acquiring banks seek to exercise certain privileges with a protracted desire of fulfilling their greed for greater power and industrial influence. There are many hypotheses, but not as many explanations on business consolidations let alone bank consolidations. This study, like so many others, has added to the existing stock of hypotheses, but very little by way of explanation. This study, however, showed that there is an associationship between bank size and acquisition premium. In addition, the merger of equals' hypothesis formulated in this study has exposed a paradigm shift in the debate on mergers and acquisitions among megabanks. Those mergers and acquisitions among the very large banks that sought to neutralize the traditional acquiree-acquirer relationship with a socio-psychological and human relation dimensions rooted in a merger of equals philosophy deserves particular attention. Such a conceptualization of merger of equals, as elucidated in this study, could rekindle an intense intellectual discussion on the question if diversity and inclusiveness as a business imperative of the future.

In this study, merger-of-equals was treated as a moderator variable. There is room for a constellation of social science research initiatives for this paradigm shift in the managerial philosophy of diversity and inclusiveness amongst the once previously recognized arch-competitors, who seek to integrate their business undertakings as single entities. In the mergers of equals situation, the acquirer is the organization that puts up the capital by way of cash or stock swaps and in so doing, inherits the ability to influence the future course of events for the new entity. It is quite plausible that an acquirer, in the merger of equals situation, will seek to integrate with an acquiree on an organizational and philosophical plateau where the diversity of ideas and inclusiveness of competing opinions are highly valued assets in the future operations of prospective consolidating business entities.

The existence of many banks in the United States is a manifestation of the historical underpinnings of a banking sector legally restricted from branching. Branching refers to the ability of a given financial entity to operate several offices away from its main office. State law did not allow banks to have the liberty to enter any geographical areas of their own choosing, nor were they permitted to do investment banking and commercial banking all at the same time. Thus, the presence of many small banks in the United States may be the result of a protective legal framework and the need to promote greater competition, which could result in lower product prices to the customers of banks. On the other hand, the presence of so many banks may be the result of lacking competition. Hence, an inefficient bank may remain in operation for the simple reason that a lower cost bank is prohibited from entering the former's area of operation.

Interstate and interregional banking advocates argue that granting banks the liberty to operate nationally in the United States will create a healthier banking environment thereby reducing the incidence of bank failures (Mishkin, 1998). After all, banks in the United States are all free to operate internationally and therefore, interstate banking should be an available option also, as the reasoning goes. Those who oppose a nationwide banking system do so for fear that a demise of the community will be inevitable, given that huge money-center banks such as those found in Chicago, New York, and San Francisco will move in and gobble up the smaller banks. With the fall of these small personal community banks, lending to small businesses, minorities and servicing the banking needs of poorer neighborhoods will dissipate, if not disappear. Another skepticism raised by the antagonist to a national banking impetus is that, over time and with consolidation and the inevitable destruction of the many community banks, the few megabanks that remain will dominate the banking industry. Fewer and larger banks, as viewed by big bank antagonists, would restrict competition and charge unconscionable fees for banking products, services, and other banking-related fees.

Currently, the bank consolidation euphoria of the 1990s has somewhat quieted down. But this may not be the end to bank consolidation as a growth model. The legal barriers that once prohibited many areas and services that banks and thrifts could have gotten into are gradually being repealed. Once bank consolidations have achieved a level where further consolidations may not be strategically or financially prudent, the banking industry will still be left with, as Allen (1997) and Mishkin (1998) have suggested, a few thousands efficient and fully operational commercial banks and thrifts inclusive of a dozen or so megabanks. The projected net effect will be that, the benefits of integration among banks will most likely outweigh the costs associated with such consolidations.

Contemporary Consolidation Issues and Future Research Initiatives

This study has helped to further illuminate the research consensus that the value creation for acquirees among megabanks involved in mergers and acquisitions is positive. What is contentious, however, and this study has sought to illuminate, is the question of value creation among the acquirer shareholders. Consistent with other studies, this study has shown that acquirers, by and large, do realize excess returns less than 0. It was clear that among some of the mergers and acquisitions, both acquirers and acquirers realized above normal returns on their equities. It was also clear that in-market megabank mergers and acquisitions have had the greatest opportunity for cost savings through synergy. In a practical sense, however, most megabanks within the United States, in the presence of a progressive relaxation of a restrictive regulatory framework, are virtual competitors in a domestic market that is decreasingly less differentiated along geographic lines. Therefore, all banks, and especially the huge ones, envisage the entire United States and possibly the entire world as a single marketplace for most of their product lines and where segmented marketing strategies constitute the modus operandi for most of these megabanks.

This study has examined, in some detail, factors that may characterize a successful merger or acquisition between two banking entities. Given the strategic and structural nature of banks in an economy, decisions and action by players in the financial services industry aimed at growing inorganically (consolidation) are subjected to intense scrutiny by all, especially bank regulators and other governmental operatives. The policy of "too big to fail" or "too important to fail" is an overarching consideration, as the urge to merge becomes increasingly obvious. Ruback (1983) articulated the view that the literature is short on the case study method of inquiry. Yin (1994) reminded researchers that a qualitative quasi-deductive inquiry could be equally scientific as any quantitative research paradigm, with the former generalizing to a theoretical proposition rather than an underlying population.

This study sought to seriously integrate aspects of a qualitative component by doing a mini case analysis of a single successful megabank merger. Seeking to follow such an additional research methodology would have taken this study outside the realm of the logic of a deductive inquiry and beyond the scope of the originally conceived theoretical framework. Using any of the measures of consolidation successes that were articulated throughout this study, future research initiatives may want to do indepth analyses as to the factors that may be responsible for the failure of some mergers and acquisitions, against a background of those that were financially successful experiments. In an expanded dialectical continuum, this study has intimated that the analysis of factors that may contribute to the failure of some of the efforts at integration among business entities could simultaneously give rise to plausible rival explanations such as, why some other efforts result in successes.

Virtual banking versus the brick and mortar facade is an issue that will continue to occupy the minds of bank regulators, academicians, and banking analysts. Similar to banking professionals and bank regulators, parallel experts in the non-financial sectors of the U.S. economy are also wrestling with the encroaching great digital divide. It follows that, in order to succeed banks should treat the Internet as a marketing opportunity by focusing on a strategy that combines traditional parts of the business with the Internet and create a brand of Internet retailing in the financial service industry. For banks, while money is still the major item in the intermediary culture of the banking industry, information and digital money such as smart cards and digital cash will represent new modes of clearance in debit and credit transactions involving banks and their customers.

The U.S. economy has, and is still enjoying modest inflation growth, low interest rates, and a window of opportunities bolstered by a favorable legal and financial environment that is definitely encouraging creative risk-taking by financial innovators. In their search for greater profits, banks are seeking out resourceful ways such as indulging in sales of collateralized debt obligations (CDOs) involving mortgage-backed securities, secondary dealings in bonds, and other credit derivatives. Indeed, banks have diversified their obligations like never before and in the process are inducing insurance companies and pension and hedge fund managers to be part of a structured credit portfolio. The concentration involving these derivatives is such that such expanding trading activities are a huge part of investment banking portfolios. For example, the largest five U.S. banks command over 90% of the derivative market, while 25% of the largest banks hold close to 99% of all derivatives.

The above recounting does suggest that the research agenda of the future will be populated with bank-related issues such as on-line banking, virtual banking, environmental problems, the rising tide of disintermediation coupled with asset-transforming financial intermediaries, off-balance sheet financing, and all the intricacies of megabanks' consolidations. In addition, service aggregation and microsegmentation (Darlington, 1998) will also be interesting and relevant conceptual models for banking professionals and researchers to examine in the future. Service aggregation simply means building an optimum customer relationship by adding successive values to the customer-bank interactions.

Microsegmantation goes beyond the mere conventional marketing demographics and seeks to categorize clients along common profiles and similar banking needs. Customer profiling may suggest, for example, that younger customers my be more interested in banking by phone and the Internet, whereas the 60 years and older customers may prefer direct and personal banking services. The areas for further inquiry mentioned in this study are only a few of the myriad of major issues that need to be addressed in this new Millennium, now that this current civilization has seemed to have gone past the once-feared Y2K technological glitches that never really happened. Thus, as financial institutions in the United States continue to integrate through mergers and acquisitions, banking professionals, bank regulators, and academicians will need to further examine the technological reality that the battle for greater market control will be waged, not in the traditional brick and mortar facade, but in faceless and placeless cyberspace.

Megabank mergers, as was highlighted in chapters 1 and 2, took place during the merger-mania decade of the 1990s. The merger of Citicorp, a bank holding company and Travelers Group, an insurance business, formed the largest financial services holding company in 1998. Citigroup, the new name for the consolidated entity, is a preeminent global financial player with some 200 million customer accounts spanning over 100 independent countries with governments, other banks, corporations, and general consumers as its clientele. In terms of assets, Citigroup holds over $1,200 billion and employs approximately 350,000 million full time employees around the world. Close to a $1 trillion in assets also are J.P. Morgan Chase & Company and Bank of America Corporation.

Currently the top 10 U.S. banks in terms of assets account for close to 58% of the bank profits and 57% of tier One capital. These high profit margins may not be due to mergers and acquisitions, or if at all, may be at most only partially.

Definitely, this question of bank size and profitability will require further investigations as the literature on the synergistic effects from megabank consolidations is yet to find empirical answers to this issue. Beginning in 2004, there seems to be an upsurge in consolidating activities among the very large banks and financial institutions. Megabanks seem heading into another "merger-mania's arms race" experimenting with merger of equals at unprecedented proportions, after a lull for about 4 years spanning the period 2000 to 2004. Perhaps having to navigate through the very much feared and so-called Millennium (Y2K) bug, banks are prepared to venture into new marriages once more. Allan Greenspan, the Federal Reserve Bank Chairman, was quick to chide bankers: "It would be a mistake to conclude that the only way to succeed in banking is through ever-greater size and diversity." Mr. Greenspan further pointed out that, "better risk management may be the only truly element of success in banking." (Balls & Wighton, 2005). As this study has shown and the pronouncement articulated by the Fed chairman, the jury is still out on the true economic value to society and shareholders and the promotion of safety and soundness of the banking system through consolidations, while simultaneously preserving competition and efficiency in the financial sector.

The research agenda of the future will require more longitudinal studies built on theoretical constructs aimed at grappling with issues of merger divorces, demergers, post merger spinoffs and divestitures, and qualitative quasi-deductive analyses of successful bank consolidation models. The term demerger means the severing of certain core businesses of a consolidated company back into its original pre-merger forms or some other underlying semi-autonomous entities. Citigroup, for example, in late 2004 began selling off some of its non-core businesses in what was called "the garage sale of peripheral activities" (Politi & Roberts, 2004). Earlier that same year, Citigroup sold its UK-based medical, construction, and industrial financial unit to another company. The reader will recall that Citigroup is the product of a huge merger involving Citicorp, a commercial bank, and Travelers Group, an insurance business.

A deeper understanding of the issues involved in successful magabank consolidations and less successful ones must be pursued with the hope of finding some of the pitfalls that potential merger players must avoid in the pre- and post-consolidation periods. Bringing two huge in-market competitors, who for that matter were most of the times acute arch-rivals to one another in their respective quests for greater market share, is no lilliputian task. Having realized the protracted savings and many shareholders wallowing in some market gains, the marriage could succeed or fail in the years following the honeymoon. The difficult task of building an integrated whole must be on the drawing board for execution long before the post-consolidation hangover has subsided. A future research initiative must seek a profound understanding and the resulting implications of the current collateralized debit obligations, given that risk-based capital ratios of many banks are no different today that they were in the pre-collateralized debt obligations boom of recent years.

REFERENCES

Adkisson, J.A., & Fraser, D.R. (1990). The effect of geographic deregulation on bank acquisition premiums. Journal of Financial Services Research, 4 (2), 145–156.

Agrawal, A., Jaffe, J.E. & Mandelker, G. (1992). The Post-merger perform of acquiring firms: A re-examination of an anomaly. Journal of Finance 42, 823–837.

Allen, P.H. (1997). Reengineering the bank: A blueprint for survival and success (2nd ed.). New York: McGraw-Hill Companies, Inc.

American Bankers Association (1991). Banking terminology (3rd ed.). Washington, D.C.: American Bankers Association.

Asquith, P., Bruner, R.F., & Mullins, D.W., Jr. (1983). The gains for bidding firms from mergers. Journal of Financial Economics, 11, 121–139.

Balls, A, & Wighton, D. (2004, October 6). Greenspan upbeat about bank merger deals. Financial Times, p. 23.

Banerjee, A. & Owers, J.E. (1992). Wealth reduction in white knight bids. Financial Management, 21, 48–57.

Brown, S.J., & Warner, J.B. (1980). Measuring security price performance. Journal of Financial Economics, 8, 205–258.

Brown, S.J., & Warner, J.B. (1985). Using daily stock returns: The case of event study. Journal of Financial Economics, 14 (1), 3–31.

Burton, M., Nesiba, R, and Lombra R. (2003). An introduction to financial markets and institutions. Mason, OH: Thomas Learning, South-Western.

Byrd, J.W., & Hickman, K.A. (1992). Do outside directors monitor managers? evidence from tender offer bids. Journal of Financial Economics, 32, 195–221.

Carow, K.A., & Larsen, Jr., G.A., (1997). The effects of FDICIA regulation on bank holding Companies. Journal of Financial Research, 20 (2), 154–174.

Chen, C.R., Lin, J.W., & Sauer, D.A. (1997). Earnings announcements, quality and quantity of information, and stock price changes. Journal of Financial Research, 20 (4), 483–502.

Cheng, D.C., Gup, B.E., & Wall, L.D. (1989). Financial determinants of bank takeovers. Journal of Money, Credit, and Banking, 21, (4), 524–537.

Cheng, S. (1998). Takeovers of privately held targets, methods of payment and bidder returns. The Journal of Finance, 53, (2), 773–784.

Calomiris, C.W. & White, E.N., The origins of federal deposit insurance in U.S. bank deregulation in historical perspective. In C.W. Calomiris (Ed.), U.S bank deregulation in historical perspective (pp. 164–211). New York, NY: Cambridge University Press.

Cooley, P.L., & Roden, P. F. (1988). Business financial management. New York: The Dryden Press.

Damodaran, A. (1994). Damodaran on valuation: Security analysis for investment and corporate finance. New York: John Wiley & Sons, Inc.

Damodaran, A. (1996). Investment valuation: Tools and techniques for determining the value of any asset. New York: John Wiley & Sons, Inc.

Damodaran, A. (1997). Corporate finance: Theory and practice. New York: John Wiley & Sons, Inc.

Damodaran, A. (2003). Investment philosophies: Successful strategies and investors who made them work. Hoboken, NJ: John Wiley & Sons, Inc.

Darlington, L. (1998). Banking without boundaries: How the banking industry is transforming itself for the digital age. In D. Tapscott, A. Lowy, & D. Ticoll (Eds.), Blueprint to the digital economy: Creating wealth in the era of e-business (pp. 113–138). New York: McGraw-Hill.

Dodd, P. (1980). Merger proposals, management discretion and stockholder wealth. Journal of Financial Economics, 8, 105–137.

Eckbo, B. E. (1983). Horizontal mergers, collusion, and stockholder wealth. Journal of Financial Economics, 11, 241–273.

Eckert, G.M. (1997). Factors affecting the probability of bank mergers and acquisitions: An empirical analysis. Unpublished Dissertation. Ann Arbor, MI: UMI Company Microfilm No. 9806932.

FDIC (2002). "Top 50 bank holding companies by Total Domestic Deposits." Retrieved 12/20/03 from http://www.fdic.gov/sod/sos/SumReport.asp?

Franks, J., Harris, M., & Titman, S. (1991). The post-merger share price Performance of Acquiring firms. Journal of Financial Economics, 29, 81–96.

Freixas, X. & Rochet, J-C. (1997). Microeconomics of banking. Cambridge, M.A.: The MIT Press.

Freund, J.E., Williams, F.J., & Perles (1993). Elementary business statistics: The modern approach. Englewood Cliff, NJ: Pentice-Hall, Inc.

Gaughan, P.A. (1996). Mergers, Acquisitions, and Corporate Restructuring. New York: John Wiley & Sons, Inc.

Granger, C.W.J. (1969). Investigating causal relations by econometric models and cross-spectral methods. Econometrica, 37, 24–36.

Halpern, P. (1983). Corporate Acquisitions: A theory of special case? A review of event studies applied acquisitions. Journal of Finance, 37 (2), 297–316.

Hanson, P. (1992). Tender offers and free cash flow: An empirical analysis. The Financial Review, 27 (2), 185–209.

Hanweck, G.A., & Shull, B. (1999). The bank merger movement: Efficiency, stability and competitive policy concern. The Antitrust Bulletin, 54 (2), 251–284.

Hatler, G.O. (1991). Bank Investments & Funds Management (2nd ed.). Washington, D.C.: American Bankers Association.

Higson, C., & Elliott, J. (1998). Post-takeover returns: The UK evidence. Journal of Empirical Finance, 5, 27–46.

Houston, J.F., & Ryngaert, M.D. (1994). The overall gains from large bank mergers. Journal of Banking and Finance, 18 (6), 1155–1177.

Jensen, M.C., & Ruback, R.S. (1983). The market for corporate control: The scientific evidence. Journal of Financial Economics, 11, 5–50.

Johnson, F.P., & Johnson, R.D. (1989). Bank Management (2nd ed.). Washington, D.C.: American Bankers Association.

Johnson, H.J. (1995). Bank mergers, acquisitions & strategic alliance (A Bankline Publication). New York: Irwin Professional Publishing.

Keller, G, Warrack, B., & Bartel, H. (1994). Statistics for management and economics (3rd ed.,). Belmont, CA: Duxbury Press.

Kincaid, H. (1996). Philosophical foundations of the social sciences: Analyzing controversies in social research. New York: Cambridge University Press.

Kohn, M. (2004). Financial institutions and markets (2nd ed.). New York, NY: Oxford University Press' Inc.

Kolari, J., & Zardkoohi, A. (1987). Bank costs, structure, and performance. Lexington, M.A.: D.C. Heath and Company.

Kover, Amy (2000). Big Banks Debunked. Fortune, February 21, (187–194).

Levine, D.M., Berenson, M.L. & Stephan, D. (1998). Statistics for managers: Using microsoft excel. Upper Saddle River, NJ: Prentice-Hall, Inc.

Loughran, T., & Vijh, A. (1997). Do long term shareholders benefit from corporate acquisitions? Journal of Finance, 52 (5), 1765–1790, December.

Maharaj, A. (2001). Bank mergers and acquisition in the United States 1990 – 1997: An Analysis of shareholders value creation and premium paid to integrate with megabanks. Ann Arbor, MI: UMI Company, A Bell & Howell Company.

Markowitz, H.M. (1991). Original (1959). Portfolio selection (2nd edition). New York, NY: Blackwell Publishers.

Mergers and Acquisitions: The Dealmakers Journal, 31 (2), September/October, 1996.

Mergerstat Review. (1998). Los Angles, CA: Houlihan Lokey Howard & Zukin.

Mergerstat Review. (1997). Los Angles, CA: Houlihan Lokey Howard & Zukin.

MergerWatch Annual 1995. (1996). Austin, TX: Sheshunoff Information Services Inc.

MergerWatch Annual 1996. (1997). Austin, TX: Sheshunoff Information Services Inc.

Miles, M.B., & Huberman, A.M. (1994). Qualitative data analysis: A sourcebook. (2nd ed.). Beverly Hills, CA: Sage Publications, Inc.

Mishkin, F.S. (1998). The economics of money, banking and financial markets (4th ed). New York: Harper Collins College Publishers.

Mishkin, F.S. (1998). Bank consolidation: A central banker's perspective. In Y. Amihud and G. Miller (Eds.), Bank mergers and acquisitions (pp. 3–19). Netherlands: Kluwer Academic Publishers.

Mueller, D.C. (1995). Mergers: Theory and evidence. In G. Mussato (Ed.), Mergers, markets and public policy (pp. 9–43). Netherlands: Klewer Academic Publishers.

New York Public Library (1997). American history desk reference. New York, N.Y.: The Stonesong Press Inc. and The New York Public Library.

Peristiani, S. (1997). Do mergers improve the x-efficiency and scale efficiency of U.S. banks? Evidence from the 1980s. Journal of Money, Credit and Banking, 29, (3), 326–337, August.

Piliotte, S. B. (1989). An Empirical examination of horizontal mergers and antitrust Enforcement: Effects on shareholder wealth and industry competition. Unpublished Dissertation. Bloomington, IN: Indiana University.

Politi, J. & Roberts, D. (2004, November 23). Citigroup sells division to GE for $4.4bn, Financial Times, p. 19.

Rau, P.R. & Vermaelen, T. (1998). Glamour, Value, and post acquisition Performance of Acquiring firms. Journal of Financial Economics, 49, 223–253.

Rhoades, S.A. (1987). Determinants of premium paid in bank acquisitions. Atlantic Economic Journal, 25 (1), 21–27, March.

Rhoades, S.A. (1993). Efficiency Effects of horizontal bank mergers. Journal of Banking and Finance, 17, 411–422

Rochet, J.C., & Tirole, J. (1996). Interbank lending and systemic risk. Journal of Money, Credit and Banking, 28 (4), 733–762.

Roll, R. (1986). The hubris hypothesis of corporate takeovers. Journal of Business, 59, 197–216.

Ruback, R.S. (1982). Conoco takeover and stochholders' returns. Sloan Management Review, 23, 13–33.

Ruback, R.S. (1983). The cities service takeovers: A case study. The Journal of Finance, 38 (2), 319–330.

Senior, H. (1999). Regionals try new charters in search for web profits. American Banker. April 29.

Sharpe, W.F. (1964). Capital asset prices: A theory of market equilibrium under conditions of risk. Journal of Finance, 19 (2), 425–442.

Sincich, T. (1996). Business statistics by example (5th ed.). Upper Saddle River, NJ: Prentice-Hall, Inc.

Sirower, M. (1997). The synergy trap: How companies lose the acquisition game. New York: The Free Press.

Smith, K.W. (1998). Comment: Beating the odds in bank mergers. American Banker. March 6, 1998.

SNL Securities LC. (1998). Bank Mergers & Acquisitions: Annual Review, 1997. Charlottesville, VA: SNL Securities, Inc.

Spiegel, J.W., & Gart, A. (1996). What lies behind the bank merger and acquisition frenzy? Business Economics, April, 1996.

Spiegel, J.W., Gart, A., & Gart, S. (1996). Banking redefined: How superregional powerhouses are reshaping financial services. Chicago, IL: Irwin Professional Publishing.

Sproull, N.L. (1995). Handbook of research methods: A guide for practitioners and students in the social sciences (2nd ed.). Metuchen, N.J.: Scarecrow Press, Inc.

Trifts, J.W., & Scanlon, K.P. (1987). Interstate bank mergers: The early evidence. The Journal of Financial Research, 10 (4), 305–311, Winter.

U. S. Bureau of the Census. (1996). Statistical Abstract of the United States: 1996 (116th ed.). Washington, D.C.

U.S. Bureau of the Census. (1998). Statistical Abstract of the United States: 1998 (118th ed.) Washington, D.C.

Varaiya, N.P. (1986). An empirical Investigation of the bidding firms' gains from corporate takeovers. Research in Finance, 6, 149–178.

Varaiya, N.P. (1988). The winner's curse hypothesis and corporate takeovers. Managerial and Decision Economics, 9, 209–220.

Wendel, C.B. (1996). The new financiers: Profiles of leaders who are shaping the financial Services industry. Chicago, IL: Irwin Professional Publishing.

Yermack, D. (1997). Good timing: CEO stock option awards and corporate news announcements. The Journal of Finance, 52 (2), 449–476, June.

Yin, R.K. (1993). Application of case study research. Newbury Park, C.A.:Sage Publications, Inc.

Yin, R.K. (1994). Case Research: Design and methods (2nd ed.). Thousand Oaks, C.A.: Sage Publications, Inc.

Appendix A: Definition of Important Terms

<u>Abnormal Return</u> the difference between an actual and expected return and is calculated by estimating the expected returns using a given stock's beta and the return identified in a market index such as Standard & Poor's 500 Index. In other words, any return not explained by the market can be considered as an abnormal return.

<u>Acquiree</u> a business entity that is being acquired by another, the latter being called the acquirer and the former sometimes being referred to as the target company in a consolidation process.

<u>Acquirer</u> the entity that is taking over another entity by purchasing or swapping the stocks and, or acquiring the assets of the acquiree in a consolidation process to form a single new entity.

<u>Acquisition</u> the process of purchasing or acquiring all or part of the assets of an entity.

<u>Acquisition Premium</u> the amount paid, whether by cash or in stocks, to acquire the company's common stock of an acquiree above and beyond the value that is dictated by the market.

<u>Adverse Selection</u>: occurs when the people who are most undesirable from the other party's viewpoint are the most likely to vigorously seek to be parties to the given financial transaction suggesting that the most undesirable may be selected.

<u>Asymmetry of information</u>: suggests that one party to a transaction may have more information about the given transaction than the other party.

<u>Balance Sheet Leveraging</u> the ability to control the amounts and rates on all items in the balance sheet with the aim of achieving and maintaining the goals of profitability, safety and liquidity.

<u>Bank Holding Company (BHC)</u> is essentially a corporation that owns several different companies with at least one of them being a bank, while the others could be engaged in activities that are very much related to banking.

<u>Bear Market</u> a situation where a market is characterized by a period of general decline in stock prices or whatever commodity is traded in a given market.

Beta in the case of a security, measures the risk a security brings to a well-diversified portfolio and measures the security's market, its systematic or its non-diversifiable risk. Beta is, in practical terms, is a coefficient which measures the relative volatility of the price of a stock and correlates positively with volatility of the market's arithmetic mean for related stocks.

Branching the ability of a given bank to operate a banking facility away from it main office. Branch banking is essentially monitored and controlled by state law.

Bull Market a situation where a market is characterized by a period of general increase in stock prices or whatever commodity is traded in a given market.

Captive Financing a corporation that runs a parallel entity in order to make loans to customers seeking to purchase the said corporations goods or services.

Collateralized Debt Obligations (CDOs) a series of complex structured financial products such as packaged loans, bonds, and credit derivatives created mainly by investment banks aimed at boosting profits and spreading risk more efficiently and effectively in the financial system.

Commercial banks institutions that accept deposits of funds and make loans to customers and to carry out a number of additional monetary activities aimed at maintaining a socially sound financial system in a given society. Commercial banks are categorized by a federally designed standard industrial classification (SIC) code.

Conglomerate Merger the process by which two or more businesses, with unrelated product lines, are joined together to form a single entity.

Consolidation the process whereby two or more entities joined together voluntarily, as in the case of a merger or involuntarily, as in the case of an acquisition, to form a new single entity.

Customer Inertia the tendency for customers to remain loyal patrons devoid of the inclination to act contrary to perceived behavior in the light of changing situations or circumstances.

Demerger the separation of certain core businesses of a consolidated company back into its original pre-merger forms or some underlying semi-autonomous entities.

Derivatives investment instruments where values are contingent upon or "derived" from the values of the underlying financial claims. Forwards, futures, and option contracts are examples of derivatives.

Disintermediation the withdrawal of money deposits from a financial institution for reasons such as the purchasing of higher yielding portfolios such as treasury bills, commercial paper, bonds and so on. In essence, the excess of withdrawals over new deposits may lead to a financial cash flow crisis in the affected financial institution and on a broader scale, to the whole banking industry.

Economically Successful to identify a consolidation, where both the stocks of one or both of the parties to a merger, is attracting abnormal returns on the common stocks at the time of or after the official announcement of a decision to merge.

Economies of Scale the tendency in a production process for long run average costs to decrease as levels of output expand.

Economies of Scope applicable, more so to financial institutions, where a given set of inputs may be utilized to produce a wider and more diversified range of services, thereby lowering long run average total costs facing a given financial institution.

Event Study a methodology used to test an occurrence or an activity that may be responsible for an adjustment in future risks or cash flows of a business undertaking. Brown and Warner (1980) have shown the market model for assessing diversified portfolio risks is a suitable technique for testing results from given activities and occurrences affecting an entity.

Financial Holding Company: is an umbrella organization for embracing bank holding companies, insurance companies, securities firms, and other financial institutions. Such a company is empowered to hold up to 100% of commercial banks and nonfinancial businesses so long as ownership is for investment purposes only and not for day-to-day management of any of the institutions, that constitutes the aggregation.

Free Cash Flow instead of allocating the excess cash, that may be the residuals of a business's cyclical activity, to pay higher dividend to stockholders the excess funds are left in the business cycle for future investments such as acquiring the assets of a close competitor.

Financial Intermediary: a financial institution that channel funds from surplus savers to deficit savers by issuing its own liabilities to surplus savers and acquiring assets and selling financial products to deficit savers and consumers generally.

Forward EPS: a relative measure that uses expected earnings per share rather than current earnings per share. (Contrast this with *trailing EPS* defined below.)

Hubris: motives driven by one's inflated ego manifesting itself as lavish presumptuousness. The desire to merge or takeover a competitor may be driven more by market share or competitiveness avoidance rather than a decision based on sound financial analysis.

In-Market entities that do business within very similar markets and within relatively close geographical areas. With rapid advances in technology geographical proximity is a depleting issue for marketing purposes.

Incremental Cash Flow the outflow and inflow of funds consonant to the additional assets within the control of the organization.

Inorganic Growth growing the size of a business by combining the equity holdings of two or more companies under a single ownership. Contrast this with organic growth.

Internal Validity truthfulness of the conjectured relationship that the presumed effect is caused or influenced by the independent variable or variables in the study.

Internet Banking the availability of checking, savings and other banking products and services through cyberspace unrestricted by geography or physical locations and utilizing a digital processing and delivery system.

Investment Portfolio various assets held by an entity for investment purposes and may include financial or real assets or both.

Last Twelve Months Earnings Per Share [(LTM) Eps$_{(x)}$] sometimes referred to as trailing-four-quarter earnings per share, measures the earnings per share for the fiscal year immediately preceding the year being considered for analysis.

Lead Study a pioneering research initiative that possesses the tendency for attracting the attention of a community of scholars.

Microsegmentation a breakdown of a business's customer base into smaller segments characterized by common customer profiles and similar banking needs, and where service aggregation defines a value-added relationship between the business and its clientele.

Moral hazard: indicates that there is a risk that one party to a transaction will exhibit a behavior, which may be deemed repulsive from the other party's point of view.

Non-Value Maximizing mergers or acquisitions that take place with the aim of having greater market share, increase total sales, increase power and influence generally or any other monopolistic tendencies that are not purely economic in nature.

Normal Return the return on a common stock conditioned upon a realized market return.

Organic Growth growing the size of a business by internally generated financing means by way of endogenous variables such as net income, and retention rate, and productive reinvestments. Contrast this with inorganic growth.

Out-Market merger involving two or more entities from diverse markets or different product lines or entities from different geographical areas.

Proxy Contest a situation where a so-called dissident individual shareholder or a group of shareholders attempts to take control of the board of directors or may seek to influence certain dramatic changes in the activities of the company.

Purchase and Assumption Method suggests that the insolvent bank will be the beneficiary of a large infusion of funds supported by the provision of a willing merger partner.

Qualitative Deductive a system of reasoning based on the premise that the collection of data connected to an underlying phenomenon is best done without any preconceived theory or hypothesis, and the analysis of which, seeks to generalize to a theoretical proposition grounded in a contextual setting.

Qualitative Quasi-Deductive a research paradigm based on the premise that the rich holistic data nested in reality similar to the qualitative inductive paradigm can be followed, while simultaneously testing and explaining the "whys" of an underlying phenomenon through systematic deductive reasoning. The purpose may be to test and verify conclusions drawn and to make predictions where necessary and desirable.

Regulation Q a United States Federal Reserve Board's guidelines which establishes the maximum interest rate that banks would pay on customers savings. This regulation was repealed in 1986.

Regulatory Forbearance: when jurisdictional regulators sidestep their obligations, that is, not to recommend an appropriate decision concerning a financial intermediary when it is most financially prudent to do so.

Savings Institutions states or federally chartered financial institutions that accept checkable deposits and savings from the public and invest mainly in mortgages and may also allocate loans to businesses and consumers.

Securitization the process of converting certain receivables with similar features, such as loans and pooling these underlying assets and selling them as securities, the secured feature being the principal and interest payments from the original loan.

Synergistic Effects the combined effort of two or more entities, working together as a single entity, will produce greater results than the sum of the results produced by the given entities working independently.

Tender Offer the offer to buy a controlling interest in a business undertaking by purchasing shares in the market at a stated price and date and is generally followed in situations when the management of the targeted entity is opposed to the takeover (American Bankers Association, 1991, p. 351). Note also that a corporation may "tender offer" its own equities if it is of the view that such an asset is underpriced, a decision that could also result in higher future dividends to shareholders on record.

Thrift institution a financial entity that primarily accepts savings and checking deposits from consumers and invests them mainly in mortgages and mortgage related securities. Thrifts may also disburse loans to business enterprises and consumers and can be organized as a mutual or capital equity institution.

Too Big to Fail Policy a policy adopted by bank regulators whereby a extra precautions will be taken to avoid the insolvency of megabanks. Therefore the purchase and assumption method would be one avenue to available to failing megabanks.

Trailing EPS: a relative measure that uses current earnings per share rather than projected earnings per share. (Contrast this with *forward EPS* defined above.)

Value Maximization the expected economic gains from an investment decision, the expectation being that the investment should earn at least a normal rate of return.

White Knight: a situation that arises when a counter offer is made by an acquirer for an acquiree's business, usually at the request of the acquiree.

X-efficiency used to signify management's indifference to a given firm's market power and generally refers to excess costs associated with the cost of producing goods or services other the costs associated by suboptimal scale or scope. In short, the higher costs due to slack management.

APPENDIX B: Mathematical Explanations

1. Percentage Returns

Let $P_{A,t-1}$ represents the price of a stock purchased on a particular day. Also let R_{At} (%) represent the return received 1 day after purchase.
Then the discrete return will be:

$$R_{At} (\%) = [(P_{At} - P_{A,t-1})(1/P_{A,t-1})] \times 100$$

$$= [(P_{At})(1/P_{A,t-1}) - 1] \times 100$$

Assuming that a dividend ($D_{At-1, t}$) is to paid over the stock holding period where t-1 and t are the day of purchase and 1 day later respectively. Then

$$R_{At} (\%) = [(P_{At} + D_{At, t})(1/P_{A,t-1}) - 1] \times 100$$

2. Standard Error and T-Statistic

The standard error (SE) of a given Average Excess Return (AER) for each level of X measured in days, months, years, etc. The calculation for SE(y.x) where y=AER can be calculated using:

$$\left[\frac{1/N(N-2) \times N\Sigma y.y - (\Sigma y)(\Sigma y) - [N\Sigma xy - (\Sigma X)(\Sigma y)][N\Sigma xy - (\Sigma X)(\Sigma y)]}{N(\Sigma x.x) - (\Sigma x)(\Sigma x)} \right]^{1/2}$$

The t-Statistic = (AER) [1/ SE(y.x)]

3. *F* Test for Differences in *k* Means

A one-way analysis of the variance or a completely randomized design model suggests that one factor of interest is considered in the model. For a single factor of influence several groups may be selected proportionately as part of a deliberate sampling process. Such subgroups will necessary entail "treatment" error, which may come to bear upon the within-group variations, whereas between-group variations entail "experimental" error.

Total Variation = within-group variations + between-group variation

$$\sum_{j=1}^{k} \sum_{i=1}^{nj} (X_{ij} - \overline{\overline{X}})^2 = \text{Sum of the squared differences between each value of the overall mean}$$

$$X_{ij} = i\text{th observation for group } j$$

$$\overline{\overline{X}} = \sum_{j=1}^{k} \sum_{i=1}^{nj} X_{ij} (1/n), \text{ the overall mean}$$

$$\sum_{j=1}^{k} \sum_{i=1}^{nj} (X_{ij} - \overline{X_j})^2 = \text{within-group variations squared}$$

$$\overline{X_j} = \text{the mean of group } j$$

$$\sum_{j=1}^{k} n_j (\overline{X} - \overline{\overline{X}})^2 = \text{the between groups variations squared}$$

$$[\sum_{j=1}^{k} n_j (\overline{X} - \overline{\overline{X}})^2] \cdot [\sum_{j=1}^{k} \sum_{i=1}^{nj} (X_{ij} - \overline{X_j})^2]^{-1} = \text{The one way ANOVA } F \text{ statistic}$$

4. Difference Between Means in Small Samples

Since the sample size is small, $Z = \dfrac{[X_2 - X_1) - (\mu_2 - \mu_1)]}{[S_1(S_2)/n_1 + S_1(S_2)/n_2]}^{1/2}$

where X_1 and X_2 = population sample means

μ_2 and μ_1 = population means

n_1 and n_2 = population sample in units

S_1 and S_2 = sample standard deviations

5. Wilcoxon Signed Rank Sum Test for n (n > 15)

Comparing matched pairs of a population or populations whose data points are considered large (n > 15) it is usual to assume that the calculated distribution of T^+ or T^- can be approximated closely with normal curves. In such situations when n is considered large the test statistic can be either T^+ or T^-. Choosing a = 0.05) level of significance the critical values from a standard normal distribution are ± 1.96. The test statistic (Z) can be approximated by:

$$Z = \dfrac{T^+ - [\underline{n}(\underline{n}+1)/4]}{\sqrt{[\underline{n}(\underline{n}+1)(2\underline{n}+1)]/24}}$$

where T^+ = the sum of assigned values that are positive.

$\underline{n}$ = number of observations

The rejection region for a one-tailed test is $Z > Z_\alpha$ or $Z < -Z_\alpha$

6. Granger Causality

Under the premise that the future cannot cause the present or the past and that y_t, a variable of the future, can be caused by x_{t-1}, a variable in a time series x_{ts} of the past, will not "Granger-cause" when the coefficients of the xs of a regression of y_t on lagged ys and lagged xs, = 0. Hence,

$$y_t = \sum_{\iota=1}^{k} \alpha_\iota \, y_{t-i} + \sum_{\iota=1}^{k} \beta_i \, x_{t-i} + \mu_i$$

Thus, assuming that $B\,i = 0$ for any $i = 0, 1, 2$, to k, x_t will fail to cause y_t.

7. Abnormal and Cumulative Abnormal Returns

Abnormal Returns (AR):

Let $AR_{A,t}$ = abnormal returns for stock A in time period t. Then

$AR_{A,t}$ = (Actual return for stock A in time t) − (Expected return for stock A in time t)

$$= \{ (P_{A,t} + D_{A,t})(1/P_{A,t-1}) - 1 \} - \{ R + [E(r_m) - R] \}\beta_A$$

where $P_{A,t}$ and $D_{A,t}$ = stock price and dividend paid relative to stock A in the current period.

$P_{A,t-1}$ = stock price of stock A in the previous period.

R = risk-free rate which may be equated to short-term T-bill rate.

$E(r_m)$ = expected market return using a comparable stock market indicator.

β_A = the beta for asset A

Cumulative Abnormal Returns (CAR):

Let $CAR_{A\pm t}$ = cumulative abnormal returns for stock A for periods on either side of the announcement date ($t = 0$).

Then $CAR_{A\pm t} = \sum_{-t}^{+t} AR_{A\pm t} = AR_{-t} + \ldots + AR_0 + \ldots + AR_{+t}$

8. Free Cash Flows, Discounting, and Risk

a. <u>Free Cash flows Discounting:</u>

$$\sum_{i=1}^{n} FCF[1/(k_{ci} - g)]$$

where n = number of years factored into the post-acquisition period

FCF = free cash flows

k_{ci} = cost of capital (%)

g = expected growth rate

b. <u>Risk is measured by:</u>

$$\left[\sum_{i=1}^{n} (k_i - \bar{k}) \times P_r(k_i) \right]^{1/2}$$

where k_i = cash flows in the ith period

$\bar{k}$ = average cash flows

P_r = the probability of the cash flows in i^{th} period

ABOUT THE AUTHOR

Dr. Ashford Maharaj's research interest in the area of bank consolidations grew out of his close association with some of the bank consolidations involving megabank mergers such as Chemical Bank and Manufacturers Hanover Trust Company, Chemical Banking Corporation and Chase Manhattan Bank N.A., and J.P. Morgan and Chase Manhattan Bank. As a former employee of the original Chemical Bank, the author held a leadership position in helping to shape a culture of diversity among previous in-market bank competitors as Chemical Bank sought to engage in a series of magabank mergers.

Currently, Dr. Maharaj is Professor of Finance at Berkeley College, White Plain NY and an adjunct business professor at the City University of New York. The author possesses firsthand knowledge on the merger and acquisition processes involving huge U.S. megabanks that integrate on a merger-of-equals basis. He holds the degrees of Bachelor of Arts with specialization in Economics, Master of Science in Education Administration, and Doctor of Philosophy with specialization in Finance. He also holds postgraduate diplomas in Banking, Business Administration, and Adult Education. Presently, the author resides in the Borough of Queens, New York with his wife and two children and is a columnist for a weekly business publication located in the south Queens area. Dr. Maharaj has also authored *Bank Mergers and Acquisitions in the United States 1990–1997* published by Dissertation.com.

INDEX

Abnormal return, 25, 31, 35, 52-54, 65-66, 76-78, 93, 95, 169 188. *See also* Excess return

Acquiree, 1, 15-17, 29, 31-32, 34, 36, 38, 40, 44, 48-49, 56, 67, 70, 81-84, 89, 103, 105-106, 114, 116-117, 119-120, 134-135, 145, 147, 150, 153-154, 169, 174

Acquirer, 10-11, 15, 17, 28-29, 31-34, 36, 38, 40, 43-44, 47-49, 54-56, 67, 76, 81-82, 89, 91, 93, 96, 98, 101-103, 105-106, 114, 116-117, 119-121, 134-135, 153-155, 169, 174

Acquisition, 15-17, 20-52, 55-57, 64, 67, 69, 72-74, 76, 79, 81-90, 92, 96, 98-104, 114, 120-122, 128, 132-135, 140, 143, 145-146, 149, 151-153, 155, 161, 164, 166-167, 169-170, 181

Acquisition premium, 15, 32-33, 36, 47, 56, 67, 82-85, 120, 128, 134-135, 146, 152-153, 169

Adverse selection, 11, 169

Announcement date, 34-36, 52, 54-56, 68, 70, 76-77, 79, 81-82, 90, 92-93, 95-97, 100, 102, 104, 108, 113-114, 153

Asymmetry of information, 11-12, 169

Average excess return, 93, 97, 175

Balance sheet leveraging, 23, 169

Bank of North America, 2

Bank of the United States, 3
  First bank, 3, 43
  Second bank, 3

Bank One, 9, 15

Banks, 26, 32-39, 41-45, 47-52, 55-56, 60-61, 64-73, 75-79, 82-83, 88-89, 91-92, 98, 101, 103-104, 107, 117, 119-121, 123, 126-128, 130, 132-134, 136, 138-140, 143-159, 164-165, 170-171, 173
  characteristics of, 105
  failure rates, 10, 13
  number of, 1, 4, 7, 9-11, 13, 16, 21-22, 41-43, 45-46, 56, 60, 68-71, 74, 78, 80, 82, 91-92, 98-100, 104, 106, 108, 115, 118, 121-123, 149, 170

Barnett Banks Inc, 15

Bear market, 28, 169

Beta, 62, 66, 169-170

Branching, 4, 7, 19, 148, 154, 170

Bull market, 28, 50, 170

Captive financing, 149, 170
Chemical Bank, 15, 19, 41, 43, 116-118, 181
Citibank, 20, 23
Collateralized Debt Obligations, 156, 170
  (CDOs), 156, 170
Commercial banks, 1, 3-6, 8-11, 13, 16, 19, 21-25, 32, 38-39, 41, 60, 67-68, 72-73, 117, 148-149, 155, 170-171
Conglomerate Merger, 5, 148, 170
Consolidation, 1, 6, 17, 19, 23, 26, 28-29, 37, 39, 42-43, 47, 116, 118, 133, 155-156, 158, 165, 169-171
  In-market, 2, 7, 19-20, 23-26, 33-35, 37-39, 41, 49, 68-72, 76, 79, 88, 90, 98, 102-103, 116, 155, 158, 172, 181
  megabank, 2, 4, 6, 8, 10, 12, 14, 16, 18, 20, 22, 24-28, 30, 32-34, 36-40, 42, 44, 46, 48, 50, 52, 54, 56, 58, 60, 62, 64, 66-68, 70-74, 76, 78-80, 82, 84, 86, 88, 90-108, 110, 112, 114, 116, 118-120, 122, 124, 126-128, 130-134, 136, 138-140, 142-144, 146, 150-158, 162, 164, 166, 170, 172, 174, 176, 178, 181, 184
Customer Inertia, 149, 170
Demerger, 158, 170
Derivatives, 156-157, 170
Disintermediation, 22, 157, 171
Dominion Bank Share, 15
Economically Successful, 25-26, 33, 35, 37, 40, 171
Economies of Scale, 7, 11, 15, 20, 29, 42, 44, 47-48, 171
Economies of Scope, 1, 10, 16, 20, 29-30, 48, 171
Enigma, 10, 15-16, 104, 153
Event Study, 27, 39, 50, 52-55, 64, 69, 72, 100, 114, 161, 171
Excess Return. *See* Abnormal return
Federal Deposit Insurance, 5-6, 13-14, 52, 65, 162
Federal Deposit Insurance Corporation, 5-6, 13-14, 52, 65, 162
Federal Deposit Insurance Corporation Improvement Act, 5-6, 13-14, 52, 65, 162
Federal Reserve Bank, 51, 158
Federal Reserve System, 4, 6
Financial Holding Company, 8, 171
Financial Intermediary, 13, 171, 173
First Union Corp, 15
Forward EPS, 171, 174
Free cash flow, 48, 163, 171
Glass-Steagall Act of 1933, 5-6, 148
Gramm-Leach-Bliley Act, 5, 8
Greenspan, Allan, 158

Growth maximization group of, 44
   theories, 12, 21, 28-29, 33, 36, 39, 41, 43-45, 47, 50-51, 149
   hubris, 2, 10-11, 29, 36-37, 43-45, 59, 85, 153, 166, 172
   management self-interest, 43-44
   monopolistic orientation, 29, 45-46
Hubris, 2, 10-11, 29, 36-37, 43-45, 59, 85, 153, 166, 172
Hypothesis, 29, 31-32, 36-37, 44-50, 52, 57, 64-65, 70-71, 76-83, 85, 89-90, 93, 97, 99-100, 102-109, 113-116, 119, 121, 128, 132-134, 140, 144-146, 149-153, 166-167, 173
   testable, xviii
   statement, 118
In-Market entities, 172
Incremental cash flow, 172
Inorganic growth, 172-173
Internal Validity, 85-86, 90, 99, 101-102, 151, 172
Internet Banking, 24, 68, 88, 172
Interstate banking, 7, 24, 47, 68, 88, 154
   Intrastate banking, 18
   Investment banking, 5, 154, 157
Investment Portfolio, 172
Last Twelve Months Earnings per share [(LTM) Eps(x)], 35, 134, 172
Lead Study, 172
Manufacturers Hanover Trust Company, 117, 181
Market concentration, 21, 43
Merger and acquisition, 15, 22, 24, 26-30, 33, 37, 42-43, 47, 51-52, 55, 67, 72-74, 76, 87, 89, 92, 99, 101, 120, 122, 146, 152-153, 167, 181
   announcements, 24-25, 36, 39, 53, 68, 86, 89, 100-101, 121, 133, 162, 167
   horizontal, 1, 19-21, 46, 50, 96, 163, 165-166
Merger of equals, 33-34, 36-37, 40-41, 48, 56, 67, 79, 81-82, 89-90, 103-109, 113-114, 116-118, 150-154, 158
   hypothesis, 29, 31-32, 36-37, 44-50, 52, 57, 64-65, 70-71, 76-83, 85, 89-90, 93, 97, 99-100, 102-109, 113-116, 119, 121, 128, 132-134, 140, 144-146, 149-153, 166-167, 173
   synthesis, 88, 102, 116, 133, 147
Microsegmentation, 157, 172
MNC Financial, 15
Moral hazard, 11-12, 14-15, 51, 172
National Banking Acts of 1863 and 1864, 3-4
NationsBank Corp, 15
Negotiable Order of Withdrawal, 13

(NOW), 5, 11, 13, 46-48, 70, 107, 115, 157
New-market bank deals, 88
Nonparametric test, 79-80, 82, 104-105
Non-value maximizing, 28, 37, 43, 51, 104, 153, 172
Normal return, 53, 173
One-stop shopping, 8, 15, 18
Optimum goal, 60
Organic growth, 172-173
Out-Market merger, 20, 173
Parallel captive finance, 19
Parametric test, 79, 105
Price offered to book value, 39, 83, 119-121, 124-128, 131-136, 138, 144-147, 151-152
Price offered to LTM Eps, 134-140, 143-147, 151
Proxy Contest, 173
Purchase and assumption method, 12, 173-174
Real-time general ledger, 24
Regulation Q, 14, 22, 24, 173
Regulatory Forbearance, 14, 173
Required rate of return, 61-62
Research paradigms, 25
   Hypothetico-deductive, 149, 151
   Qualitative deductive, 173
   Qualitative quasi-deductive, 25-27, 33, 38, 40, 53, 156, 158, 173
   Quantitative, 25-26, 33, 47, 53, 68, 72, 76, 79, 90, 105-106, 156
Revenue enhancement, 29-30, 49, 134
Sample selection, 73
Savings and Loan Associations, 10-11, 13, 15-16
Savings and Loan Associations crisis, 13
Savings Institutions, 72-73, 173
Securitization, 14, 173-174
Significance of the study, 37, 39
Synergistic Effects, 30, 32, 83, 158, 174
Synergy, 20, 23, 29-32, 34, 39, 47-48, 83, 117, 155, 166
Thrift institution, 33, 104, 174
Too Big to Fail Policy, 174
Too important to fail, 156
Trailing EPS, 171, 174
Travelers Group, 5, 20, 23, 148, 157-158
Type I error, 101, 132, 144, 146, 151
Type II error, 151

Valuation Process, 31, 61-62
Value Creation, 1, 16, 26, 30, 34, 44, 49, 51, 53, 76, 81, 86, 89-91, 98, 102, 105, 117, 150, 152-153, 155, 164
Value Maximization, 30, 32, 44, 47, 55, 58-61, 104, 149, 174
   Shareholders, 1, 6, 10, 15-17, 23, 26, 30-36, 44, 47, 49, 51-53, 57-61, 65, 67, 70, 76, 81, 86, 88-91, 96, 98, 102-103, 105, 116-117, 134, 149-150, 152-153, 155, 158, 164, 173-174
   Stakeholders, 58-59
Value maximization group of theories, 47
   Economies of scale, 7, 11, 15, 20, 29, 42, 44, 47-48, 171
   Reengineering initiatives, 44, 50
   Revenue Enhancement, 29-30, 49, 134
Virtual banking, 24, 39, 149, 156-157
White Knight, 15, 161, 174
Wilcoxon signed rank sum test, 80, 82, 105-108, 113-115, 151, 177
X-efficiency, 49, 165, 174
Y2K, xvi-xvii, 157-158
Zero-sum game, 59

978-0-595-81419-0
0-595-81419-0

Printed in the United States
39848LVS00004B/132